Introducing
Phonetics and
Phonology

third edition

Mike Davenport
S.J. Hannahs

Introducing
Phonetics and
Phonology

third edition

Routledge
Taylor & Francis Group

LONDON AND NEW YORK

First edition published 1998
Second edition published 2010
by Hodder Education

Published 2013 by Routledge
2 Park Square, Milton Park, Abingdon, Oxon OX14 4RN
711 Third Avenue, New York, NY, 10017, USA

Routledge is an imprint of the Taylor & Francis Group, an informa business

The advice and information in this book are believed to be true and
accurate at the date of going to press, but neither the authors nor the publisher
can accept any legal responsibility or liability for any errors or omissions.

British Library Cataloguing in Publication Data
A catalogue record for this title is available from the British Library

Library of Congress Cataloging-in-Publication Data
A catalog record for this book is available from the Library of Congress

ISBN 13: 978-1-444-10988-7 (pbk)

Typeset in 10/12 Stone Serif by Phoenix Photosetting, Chatham, Kent *for Lesley and Maggie*

Contents

List of tables

List of figures

Preface

This textbook is intended for the absolute beginner who has no previous knowledge of either linguistics in general or phonetics and phonology in particular. The aim of the text is to serve as an introduction first to the speech sounds of human languages – that is phonetics – and second to the basic notions behind the organisation of the sound systems of human languages – that is phonology. It is not intended to be a complete guide to phonetics nor a handbook of current phonological theory. Rather, its purpose is to enable the reader to approach more advanced treatments of both topics. As such, it is primarily intended for students beginning degrees in linguistics and/or English language.

The book consists of two parts. After looking briefly at phonetics and phonology and their place in the study of language, Chapters 2 through 6 examine the foundations of articulatory and acoustic phonetics. Chapters 7 through 12 deal with the basic principles of phonology. The final chapter of the book is intended as a pointer towards some further issues within contemporary phonology. While the treatment does not espouse any specific theoretical model, the general framework of the book is that of generative phonology and in the main the treatment deals with areas where there is some consensus among practising phonologists.

The primary source of data considered in the book is from varieties of English, particularly Received Pronunciation and General American. At the same time, however, aspects of the phonetics and phonology of other languages are also discussed. While a number of these languages may be unfamiliar to the reader, their inclusion is both justifiable and important. In the first place, English does not exemplify the full range of phonological processes that need to be considered and exemplified. Second, the principles of phonology discussed in the book are relevant to all human languages, not just English.

At the end of each chapter there is a short section suggesting further readings. With very few exceptions the suggested readings are secondary sources, typically intermediate and advanced textbooks. Primary literature has generally not been referred to since the intended readership is the beginning student.

Exercises are included at the end of Chapters 2 through 12. These are intended to consolidate the concepts introduced in each chapter and to afford the student the opportunity to apply the principles discussed. While no answers are provided, the data from a number of the exercises are given fuller accounts in later chapters.

As with any project of this sort, thanks are due to to a number of colleagues, friends and students. In particular we'd like to thank Michael Mackert for his comments and critique. A number of other people have also given us the benefit of their comments and suggestions, including Maggie Tallerman, Lesley Davenport, Roger Maylor and Ian Turner. None of these people is to be blamed, individually or collectively, for any remaining shortcomings. Thanks also to generations of students at the universities of Durham, Delaware, Odense and Swarthmore College, without whom none of this would have been necessary!

Mike Davenport
S. J. Hannahs
Durham
March 1998

Preface to the second edition

Whilst maintaining the basic structure and order of presentation of the first edition, we have added a new chapter on the syllable, stress, tone and intonation, as well as adding or expanding sections in existing chapters, including a section on recent developments in phonological theory. We have also made numerous minor changes and corrections. We have been helped in this endeavour by many colleagues, students, reviewers and critics. For his specialist help on the anatomy of the vocal tract we'd like to express our thanks to James Cantrell. For help, encouragement, and apposite (and otherwise!) criticism we'd also like to thank (in alphabetical order): Loren Billings, David Deterding, Laura J. Downing, Jan van Eijk, Mária Gósy, András Kertész, Thomas Klein, Ken Lodge, Annalisa Zanola Macola, Donna Jo Napoli, Kathy Riley, Jürg Strässler, Maggie Tallerman, Larry Trask, and anonymous reviewers for Hodder Arnold. We'd also like to acknowledge the help (and considerable patience) of staff at Hodder Arnold: Eva Martinez, Lesley Riddle, Lucy Schiavone and Christina Wipf Perry. We apologise to anyone we've left out (and to anyone who didn't want to be included). None of these people can be assumed to agree with (all of) our assumptions or conclusions; nor (unfortunately) can they be held responsible for any remaining infelicities.

Mike Davenport & S. J. Hannahs
Durham & Newcastle
December 2004

Preface to the third edition

We are gratified and flattered that this book has maintained its popularity. We've tried in this edition to correct further errors and to update and expand the content in the light of recent developments in phonological theory. We have added a chapter on Optimality Theory and drawn explicit parallels between derivational analysis and optimality accounts. We have also included a glossary of terms.

In preparing this edition, we've had the benefit of various comments from colleagues and students over the past few years. These include, in no particular order, Mais Sulaiman, Tina Fry, Clare Wright, Magda Sztencel, Gosia Krzek, Paksiri Tongsen, Yousef Elramli, Mohana Dass Ramasamy, Alex Leung, Robert Bell, Alison Pennell. We would also like to thank staff at Hodder Education, in particular Bianca Knights and Liz Wilson. We'd also like to thank Caroline McPherson for her invaluable assistance in preparing the glossary. We apologise to any helpful souls we have missed out, or any we have included against their will.

Mike Davenport & S. J. Hannahs
Durham & Newcastle
June 2010

THE INTERNATIONAL PHONETIC ALPHABET (revised to 2005)

CONSONANTS (PULMONIC)   © 2005 IPA

	Bilabial	Labiodental	Dental	Alveolar	Postalveolar	Retroflex	Palatal	Velar	Uvular	Pharyngeal	Glottal
Plosive	p b			t d		ʈ ɖ	c ɟ	k ɡ	q ɢ		ʔ
Nasal	m	ɱ		n		ɳ	ɲ	ŋ	N		
Trill	ʙ			r					ʀ		
Tap or Flap		ⱱ		ɾ		ɽ					
Fricative	ɸ β	f v	θ ð	s z	ʃ ʒ	ʂ ʐ	ç ʝ	x ɣ	χ ʁ	ħ ʕ	h ɦ
Lateral fricative				ɬ ɮ							
Approximant		ʋ		ɹ		ɻ	j	ɰ			
Lateral approximant				l		ɭ	ʎ	ʟ			

Where symbols appear in pairs, the one to the right represents a voiced consonant. Shaded areas denote articulations judged impossible.

CONSONANTS (NON-PULMONIC)   VOWELS

Clicks	Voiced implosives	Ejectives
ʘ Bilabial	ɓ Bilabial	ʼ Examples:
ǀ Dental	ɗ Dental/alveolar	pʼ Bilabial
ǃ (Post)alveolar	ʄ Palatal	tʼ Dental/alveolar
ǂ Palatoalveolar	ɠ Velar	kʼ Velar
ǁ Alveolar lateral	ʛ Uvular	sʼ Alveolar fricative

Where symbols appear in pairs, the one to the right represents a rounded vowel.

OTHER SYMBOLS

ʍ Voiceless labial-velar fricative	ɕ ʑ Alveolo-palatal fricatives
w Voiced labial-velar approximant	ɺ Voiced alveolar lateral flap
ɥ Voiced labial-palatal approximant	ɧ Simultaneous ʃ and x
ʜ Voiceless epiglottal fricative	
ʢ Voiced epiglottal fricative	Affricates and double articulations can be represented by two symbols joined by a tie bar if necessary.
ʡ Epiglottal plosive	k͡p t͡s

SUPRASEGMENTALS

ˈ	Primary stress
ˌ	Secondary stress
ː	Long ˌfoʊnəˈtɪʃən
ˑ	Long eː
̆	Half-long eˑ
	Extra-short ĕ
ǀ	Minor (foot) group
ǁ	Major (intonation) group
.	Syllable break ɹi.ækt
‿	Linking (absence of a break)

DIACRITICS   Diacritics may be placed above a symbol with a descender, e.g. ŋ̊

̥	Voiceless	n̥ d̥	̤	Breathy voiced	b̤ a̤	̪	Dental	t̪ d̪
̬	Voiced	s̬ t̬	̰	Creaky voiced	b̰ a̰	̺	Apical	t̺ d̺
ʰ	Aspirated	tʰ dʰ	̼	Linguolabial	t̼ d̼	̻	Laminal	t̻ d̻
̹	More rounded	ɔ̹	ʷ	Labialized	tʷ dʷ	̃	Nasalized	ẽ
̜	Less rounded	ɔ̜	ʲ	Palatalized	tʲ dʲ	ⁿ	Nasal release	dⁿ
̟	Advanced	u̟	ˠ	Velarized	tˠ dˠ	ˡ	Lateral release	dˡ
̠	Retracted	e̠	ˤ	Pharyngealized	tˤ dˤ	̚	No audible release	d̚
̈	Centralized	ë	̴	Velarized or pharyngealized	ɫ			
̽	Mid-centralized	ě̽	̝	Raised	e̝ (ɹ̝ = voiced alveolar fricative)			
̩	Syllabic	n̩	̞	Lowered	e̞ (β̞ = voiced bilabial approximant)			
̯	Non-syllabic	e̯	̘	Advanced Tongue Root	e̘			
˞	Rhoticity	ɚ a˞	̙	Retracted Tongue Root	e̙			

TONES AND WORD ACCENTS

LEVEL		CONTOUR	
e̋ or ˥	Extra high	ě or ˇ	Rising
é ˦	High	ê ˆ	Falling
ē ˧	Mid	e᷄ ᷄	High rising
è ˨	Low	e᷅ ᷅	Low rising
ȅ ˩	Extra low	e᷈ ᷈	Rising-falling
↓	Downstep	↗	Global rise
↑	Upstep	↘	Global fall

Introduction

This book is about the sounds we use when we speak (as opposed to the sounds we make when we're doing other things). It's also about the various kinds of relationship that exist between the sounds we use. That is, it's about 'phonetics' – the physical description of the actual sounds used in human languages – and it's about 'phonology' – the way the sounds we use are organised into patterns and systems. As speakers of a particular language (English, say, or Hindi or Gaelic or Mohawk) we obviously 'know' about the *phonetics* and *phonology* of our language, since we use our language all the time, and unless we are tired or not concentrating (or drunk), we do so without making errors. Furthermore, we always recognise when someone else (for example a non-native speaker) pronounces something incorrectly. But, equally obviously, this knowledge is not something we are conscious of; we can't usually express the knowledge we have of our language. One of the aims of this book is to examine some ways in which we can begin to express what native speakers know about the sound system of their language.

1.1 Phonetics and phonology

Ask most speakers of English how many vowel sounds the language has, and what answer will you get? Typically, unless the person asked has taken a course in phonetics and phonology, the answer will be something like 'five; A, E, I, O and U'. With a little thought, however, it's easy to see that this can't be right. Consider the words 'hat', 'hate' and 'hart'; each of these is distinguished from the others in terms of the vowel sound between the 'h' and 't', yet each involves the vowel letter 'a'. When people answer that English has five vowels, they are thinking of English *spelling*, not the actual *sounds* of English. In fact, as we will see in Chapter 4, most kinds of English have between 16 and 20 different vowel sounds, but most speakers are completely unaware of this, despite constantly using them.

In a similar vein, consider the words 'tuck', 'stuck', 'cut' and 'duck'. The first three words each contain a sound represented in the spelling by the letter 't', and most speakers of English would say that this 't' sound is the same in each of these words. The last word begins with a 'd' sound, and in this case speakers would say that this was a quite different sound to the 't' sounds.

An investigation of the physical properties of these sounds (their phonetics) reveals some interesting facts which do not quite match with the ideas of the native speaker. In the case of the 't' sounds we find that there are quite noticeable differences between the three. For most speakers of English, the 't' at the beginning of 'tuck' is accompanied by an audible outrush of air (a little like a very brief 'huh' sound), known as **aspiration**. There is no such outrush for the 't' in 'stuck', which actually sounds quite like the 'd' in 'duck'. And the 't' in 'cut' is different yet again; it may not involve any opening of the mouth, or it may be accompanied by, or even replaced by, a stoppage of the air in the throat, similar to a very quick cough-like sound, known as a 'glottal stop'. When we turn to the 'd' sound, the first thing to notice is that it is produced in a very similar way to the 't' sounds; for both 't' and 'd' we raise the front part of the tongue to the bony ridge behind the upper teeth to form a blockage to the passage of air out of the mouth. The difference between the sounds rests with the behaviour of what are known as the vocal cords (in the Adam's apple), which vibrate when we say 'd' and do not for 't'. (We shall have much more to say about this kind of thing in Chapters 2, 3, 4 and 5.)

That is, **phonetically** we have four closely related but slightly different sounds; but as far as the speaker is concerned, there are only two, quite different, sounds. The speaker is usually unaware of the differences between the 't' sounds, and equally unaware of the similarities between the 't' and 'd' sounds. This reflects the **phonological** status of the sounds: the 't' sounds behave in the same way as far as the system of English sounds is concerned, whereas the 't' and 'd' sounds behave quite differently. There is no contrast among the 't' sounds, but they as a group contrast with the 'd' sound. That is, we cannot distinguish between two different words in English by replacing one 't' sound with another 't' sound: having a 't' without aspiration (like the one in 'stuck') at the beginning of 'tuck' doesn't give us a different English word (it just gives us a slightly odd pronunciation of the *same* word, 'tuck'). Replacing the 't' with a 'd', on the other hand, clearly does result in a different English word: 'duck'.

So where phonetically there are four different sounds, phonologically there are only two contrasting elements, the 't' and the 'd'. When native speakers say that the 't's are the same, and the 'd' is different, they are reflecting their knowledge of the phonological system of English, that is, the underlying organisation of the sounds of the language.

In a certain respect phonetics and phonology deal with many of the same things since they both have to do with speech sounds of human language. To an extent they also share the same vocabulary (though the specific meanings of the words may differ). The difference between them will become clear as the book progresses, but it is useful to try to recognise the basic difference from the outset. Phonetics deals with speech sounds themselves, how they are made (*articulatory phonetics*), how they are perceived (*auditory phonetics*) and the physics involved (*acoustic phonetics*). (Note that terms in bold and italics are listed in the glossary). Phonology deals with how these speech sounds are organised into systems for each individual language; for example: how the sounds can be combined, the relations between them and how they affect each other.

Consider the word 'tlip'. Most native speakers of English would agree that this is clearly not a word of their language, but why not? We might think that there is a phonetic reason for this, for instance that it's 'impossible to pronounce'. If we found that there are no human languages with words beginning 'tl...', we might have some evidence for claiming that the combination of 't' followed by 'l' at the beginning of a word is impossible. Unfortunately for such a claim, there are human languages that happily combine 'tl' at the beginnings of words, e.g. Tlingit (spoken in Alaska), Navajo (spoken in Southwestern USA); indeed, the language name Tlingit itself begins with this sequence. So, if 'tl...' is phonetically possible, why doesn't English allow it? The reason is clearly not phonetic. It must therefore be a consequence of the way speech sounds are organised in English which doesn't permit 'tl...' to occur initially. Note that this sequence can occur in the middle of a word, e.g. 'atlas'. So, the reason English doesn't have words beginning with 'tl...' has nothing to do with the phonetics, since the combination is perfectly possible for a human being to pronounce, but it has to do with the systematic organisation of speech sounds in English, that is the phonology.

Above we noted that phonetics and phonology deal with many of the same things. In another very real sense, however, phonetics and phonology are only accidentally related. Most human languages use the voice and vocal apparatus as their primary means of expression. Yet there are fully fledged human languages which use a different means of expression, or 'modality'. Sign languages – for example British Sign Language, American Sign Language, Sign Language of the Netherlands and many others – primarily involve the use of manual rather than vocal gestures. Since these sign languages use modalities other than speaking and hearing to encode and decode human language, we need to keep phonetics – the surface manifestation of spoken language – separate from phonology – the abstract system organising the surface sounds and gestures. If we take this division seriously, and we have to on the evidence of sign language, we need to be careful to distinguish systematically between phonetics and phonology.

1.2 The generative enterprise

We have seen that we can make a distinction between on the one hand the surface, physical aspects of language – the sounds we use or, in the case of sign languages, the manual and facial gestures we use – and on the other hand the underlying, mental aspects that control this usage – the system of contrasting units of the phonology. This split between the two different levels is central to the theory of linguistics that underpins this book – a theory known as **Generative grammar**. Generative grammar is particularly associated with the work of the American linguist Noam Chomsky, and can trace its current prominence to a series of books and articles by Chomsky and his followers in the 1950s and 1960s.

A couple of words are in order here about the terms 'generative' and 'grammar'. To take the second word first, 'grammar' is here used as a technical term. Outside linguistics, 'grammar' is used in a variety of different ways, often being concerned only with certain aspects of a language, such as the endings on nouns and verbs in a language like German. In generative linguistics, its meaning is something like 'the complete description of a language', that is, what the sounds are and how they combine, what the words are and how they combine, what the meanings of the words are, etc. The term 'generative' also has a specific meaning in linguistics. It does not mean 'concerning production or creation'; rather, adapting a usage from mathematics, it means 'specifying as allowable or not within the language'. A generative grammar consists of a set of formal statements which delimit all and only all the possible structures that are part of the language in question. That is, like a native speaker, the generative grammar must recognise those things which are allowable in the language and also those things which are *not* (hence the rather odd 'all and only all' in the preceding sentence).

The basic aim of a generative theory of linguistics is to represent in a formal way the tacit knowledge native speakers have of their language. This knowledge is termed **native speaker competence** – the idealised unconscious knowledge a speaker has of the organisation of his or her language. **Competence** can be distinguished from **performance** – the actual use of language. Performance is of less interest to generative linguists since all sorts of external, non-linguistic factors are involved when we actually use language – factors like how tired we are, how sober we are, who we are talking to, where we are doing the talking, what we are trying to achieve with what we are saying, etc. All these things affect the way we speak, but they are largely irrelevant to our knowledge of how our language is structured, and so are at best only peripheral to the core generative aim of characterising native speaker competence.

So what exactly are the kinds of things that we 'know' about our language? That is, what sort of things must a generative grammar account for? One important thing we know about languages is that they do indeed have structure; speaking a language involves much more than randomly combining bits of that language. If we take the English words 'the', 'a', 'dog', 'cat' and 'chased', native speakers know which combinations are permissible (the term is *grammatical*) and which are not (*ungrammatical*); so 'the dog chased a cat' or 'the cat chased a dog' are fine, but *'the cat dog a chased' or *'a chased dog cat the' are not (an asterisk before an example indicates that the example is judged to be ungrammatical by native speakers). So one of the things we know about our language is how to combine words together to form larger constructions like sentences. We also know about relationships that hold between words in such sentences; we know, for example, that in 'the dog chased a cat' the words 'the' and 'dog' form a unit, and are more closely related than say 'dog' and 'chased' in the same sentence. This type of knowledge is known as **syntactic knowledge**, and is the concern of that part of the grammar known as the *syntax*.

We also know about the internal make-up of words. In English a word like 'happy' can have its meaning changed by adding the element 'un'

4

at the beginning, giving 'unhappy'. Or it could have its function in the sentence changed by adding 'ly' to the end, giving 'happily'. Indeed, it could have both at once, giving 'unhappily', and again, native speakers 'know' this and can recognise ungrammatical structures like *'lyhappyun' or *'happyunly'. In the same way, speakers recognise that adding 's' to a word like 'dog' or 'cat' indicates that we are referring to more than one, and they know that this plural marker must be added at the end of the word, not the beginning. This type of knowledge about how words are formed is known as *morphology*, and is the concern of the morphological component of the grammar.

The grammar must also account for our knowledge about the meanings of words, how these meanings are related and how they can be combined to allow sentences to be interpreted. This is the concern of the *semantics*.

Finally, as we have seen in this chapter, we as native speakers have knowledge about the sounds of our language and how they are organised, that is, **phonological** knowledge. This is the concern of the **phonological component** of the grammar (and, of course, of this book).

So a full generative grammar must represent all of these areas of native speaker knowledge (syntactic, morphological, semantic and phonological). In each of these areas there are two types of knowledge native speakers have: that which is predictable, and that which is not. A generative grammar must therefore be able to characterise both these sorts of knowledge. As an example, it is not predictable that the word in English for a domesticated feline quadruped is 'cat'; the relationship between the animal and the sequence of sounds we use to name it is arbitrary (if it wasn't arbitrary then presumably all languages would have the same sequence of sounds for the animal). On the other hand, once we know what the sounds are, it *is* predictable that the first sound will be accompanied by the outrush of air known as aspiration that we discussed above, whereas the last sound will not. Our model of grammar must also make this distinction between the arbitrary and the predictable. This is done by putting all the arbitrary information in a part of the grammar known as the *lexicon* (which functions rather like a dictionary). The predictable facts are then expressed by formal statements known as rules or constraints, which act on the information stored in the lexicon.

So, to return to our feline quadruped, the lexicon would contain all the arbitrary facts about this word, including information on its syntactic class (that it is a noun), on its meaning (a domesticated feline quadruped!) and on its pronunciation (a 'c' sound followed by an 'a' sound followed by a 't' sound). This information, known as a lexical entry, is then available to be acted upon by the various sets of statements in the components of the grammar. So, the syntax might put the word in the noun slot in a structure like 'the big NOUN', the phonology would specify the actual pronunciation of each of the three sounds in the word, the semantics link the word to its meaning, etc. In this way, the grammar as a whole serves to 'generate' or specify allowable surface structures that the lexical entries can be part of, and can thus make judgements about what is or is not part of the language, in exactly the same way that a native speaker can. If faced with a structure like *'the very cat dog' the syntactic component of the grammar would reject this as ungrammatical because the word 'cat' (a noun) is occupying an adjective slot, not a noun slot; if faced with a pronunciation which involves the first sound of 'cat' being accompanied by a 'glottal stop' (see Section 3.1.5), the phonological component would similarly reject this as ungrammatical, since this is not a characteristic of such sounds at the beginning of words in English. The components of the grammar thus serve to mediate between, or link, the two levels of structure: (1) the underlying, mental elements of the language (that is, linguistic structures in the speaker's mind which the speaker is not consciously aware of) and (2) the surface, physical realisations of these elements (that is, the actual sounds made by the speaker when uttering a word).

The nature of the organisation of the phonological component of a generative grammar is the concern of the second part of this book, Chapters 7 to 13. To begin with, however, we concentrate in Chapters 2 to 6 on the description, classification and physical characteristics of speech sounds, that is, phonetics.

Further reading

For general introductions to generative linguistic theory, including phonetics and phonology, see for example Fromkin, Rodman and Hyams (2006), Akmajian, Demers, Farmer and Harnish (2001), O'Grady, Dobrovolsky and Katamba (1997), Kuiper and Allan (2003), Napoli (1996), Yule (2006).

2

Introduction to articulatory phonetics

The medium through which most of us experience language most of the time is sound; for all non-deaf language users, the first exposure to language is through sound, and in non-literate, hearing societies it is typically the only medium. Humans have a variety of ways of producing sounds, not all of which are relevant to language (for example: coughing, burping, etc.). How sound is *used* in language, that is, speech sounds, is the focus of this book, and one obvious place to start out is to look at the physical processes involved in the production of speech sounds by speakers – the study of articulatory phonetics.

This chapter examines the major aspects of speech production:

❑ the airstream mechanism – where the air used in speech starts from, and which direction it is travelling in
❑ the state of the vocal cords – whether or not the vocal cords are vibrating, which determines voicing
❑ the state of the velum – whether it is raised or lowered, which determines whether a sound is oral or nasal
❑ the place and manner of articulation – the horizontal and vertical positions of the tongue and lips.

In Chapters 3 and 4 we look in some detail at different speech sounds, beginning with the various types of consonant and then moving on to vowels. The primary focus is on speech sounds found in different varieties of English, particularly Received Pronunciation (RP) and General American (GenAm). RP refers to a non-regional pronunciation found mainly in the United Kingdom, sometimes known non-technically as 'BBC English' or 'the Queen's English'. General American refers to a standardised form of North American English, often associated with broadcast journalism and, thus, sometimes known as 'network English'. Although the focus is on English, exemplification will also come from other languages.

2.1 Overview

Speech sounds are created by modifying the volume and direction of a flow of air using various parts of the human respiratory system. We need to consider the state of these parts in order to be able to describe and classify

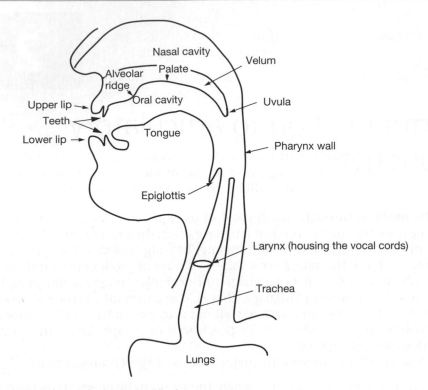

Fig. 2.1 The vocal tract and articulatory organs

the sounds of human languages. Figure 2.1 illustrates the parts of anatomy we need to examine.

2.1.1 Airstream mechanism

We can start with the airflow itself – where is it initiated and which direction is it travelling in? The major 'initiator' is the lungs and the most common direction is for the air to flow out from the lungs through the trachea (windpipe), larynx (in the Adam's apple) and *vocal tract* (mouth and nose); all human languages involve this type of airstream mechanism, known as 'pulmonic egressive' (= from the lungs outwards) and for many, including English, it is the sole airstream mechanism employed for speech sounds. A number of languages also employ other possibilities; the air may be moving inwards (an ingressive airstream mechanism), the flow itself may begin at the *velum* (soft palate) or the *glottis* (the space between the vocal cords) – velaric and glottalic airstreams respectively. This gives a possible six airstream mechanisms:

❑ pulmonic egressive – used in all human languages
❑ pulmonic ingressive – not found
❑ velaric egressive – not found

- ❏ velaric ingressive – used in e.g. Zulu (S. Africa)
- ❏ glottalic egressive – used in e.g. Navajo (N. America)
- ❏ glottalic ingressive – used in e.g. Sindhi (India).

However, as can be seen from the list above, two of the possible types – pulmonic ingressive and velaric egressive – are not found in any human language (it is unclear why this is so).

Having established the starting point of the airflow and the direction it is travelling in, we can then look at what happens to it as it moves over the other organs involved in speech sound production. For what follows, we will assume a pulmonic egressive airstream mechanism; sounds produced with other airstream types will be discussed in later sections.

2.1.2 The vocal cords

As air is pushed out from the lungs, it moves up the trachea into the larynx. In the larynx the airflow encounters the vocal cords. The vocal cords are actually two folds of tissue, but when visualized from above (as in laryngeal examination), they appear as white cords surrounded by pinkish areas (hence the popular term 'vocal cords'). These flaps run from the arytenoid cartilages in the back to a point on the inner surface of the thyroid cartilage in the front. When the vocal cords are apart, as in Figure 2.2 (which shows an open glottis), then the air passes through unhindered, resulting in what is known as a **voiceless** sound, such as in the initial and final sounds in the word 'pass.' (Since English orthography is not a system of phonetic representation, a single sound may be represented by more than one orthographic symbol, as in the final sound in 'pass'.) Lying above the true vocal folds are the false folds. The false vocal folds can also be set into vibration to produce some sounds, such as with a hard cough, but are not normally associated with speech production. The thyroid cartilage, located at the front of the larynx, causes the protrusion known as the Adam's apple in the front of the throat.

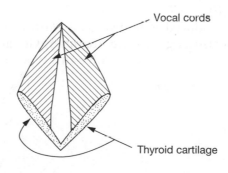

Fig. 2.2 Open glottis

Note: In this and subsequent figures showing states of the glottis the bottom of the diagram corresponds to the front of the larynx. Note that all the figures in this chapter are schematic rather than anatomically accurate representations.

If, however, the vocal cords are brought together by muscular contractions, as in Figure 2.3 (which shows a narrowed glottis), then as the air is forced through, air pressure causes the vocal cords to vibrate. This vibration (voicing) is maintained by aerodynamic and elastic forces until movement of the arytenoid cartilages separates the vocal cords. (This is a simplification of the complexities involved in the production of voicing; the reader interested in greater detail should consult one of the works listed in the Further Reading section at the end of this chapter.)

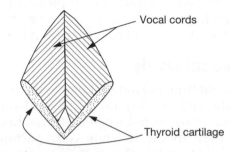

Fig. 2.3 Narrowed vocal cords

This vibration results in a **voiced** sound, as in all three sounds in 'buzz'. You can feel (as well as hear) the difference between voiceless and voiced sounds by placing your finger against your Adam's apple and then making prolonged 'sss' (as in 'hi<u>ss</u>') and 'zzz' (as in 'hi<u>s</u>') sounds: for the 'zzz' sound you should be able to feel the vibration of the narrowed vocal cords, while for 'sss' the vocal cords are wide apart and there is no such vibration.

These two positions – open and narrowed – are the most common in the languages of the world, but the vocal cords may take on a number of other configurations which can be exploited by languages. For instance, they may be completely closed (see Figure 2.4), not allowing air to pass through at all and thus causing a build-up of pressure below the vocal cords; when they are opened, the pressure is released with a forceful outrush of air (similar to a cough).

The sound so produced is known as a **glottal stop** which is found in many kinds of British English – e.g. Cockney, Glasgow, Manchester, etc. –

Fig. 2.4 Closed glottis   **Fig. 2.5** Creaky voice aperture

as the final sound of words like 'what'. Alternatively, the vocal cords may be open only at one end, as in Figure 2.5, resulting in what are known as **creaky voice** sounds, found in languages such as Hausa (spoken in Nigeria). Imitating the sound of an unoiled door closing slowly involves creaky voice.

Finally, the vocal cords may be apart (much as for voiceless sounds), but the force of air may still cause some vibration, giving what are known as **breathy voice** or 'murmured' sounds, found in Hindi (spoken in India) or, for many speakers of English, in the 'h' of 'ahead'.

2.1.3 The velum

The position of the velum is the next consideration. The **velum**, or soft palate, is a muscular flap at the back of the roof of the mouth; this may be raised – cutting off the nasal tract – or lowered – allowing air into and through the nose (see Figure 2.6). When the velum is raised (known as 'velic closure'), the air can only flow into the oral tract, that is, the mouth; sounds produced in this way are known as *oral sounds* (all those in 'frog', for example). When the velum is lowered, air flows into both mouth and nose, resulting in *nasal sounds* (the first and last sounds in 'man', or the vowel in French *pain* 'bread', for example).

2.1.4 The oral tract

We have thus far considered the type of airstream mechanism involved in the production of a speech sound, the state of the vocal cords (whether the sound is voiced or voiceless, for instance) and the state of the velum (whether the sound is nasal or oral). We must now look at the state of the oral tract; in particular, the position of the *active articulators* (lower lip and tongue) in relation to the *passive articulators* (the upper surfaces of the oral tract).

The **active articulators** are, as their name suggests, the bits that move – the lower lip and the tongue. It is convenient to consider the tongue as consisting of a number of sections (though these cannot move entirely independently, of course). These are: the tip, blade, front, back and root; the front and back together are referred to as the body (see Figure 2.6). The **passive articulators** are the non-mobile parts – the upper lip, the teeth, the roof of the mouth and the pharynx wall. The roof of the mouth is further subdivided into alveolar ridge, hard palate, soft palate (or velum) and uvula (see, again, Figure 2.6).

Consideration of the relative position of active and passive articulators allows us to specify what are known as the *manner of articulation* and the *place of articulation* of the speech sound. These will be discussed in detail in the following two chapters; for the moment, a brief survey will suffice.

2.1.5 Manner of articulation

Manner of articulation refers to the vertical relationship between the active and passive articulators, i.e. the distance between them (usually

11

1 Oral cavity
2 Nasal cavity
3 Lips – labial
   3a Upper lip
   3b Lower lip
4 Teeth – dental
5 Alveolar ridge – alveolar
6 Palate – palatal
7 Velum – velar
8 Uvula – uvular
9 Pharynx – pharyngeal
10 Tongue tip
11 Tongue blade
12 Tongue front⎤
13 Tongue back⎦ = Tongue body
14 Tongue root

Fig. 2.6 Sagittal section

Note: The name of the position is given, followed (where appropriate) by its corresponding adjective.

known as **stricture**); anything from being close together, preventing air escaping, to wide apart, allowing air to flow through unhindered.

When the articulators are pressed together (known as **complete closure**), a blockage to the airflow is created, causing air pressure to build up behind the blockage. When the blockage is removed, the air is released in a rush. The sounds produced in this way are known as *stops*; these may be oral (with velum raised), as in the first and last sounds in 'b̲a̲d̲', or nasal (lowered velum), as in the first and last sounds in 'm̲a̲n' – the only difference between these words is the position of the velum, since the active articulators are in the same positions for both words.

The first and last sounds in 'ch̲urch̲' also involve complete closure, but have a different release of air. In the oral stops we have looked at so far, the active articulator is lowered completely, giving a wide 'escape hole' for the air, as for the stop sounds in 'b̲a̲d̲'; for the first and last sounds in 'ch̲urch̲' the active articulator is lowered only slightly, giving a slower release of the air through a narrow channel between the articulators. As the air passes through this narrow space there is friction (see fricatives in the next paragraph). Sounds produced in this way are known as *affricates*.

When the articulators are close together, but without complete closure (a stricture known as *close approximation*), the air is forced through the narrow gap between the articulators, causing some turbulence; sounds so produced are known as *fricatives* (the first and last sounds in 'f̲ez̲').

For the other major sound types – *liquids*, *glides* and *vowels* – there is free passage of air through the oral tract, though the exact relation between the articulators will vary. For vowels (the middle sounds in 'c<u>a</u>t', 'd<u>o</u>g', 'm<u>ea</u>t', etc.) and glides (sometimes known as 'semi-vowels') (the initial sounds in '<u>y</u>ak' and '<u>w</u>arthog'), the articulators are wide apart and the air flows out unhindered (this is known as ***open approximation***). For liquids (the first and last sounds in '<u>r</u>ai<u>l</u>'), there is both contact and free air passage: for the 'r' sound, the sides of the tongue are in contact with the gums, but the air flows freely down the centre of the tongue, and for the 'l' sound, the centre of the tongue is in contact with the alveolar ridge but the air flows out freely over the lowered sides of the tongue – see Section 3.5.

2.1.6 Place of articulation

Place of articulation refers to the horizontal relationship between the articulators. It specifies the position of the highest point of the active articulator (usually some part of the tongue, but the lower lip may also be the active articulator) in relation to the passive articulator. The passive articulator involved typically gives its name to the place of articulation. The major places of articulation are shown in Table 2.1.

Table 2.1 The major places of articulation

Place of articulation	Active articulator	Passive articulator	Example
bilabial	lower lip	upper lip	<u>b</u>at
labiodental	lower lip	upper teeth	<u>f</u>ish
dental	tongue tip or blade	upper teeth	mo<u>th</u>
alveolar	tongue tip or blade	alveolar ridge	<u>d</u>og
retroflex	curled tongue tip	area immediately behind alveolar ridge	Malayalam [ku<u>tt</u>i] 'child'
palato-alveolar (or alveo-palatal)	tongue blade	area immediately behind alveolar ridge	<u>sh</u>ark
palatal	tongue front	hard palate	<u>y</u>ak
velar	tongue back	velum	<u>g</u>oat
uvular	tongue back	uvula	French <u>r</u>at 'rat'
pharyngeal	tongue root	pharynx wall	Arabic [ʕamm] 'uncle'
glottal	vocal cords	vocal cords	<u>h</u>are

In Table 2.1 most places of articulation are self-explanatory to the English speaker (see Figure 2.6). Let us mention here two that are not: retroflex and pharyngeal. A ***retroflex sound*** involves a particular shape of the tongue as well as a horizontal relationship between the articulators. The tongue tip is curled towards the back of the mouth. Such sounds may be heard in Indian

13

English for 't' and 'd', due to the influence of native languages of the Indian subcontinent, many of which have retroflex consonants. A **pharyngeal** sound involves moving the root of the tongue towards the back of the throat, i.e. the pharynx wall. Such sounds are common in many varieties of Arabic and Hebrew.

It is also possible for a speech sound to have two places of articulation simultaneously, known as 'dual articulations'. The articulations may be of equal importance, as in the initial labial-velar sound in 'wombat', involving as active articulators the lower lip and the back of the tongue, or one place may be 'added on' to another (primary) place. This latter situation is found, for example, in the palatalised stops of Slavic languages such as Polish or Russian, where a raising of the tongue body towards the hard palate accompanies the main place of articulation of the stop, as in Russian [bratʲ] 'to take'.

2.2 Speech sound classification

We now have a method of describing the articulation of any speech sound by specifying (1) the airstream mechanism, (2) the state of the vocal cords, (3) the position of the velum, (4) the place of articulation and (5) the manner of articulation. Thus, the first sound in 'pig' could be classified – using these five features – as a pulmonic egressive, voiceless, oral, bilabial stop.

In fact, for consonants, it is more usual to use a three term classification, referring to voicing, place and manner, with airstream and velum only referred to when they are not pulmonic egressive and oral respectively; thus the 'p' sound in 'pig' is normally referred to as a voiceless bilabial stop, 'z' as in 'fez' is a voiced alveolar fricative.

For vowels, the classification is slightly different; voicing is typically irrelevant, since in most languages, vowels are always voiced, and the vertical (manner for consonants) and horizontal (place for consonants) dimensions are more restricted. All vowels are produced with a stricture of open approximation, so manner as such is irrelevant; however, different vowels do involve differences in the highest point of the tongue; for the vowel sound in 'sit' the tongue is higher than for the vowel sound in 'sat'; we refer to 'high', 'mid' and 'low' vowels. Horizontally, vowels are restricted to the palatal and velar regions; compare the vowels in 'fee' (made in the palatal area) and 'far' (made further back in the velar area); in this dimension we refer to vowels as 'front', 'central' and 'back'. There is a further consideration for vowels, however, not usually relevant for consonants; that of lip rounding. (Note that even though the upper lip is considered a passive articulator, it does participate in lip rounding.) The vowel sound in 'see' involves no lip rounding, while the lips are rounded for the vowel sound in 'sue'; you can check this by looking in a mirror as you say these sounds. Thus the vowel sound in 'see' can be referred to as a high front unround vowel, that in 'sort' as a mid back round vowel.

2.3 Supra-segmental structure

Thus far, we have considered speech sounds, or segments, as individual units. When we use speech, however, we do not produce segments as individual items; rather, they are part of larger constructions. One such 'larger construction' that sounds can be combined together to form is the *syllable*. Coming up with a straightforward definition of the syllable is no easy task (but see Section 6.1.1 for some discussion); speakers nonetheless have an intuitive idea of what the syllable is. We can, for instance, count them, or tap in time to them, quite easily; most speakers of English would agree that the word 'rabbit' has two syllables, that 'elephant' has three syllables and that 'armadillo' has four. While all these syllables are different, in the sense that they are made up of different segments, they nonetheless share certain structural properties; they all have a vowel, and this vowel may be preceded and/or followed by one or more consonants; the first syllable of 'elephant' is just the vowel represented orthographically as 'e', the second is a vowel preceded by a consonant 'le', and the third is a vowel preceded by one consonantal sound (orthographically 'ph') and followed by two consonant segments. So, while consonants appear to be optional in syllable structure, vowels seem to be obligatory. The facts are actually more complex than this, since many languages, including English, allow nasals and liquids to form a syllable without a vowel, e.g. 'bott<u>le</u>'. These liquids and nasals are known as **syllabic**. The vowel is said to be the **peak** or *nucleus* of the syllable, with any consonants preceding the nucleus said to be in the syllable *onset*, and any following the nucleus said to be in the syllable *coda*. So the first syllable in 'rabbit' has an 'r' sound in the onset, the vowel represented by 'a' in the nucleus, and no coda; the second syllable has a single consonant in the onset (even though the orthography has two symbols, 'bb'), the vowel represented by 'i' as the nucleus, and a single coda consonant 't'.

As well as being aware of how many syllables there are, speakers can usually also recognise that when we have a sequence of syllables, making up a word or a sentence, some syllables are 'stronger' or 'more noticeable' than others. Thus, in 'rabbit' and 'elephant' the first syllable is more noticeable than the others, whereas in 'armadillo' it's the third syllable that is most noticeable; in a sentence like 'Albert went to the zoo' we can usually agree that the final syllable ('zoo') is more prominent than any of the others. That is, we can recognise that some syllables carry more *stress* than others. Stressed syllables are produced with more muscular effort, and are louder and longer than unstressed syllables. We shall have more to say about syllables and stress in Chapter 6.

2.4 Consonants vs. vowels

Syllable structure plays a role when we attempt to clarify a major distinction between speech-sound types that we have thus far simply been assuming: that between *consonants* and *vowels*. This is not as straightforward as it might at first appear; at first glance, the essential difference would seem to have to

15

do with degree of stricture, i.e. the distance between the active and passive articulators. For consonants there is some kind of obstruction in the oral tract, whereas for vowels there is no such hindrance to the outflow of the air. Thus, stops (oral and nasal), fricatives and liquids all involve a stricture of at least close approximation. Liquids and nasals might appear to be counterexamples to this claim, since the air flows out freely for these sound types. In each case, however, there is some obstruction in the oral tract; for nasals, complete closure (since they are stops). For liquids, there is some contact between articulators, but this does not extend across the full width of the oral tract – so, for the 'l' in 'lion', the middle of the tongue tip is in contact with the alveolar ridge, but the sides of the tongue are lowered, allowing free airflow.

The class of glides is a problem for this definition, however, since for them there is a stricture of open approximation. For these sounds, the consonant/vowel distinction rests not so much with the phonetics as with the phonology. That is, it has to do with how the sounds function in the language, rather than with the details of their articulation. True vowels like the 'i' in 'pig' are syllabic; that is, they comprise the essential part of the syllable, known as the nucleus, and without which there would not be a syllable (for details of syllable structure, see Section 2.3 and Chapter 6). Glides, on the other hand, behave like consonants in that they do not form the nuclei of syllables, but rather occur on the edges of syllables. That is, the main difference between the 'y' in 'yak' and the 'i' in 'pig' is not so much the articulation (which is much the same, though the 'y' may well be somewhat shorter), but the function of the two sounds. In 'pig' the segment represented by 'i' is the nucleus (or head) of its syllable; in 'yak' the segment represented by 'y' is not the nucleus (the 'a' is), but rather the onset. So we might say for English and many other languages that a vowel is a sound produced with open approximation and which is a syllable nucleus; this will exclude glides, which are not nuclei, and will also exclude syllabic liquids and nasals (as in the final sounds of 'throstle' and 'mutton') since these are not produced with open approximation.

Further reading

For greater detail of the anatomical side of speech production see Clark, Yallop and Fletcher (2008). The standard linguistics textbook for articulatory (and acoustic) phonetics is Ladefoged (2005), see especially Chapter 1. Catford (2001) is an accessible general introduction to phonetics. Laver (1994) is a very full treatment of phonetic principles. Also useful are Ball & Rahilly (1999), Johnson (2002), Ladefoged (2001), Lodge (2009) and the IPA handbook (1999).

Exercises

1 In each of the following words a sound is underlined. For each sound state (i) its voicing, (ii) whether it is oral or nasal, (iii) its place of articulation and (iv) its manner of articulation.

   a. bee   b. reason   c. hang   d. jungle
   e. vine   f. leech   g. listen   h. lark

2 Name the active articulator for each of the underlined sounds below.

   a. those   b. keep   c. mess   d. rich
   e. revile   f. final   g. pet   h. yacht

3 Each of the words below has a sound underlined. For each of the pairs of words state what the difference is between the underlined sounds. For example the underlined sounds in in and ink differ in place of articulation (alveolar vs. velar); those in pop and bop differ in voicing (voiceless vs. voiced).

   a. toe / doe   b. sick / tick   c. luck / lug   d. lip / lick
   e. rift / wrist   f. cad / can   g. measure / mesher h. bag / gag

4 For each of the words below describe the sequence of events required to produce the consonants in the word. For example, for the word 'tab': (1) for 't' the tip of the tongue rises to touch the alveolar ridge making complete closure, (2) the tip of the tongue lowers allowing release of the closure, (3) there is no voicing, (4) for 'b' voicing continues (from the vowel), (5) the lower lip rises to form complete closure with upper lip and (6) lower lip lowers to allow release of closure.

   a. sag   b. think   c. fell   d. dreamt

5 For each of the following words identify the number of syllables and indicate which syllable bears the main stress:

   a. recipient   b. envelope   c. natural   d. survey (noun)
   e. diametrical   f. intellectual   g. survey (verb)   h. diameter

3

Consonants

As we saw in Chapter 2, the class of consonants can be divided into a number of sub-groupings on the basis of their manner of articulation. The first division we will consider here is *obstruent* vs. *sonorant*. For obstruents, the airflow is noticeably restricted, with the articulators either in complete closure or close approximation. For sonorants, either there is no such restriction in the oral tract, or the nasal tract is open; either way, the air has free passage through the vocal tract. The class of obstruents can be further subdivided into *stops*, *fricatives* and *affricates*, again on the basis of stricture type. The class of **sonorant consonants** can be subdivided into *nasals*, *liquids*, and *glides* (vowels are also sonorants, but not sonorant consonants).

A further important distinction between obstruents and sonorants is that, while the various obstruent subtypes listed above may have both voiced and voiceless counterparts in most languages, sonorant subtypes are typically only voiced. Thus English can distinguish 'pad' from 'bad' due to the voicing contrast of the initial bilabial obstruents (stops) represented orthographically by 'p' and 'b'. With sonorants no such pairs exist; for the nasals, for example, there is only one bilabial – the (voiced) nasal found in 'mad' – and no voiceless bilabial nasal.

This chapter looks in some detail at consonantal articulation types, starting with those having the narrowest stricture, the stops and affricates, moving through more open strictures to the fricatives and then to nasals and liquids, ending with the class with the widest stricture setting, the glides. For each class of consonant, there is a description of its production at different places of articulation and a discussion of any significant variation exhibited (both positional variation, in terms of what happens when the sound occurs in different positions within a sequence of sounds, and regional variation, with respect to different varieties of English around the world). Though the discussion focusses on (varieties of) English, there is also some consideration of each class as it occurs in other languages.

In the discussion on how the sounds are used in languages, the position in which a sound occurs in a word is described: it may occur word-initially (i.e. at the start of a word), word-medially (i.e. within the word) or word-finally.

At the appropriate points, typically towards the beginning of each section, the phonetic symbols relevant to the sounds under discussion will be introduced. The phonetic symbols used will be those of the International Phonetic Alphabet (IPA); a chart of IPA symbols can be found on page xviii.

Note that whenever a symbol is intended as a phonetic representation, it will be enclosed in square brackets; thus [dɪg] represents the pronunciation of the word spelled 'dig' – that is, 'dig' can be transcribed as [dɪg] – and [θɪŋ] represents the pronunciation of 'thing'. Orthographic (spelling) forms will be indicated by quotes, as in the previous sentence.

Some symbols for vowels (see Chapter 4) are introduced in this chapter and examples of their pronunciation are given as they occur.

3.1 Stops

As was outlined in Section 2.1.5, stops are characterised by involving complete closure in the oral tract, preventing the airflow from exiting through the mouth. They may be oral (velum raised) or nasal (velum lowered, allowing air to pass freely out through the nose). Pulmonic egressive oral stops are often also known as plosives and, as expected for obstruents, are either voiced or voiceless. Nasal stops, being sonorants, are in most languages voiced only. (Nasal stops will be dealt with in Section 3.4.)

In common with most other languages, English has three pairs of voiceless/voiced stops, shown in Table 3.1.

Table 3.1 Stops in English

Place of articulation	Voice	Symbol	Example
bilabial	–	[p]	'pig'
	+	[b]	'bear'
alveolar	–	[t]	'tiger'
	+	[d]	'dog'
velar	–	[k]	'cat'
	+	[g]	'gorilla'

Note: '+' indicates the presence of voicing; '–' indicates the absence of voicing.

There is also the glottal stop [ʔ], heard for example in many British English varieties (e.g. London, Manchester, Glasgow, Edinburgh as well as newer varieties of RP) and some varieties of North American English (e.g. New Jersey, metropolitan and upstate New York) as the final sound in 'rat', or for most speakers in the negative 'uh-uh', or at the beginning of a voluntary cough. The glottal stop is voiceless; it has no voiced counterpart, since the vocal cords cannot vibrate when they are in contact.

As suggested above, most languages have bilabial, alveolar and velar stops; a number may well have stops at other places of articulation too, such as palatal [c] and [ɟ], e.g. Malayalam (India), or uvular [q] and [ɢ], e.g. Quechua (Bolivia, Peru). Note that when pairs of sounds with the same place of articulation are presented, the convention is that the first member is voiceless, the second voiced; so Quechua [q] is voiceless and [ɢ] is voiced.

19

A not insignificant number of languages have some stops produced with an airstream mechanism other than pulmonic egressive; such stops are not plosives. If the glottis is closed then raised, the air above it (in the vocal tract) will be pushed upwards, becoming compressed behind the blockage in the oral tract; this air exits on release of the closure in the oral tract. This airstream mechanism is known as glottalic egressive, and the stops so produced are known as *ejectives*. Ejectives are indicated by an apostrophe following the stop symbol, as in [p'], [t'], [k']. Given that they are produced with a closed glottis, only voiceless ejectives are possible. Ejectives are found in a number of African, Native American and Caucasian languages, as well as elsewhere; just under 20 per cent of all the world's languages have ejectives of one sort or another.

Implosives also involve a glottalic airstream mechanism, but in this case the glottis is lowered, not raised, drawing the air in the vocal tract downwards. For most implosives, the glottis is narrowed, i.e. they are voiced, but a small number of languages – e.g. some varieties of Igbo (Nigeria) – have an articulation involving a closed glottis, giving voiceless implosives. About 10 per cent of the world's languages have implosives, many in West Africa. Implosives have their own set of IPA symbols, including [ɓ] (bilabial), [ɗ] (dental or alveolar) and [ɠ] (velar). The preceding are voiced; voicelessness (in general, not just for implosives) may be indicated by a diacritic [̥], as in [ɓ̥] for a voiceless bilabial implosive.

The remaining type of stop involves a velaric ingressive airstream mechanism, and is known as a *click*. Click sounds involve dual closure in the oral tract – one velar and one forward of the velum – trapping a body of air. The more forward occlusion is released before the velar closure, drawing the air inwards. The subsequent release of the velar closure results in the click. Given the method of articulation, clicks can only have places of articulation forward of the velum, e.g. bilabial [ʘ], dental [ǀ] (or [ʇ]), alveolar [ǃ] (or [ʗ]), alveolar lateral [ǁ]. Such sounds are common in, and (as speech sounds) exclusive to, the languages of Southern Africa, such as Nama, Zulu and Xhosa (the first sound of which is a lateral click). Languages like English have clicks as non-linguistic sounds, such as the one we use to attract the attention of a horse, or to express disapproval.

3.1.1 The production of stops

Produced in isolation, all pulmonic egressive oral stops involve three clearly identifiable stages; first, there is the **closing stage**, when the active articulator is raised to come into contact with the passive articulator – for example, for the initial sound in 'dog' the blade of the tongue must be raised to the alveolar ridge. Second, there is the **closure stage**, when the articulators remain in contact and the air builds up behind the blockage. Third, there is the **release stage**, when the active articulator is lowered, allowing the air to be released with some force (hence the term 'plosives' for oral stops).

Usually, however, we do not produce stops (or any other speech sound) in isolation. When oral stops are produced in ordinary connected speech, the closing stage and/or the release stage may be missing, due to the influence of neighbouring sounds. Only the closure stage is necessary for all stops in all positions – if there is no period of closure, the sound isn't a stop.

In connected speech, stops may be produced without the closing stage when they follow another stop with the same place of articulation – that is, when they follow a **homorganic** stop. Thus the bilabial plosive [p] of 'shrimp' has no separate closing stage, since the articulators have already been raised to complete closure for the nasal stop (for which the symbol is [m]), which is also bilabial. The change from [m] to [p] is effected by raising the velum (nasal → oral) and widening the space between the vocal cords (voiced → voiceless). Similarly, there is no closing stage for the alveolar [d] in the sequence 'hot dog'; again the articulators are already in the appropriate position because of the [t] of 'hot'.

When we have a sequence of homorganic stops such as those in 'hot dog' or 'big cat', it is not only the second stop that lacks a stage; the first stop in each lacks not a closing stage, but a release stage. Rather than lowering then raising the active articulator, it simply remains in contact with the passive articulator during the production of both stops. Compare the [g]-sounds in (careful) pronunciation of 'big' in isolation with the same word in 'big cat'; in the latter case, the back of the tongue only lowers for the beginning of the 'a' in 'cat', not for the end of the 'g' in 'big'.

The release stage may also be absent in non-homorganic clusters (i.e. a sequence of sounds which are produced at different places of articulation). In a sequence such as that underlined in 'duct', the velar stop [k], here spelt 'c', has no release stage. Compare the velar stop in 'duct' with that in a careful pronunciation of 'duck'; in the latter, the release of the velar stop [k] (orthographically 'ck') is likely to be clearly audible, where for 'duct' only the release of the [t] will be heard. The lack of release for [k] here is due to the fact that the articulators are already in complete closure position at the alveolar ridge for the [t] before the back of the tongue is lowered at the end of the [k]; the air thus cannot escape from the mouth before the release of the second stop [t].

When a stop occurs at the end of a word, i.e. word-finally, before a pause, there is also often no audible release stage. This is indicated with the diacritic symbol [˥] following the symbol in question. The articulators simply remain in contact until the next chunk of speech is initiated, or until the air has dissipated in some other way (by breathing out, for example); so in a question like 'Was it a dog?' the back of the tongue may remain in complete closure with the velum for some time (e.g. for the final [g˥] of 'dog'). It should be noted that this lack of release is not found in all languages; French, for instance, tends to have fully released final stops.

3.1.2 The release stage

When there is a release stage, it may not always involve a straightforward lowering of the active articulator; the actual release may depend on the following sound in a number of ways. So, in a word like 'mutton' the [t] is released not via the lowering of the tongue tip, since this stays in place for the alveolar nasal (represented phonetically as [n]); rather, the release of the oral stop occurs when the velum is lowered for the nasal, allowing the air to escape through the nose (compare the [t] in 'mutton' with that in a careful pronunciation of 'mutt', where the alveolar stop is released orally). Release of stops via the lowering of the velum is known as nasal release, and occurs when an oral stop precedes a nasal stop.

In a similar way, when the alveolar stops [t] or [d] precede the lateral liquid [l], in words like 'beetle' and 'badly', the release is known as lateral release. In this case, the centre of the tongue tip remains in contact with the alveolar ridge for the [l], and the built-up air is released when the sides of the tongue lower (compare the [d] in 'badly' with that in 'bad').

3.1.3 Aspiration

A further important aspect of the release stage of plosives, particularly associated with voiceless stops, is the phenomenon known as *aspiration*. Compare the stops in the pairs 'pie – spy', 'tie – sty' and 'core – score'. For most English speakers (though not all from the North of England or from Scotland, for example), these should sound quite different. When the voiceless stop begins the word, as in the first member of each pair, there is likely to be an audible puff of air following the release. When the stop follows [s], as in the second member, there is no such puff of air (indeed, the stop may well sound more like its voiced counterpart in 'buy', 'die' and 'gore' respectively). Stops like those in 'pie', 'tie' and 'core', which have this audible outrush of air, are known as aspirated stops; those in 'spy', 'sty' and 'score' are known as unaspirated. Aspiration is indicated by a superscript [ʰ] following the symbol for the stop, e.g. [pʰ], [tʰ], [kʰ].

Articulatorily, what is happening is that for aspirated stops, the vocal cords remain wide open after the release of the plosive and into the initial articulation of the following segment. This means that the first part of the vowel in, say, 'pie' is actually produced without vibrating vocal cords, i.e. without voicing. Vocal cord vibration (voicing) thus only begins at some point into the production of the vowel; the onset of voicing is delayed. For unaspirated stops, such as that in 'spy', the vocal cords begin vibrating immediately upon the release of the stop; there is no delay in the onset of voicing and the following vowel segment is thus fully voiced throughout. This difference is illustrated in Figure 3.1, where a straight horizontal line indicates voicelessness, a zigzag voicing, and a vertical line the release stage of the stop (see also Section 5.2.4.4). The vowel in 'pie' and 'spy' is represented in phonetic symbols as [aɪ]; see Chapter 4.

Fig. 3.1 Aspirated [pʰ] vs. unaspirated [p]

In English, aspiration is strongest (i.e. most noticeable) in voiceless stops which occur at the beginning of stressed syllables (like those exemplified above). It may also be present, though more weakly, if the stops begin unstressed syllables, as in 'patrol', 'today' or 'consist' – compare the [p]s in 'petrol' (stressed syllable, strong aspiration) and 'patrol' (unstressed syllable, weak aspiration). Word-finally, as in 'hop', there may again be aspiration (if the stop has a release stage – see Section 3.1.1), the strength of which may vary according to accent or individual (Liverpool accents, for instance, often have strongly aspirated word-final voiceless stops). Aspiration does not, however, occur with stops that follow initial [s], as we have seen above. Aspiration thus contributes to the set of factors distinguishing potentially ambiguous sequences, such as 'peace talks' and 'pea stalks'. In a **broad phonetic transcription** (that is, one which lacks detail of phenomena such as aspiration) these two phrases have the same set of segments (RP [piːstɔːks]; symbols for vowels are introduced in Chapter 4). Despite this, they do not sound the same; hearers can usually distinguish them without too much trouble. This is in part due to the fact that in 'peace talks' the 't' is aspirated ([tʰ]), since it is in initial position in a stressed syllable, whereas in 'pea stalks' it follows [s], and thus is not aspirated ([t]).

When an aspirated stop is followed by a liquid or glide ([l], [r], [j] or [w]), in words such as 'platypus', 'crocodile', 'cue' or 'twit' respectively, the aspiration is realised as the devoicing of the sonorant. That is, the vocal cords remain open through the articulation of the liquid or glide, narrowing (and thus beginning to vibrate) only when the articulation of the vowel starts.

Phonetically, then, English has three kinds of stop: voiced, e.g. [b], voiceless unaspirated, e.g. [p] and voiceless aspirated, e.g. [pʰ]. In terms of contrasts, however, aspiration is not significant; no words are distinguished from others solely by virtue of having an aspirated versus unaspirated stop, since aspiration is entirely predictable from the position of a voiceless stop. That is, we do not distinguish [pɪt] from [pʰɪt] or [bɪt] ([ɪ] stands for the 'i' sound in 'pit'); we simply know that [pɪt] is unlikely in most forms of English, since we expect aspiration of voiceless stops in this position. This is not so for all languages, however. Languages such as Thai or Korean make a three-way distinction, so that [baa] 'shoulder', [paa] 'forest' and [pʰaa] 'to split' are all different words in Thai ([a] stands for an 'a' sound not unlike that in English 'cat'). Differences in the patterning of sounds, as in Thai and English above, will be dealt with in Chapter 8.

3.1.4 Voicing

As we have already noted, in common with other obstruents, plosives may be either voiceless (produced with an open glottis) or voiced (produced with a narrowed glottis). This gives us contrasts in English such as 'lopping' vs. 'lobbing', 'lacking' vs. 'lagging' and (in British and Southern Irish English, but not North American or Northern Irish English – see Section 3.1.6) 'latter' vs. 'ladder', where there is a difference in the voicing of the medial plosive.

While the difference is clear in these instances, it is not always so obvious. Voiceless stops remain voiceless throughout their articulation in English, but voicing is not always constant for voiced stops. Only in instances like those above, i.e. between two other voiced sounds, is an English voiced stop fully voiced. Elsewhere, such stops are likely to be wholly or partly devoiced. When in initial position, vocal cord vibration may not begin until well into the articulation of the stop; similarly, in final position, vocal cord vibration may cease well before the end of the articulation. This is indicated in transcription by the diacritic [̥] (or [°] if the symbol has a tail), as in '[b̥]eetle' or 'do[g̊]'. For some accents (West Yorkshire, for instance) there is no voicing at all in final position. This is also true in a number of other languages, such as Danish or German, but by no means for all; French, for instance, has fully voiced final stops.

The presence or absence of voicing in a plosive in English (irrespective of any positional devoicing) may affect the preceding sound in a significant way. When a voiced stop follows a liquid, nasal or vowel it causes that sound (or 'segment') to lengthen (to last longer); compare the duration of the penultimate segments in 'gulp' vs. 'bulb', 'sent' vs. 'send' and 'back' vs. 'bag'. In each case, the segment preceding the voiced stop is noticeably longer than that preceding the voiceless stop, even though the voiced stop may in fact be partly or fully devoiced due to being in final position. This means, in fact, that for many hearers, one of the main cues for deciding whether a final stop in English is voiced or voiceless is the duration of the preceding segment, rather than the realisation of the plosive segment itself.

3.1.5 Glottalisation and the glottal stop

In many kinds of English, voiceless stops may be subject to 'glottalisation' or 'glottal reinforcement'. This means that as well as closure in the oral tract, there is an accompanying (brief) closure of the vocal cords, resulting in a kind of dual articulation. This glottalisation is particularly likely for final stops in emphatic utterances, such as 'stop that!', where the final [p] and [t] may well be glottalised, but is common to some degree for many word-final voiceless stops. This sound is often transcribed in IPA by using a superscript [ʔ] after the stop symbol: [pʔ] or [tʔ]. In some kinds of English, notably North East English English (known colloquially as 'Geordie'), this glottalisation is very salient not only on final voiceless stops, but also voiceless stops occurring intervocalically (that is, between two vowels); the 'p' in a word like 'super' is heavily glottalised in this type of English, and might appropriately be transcribed [ʔp], though this is also found as a transcription for the weaker glottal reinforcement described above.

As well as being glottalised, voiceless stops may under some circumstances be replaced by a glottal stop. That is, there will be no oral closure at all, only glottal closure. The extent to which this occurs will depend on the accent of the speaker, the particular stop involved and the position of the stop. Thus, for many speakers of most kinds of British English (including RP), a [t] can be replaced by [ʔ] before a nasal, as in 'a[ʔ n]ight' ('at night') or 'Bri[ʔn̩]' ('Britain'), where the subscript [ˌ] indicates a syllabic consonant (see Sections 2.3 and 6.1). Similarly, a voiceless stop may be replaced by [ʔ] when preceding a homorganic obstruent; 'grea[ʔ s]mile' ('great smile') or 'gra[ʔ f]ruit' ('grapefruit'). Somewhat more restrictedly (though still true for many types of more recent RP), word-final [t] may be [ʔ], as in 'ra[ʔ]' ('rat'). [ʔ] for word-final [p] or [k] is not a feature of standard varieties, but does occur in a number of non-standard Englishes, such as Cockney, where [ræʔ] could represent any of 'rap', 'rat' or 'rack'. More restrictedly still, in terms of varieties though not numbers of speakers, intervocalic [t] may be a glottal stop, as in 'wa[ʔ]er' ('water') or 'bu[ʔ]er' ('butter').

Vowels may also be subject to glottal reinforcement when they occur word-initially, especially if emphatic, as 'go [ʔ]away!' or 'it's [ʔ]over!', or if there is hiatus (two juxtaposed vowels in consecutive syllables), as in 'co-[ʔ]authors'. It may also be found in a position where there might otherwise be an intrusive or linking 'r' in non-rhotic accents (i.e. accents in which an orthographic 'r' after a vowel, as in 'cart, is not pronounced) such as many kinds of English spoken in England or Australia (see Section 3.5.2.1), as in 'law [ʔ] and order' (as opposed to 'law [ɹ] and order', where [ɹ] represents an 'r' sound).

This pre-vocalic glottal stop is also found in German, though there are no restrictions on its occurrence; any vowel in initial position will be preceded by [ʔ], as in [ʔ]*Adler* ('eagle').

3.1.6 Variation in stops

As we have seen in the previous two sections, the position of a sound may well influence the exact nature of the production of the sound (nasal or lateral release, aspiration, glottalisation, etc.). When the particular realisation is due to the character of a neighbouring sound, as in the nasal or lateral release of stops, we say that the sound has **assimilated** to its neighbour(s). This section looks at some of the other ways stops, and in particular the alveolars [t] and [d], assimilate to their context.

The bilabials [p] and [b] show no significant **assimilation**, typically remaining bilabial irrespective of context. The velars similarly are relatively stable, except that they are fronted – that is, with contact closer to palatal than velar – in the context of front vowels. Compare the position of closure for the stops in 'kick' and 'cook'; the stops in 'kick' are produced noticeably further forward than the corresponding stops in 'cook'.

Unlike the bilabials and velars, the alveolars [t] and [d] show considerable variation depending on context. Monitor carefully the position of the closure for the underlined stops in the following words (spoken at normal tempo, but without the [t]s being replaced by glottal stops):

hot potato	bad boy	sad man
hot crumpet	bad girl	sad king
hot thing	bad though	sad thought

In each case, the closure for the 't' or 'd' will not be alveolar but will be at the place of articulation of the following segment. Preceding a bilabial, the closure for the 't/d' is also bilabial: 'ho[p p]otato', 'ba[b b]oy', 'sa[b m]an'; preceding velars, we get velar closure: 'ho[k k]rumpet', 'ba[g g]irl', 'sa[g k]ing'; and before dentals, closure at the teeth (indicated by a diacritic [̪]): ho[t̪ θ]ing', 'ba[d̪ ð]ough', 'sa[d̪ θ]ought'.

As well as being influenced by surrounding consonants, the alveolar stops also show variation between vowels in a number of varieties of English, though here the assimilation involves manner rather than place of articulation. A well-known instance of this is the phenomenon of 'flapping' found in many North American and Northern Irish accents of English, in which the distinction between [t] and [d] is lost (the technical term is **neutralised**) between vowels, both [t] and [d] being replaced by a sound involving voicing and a very brief contact between tongue tip and alveolar ridge. This sound is known as a voiced alveolar flap, and is transcribed as [ɾ]. Thus, for many American and Northern Irish speakers 'Adam' and 'atom' may be *homophones*, i.e. sound identical, both words having the flap for the intervocalic 't' and 'd'. Flapping occurs whenever what would be [t] or [d] in other accents occurs between two vowels, both within words as in the examples above and across word boundaries as in 'ge[ɾ] away' ('get away') or 'hi[ɾ] it' ('hit it'). One important exception to this is when the stop begins a stressed syllable, as in 'a[tʰ]end' ('attend'), where the second syllable carries the stress (compare this with the 't' in 'atom', which is flapped).

A similar process is found in many Northern English accents, affecting only the voiceless alveolar stop [t]. In these accents, the [t] is replaced by an r-sound [ɹ] when it occurs after a short vowel and the next sound is a vowel, as in 'lo[ɹ] of fun', 'ge[ɹ] off' or 'shu[ɹ] up'. Unlike flapping, this 't → r' process only rarely occurs word internally (a couple of examples being 'be̲t̲t̲er' and 'ma̲t̲t̲er'). It typically only happens across word boundaries, and even then not with all words; there is no replacement of [t] by [ɹ] across the word boundary in 'hot iron', for example.

While these processes do not involve assimilation in terms of place of articulation, which remains alveolar, it might be said that there is manner assimilation, in that the sounds replacing [t] are 'more vowel-like', being voiced (like vowels) and, at least for [ɹ], sonorant (again, like vowels) rather than obstruent. Discussion of this phenomenon will be taken up again in Chapter 10.

3.2 Affricates

Affricates are produced like plosives, in that they involve a closing stage, a closure stage and a release stage. The difference lies in the nature of the release: where for a 'standard' plosive, the active articulator is lowered swiftly and fully, allowing a sudden, unhindered explosion of air, for affricates the active articulator remains close to the passive articulator, resulting in friction as the air passes between them, as for fricatives (see Sections 2.1.5 and 3.3). Phonetically, then, affricates are similar to a stop followed by a fricative; they do not, however, behave like a sequence of two segments. Consider 'catch it' and 'cat shit'; the sound represented by 'tch' ([tʃ]) is noticeably shorter than the sequence of sounds represented by 't sh' ([t + ʃ]).

English has only two affricates, the voiceless palato-alveolar [tʃ], as in 'chimpanzee', and its voiced counterpart [dʒ] as in 'jaguar'. Both affricates can appear in all positions; word-initially, word-medially and word-finally; '[tʃ]eetah' ('cheetah'), 'lo[dʒ]er' ('lodger'), 'fu[dʒ]' ('fudge'). (The symbols [č] and [ǰ] may also be encountered for these sounds, as may [tʃ] and [dʒ].)

Affricates at other places of articulation are found in many languages; German has voiceless labio-dental [pf] in *Pferd* 'horse', and voiceless alveolar [ts] in *Zug* 'train'; Italian has a voiced alveolar [dz] in *zona* 'zone'.

3.2.1 Voicing and variation

As with all obstruents, the voiced affricate lengthens a preceding sonorant segment (nasal, liquid or vowel); compare the sonorants underlined in 'lunch' vs. 'lunge', 'belching' vs. 'Belgian', 'aitch' vs. 'age'.

There is little assimilation of the affricates in English, though the oral stop part of the articulation may be missing when they follow [n], as 'lun[ʃ]' (vs. 'lun[tʃ]') or 'spon[ʒ]' (vs. 'spon[dʒ]'). There is also some variation among speakers between word final [dʒ] and [ʒ] in loan words like 'garage', 'beige'.

3.3 Fricatives

Fricatives are produced when the active articulator is close to, but not actually in contact with, the passive articulator. This position, close approximation, means that as the air exits, it is forced through a narrow passage between the articulators, resulting in considerable friction, hence the term 'fricative'. As with the plosives, fricatives can be voiceless or voiced.

Table 3.2 Fricatives in English

Place of articulation	Voice	Symbol	Example
labio-dental	−	[f]	'fox'
	+	[v]	'vixen'
dental	−	[θ]	'moth'
	+	[ð]	'this'
alveolar	−	[s]	'snake'
	+	[z]	'zebra'
palato-alveolar	−	[ʃ]	'shrew'
	+	[ʒ]	'measure'
glottal	−	[h]	'haddock'

Note: '+' indicates the presence of voicing; '−' indicates the absence of voicing.

The majority of varieties of English have the fricatives given in Table 3.2. The glottal fricative [h] has no voiced counterpart in many Englishes, though some speakers have a breathy voice (see Section 2.1.2) [ɦ] where the sound begins a stressed syllable which follows a vowel-final non-stressed syllable, as in 'beh̲ave' or 'reh̲earsal'. The sound [h] does not occur at all, or occurs only sporadically, in many non-standard English Englishes, which thus make no distinction between words such as 'hill' and 'ill'.

A number of varieties also have a voiceless velar fricative [x]; this is particularly true of the 'Celtic' Englishes (Irish, Scottish and Welsh English) in words such as Scottish and Irish 'loc̲h̲/lough', Scottish 'dreic̲h̲' (dreary) and Welsh 'bac̲h̲' (dear).

Other languages have fricatives in other places of articulation, such as bilabial (Spanish voiced [β] in *Cub̲a*), palatal (German voiceless [ç] in *nic̲h̲t* 'not'), uvular (Afrikaans voiceless [χ] in *gog̲ga* (a small insect)) and pharyngeal (Arabic voiced [ʕ] [ʕamm] 'uncle'). A small number of languages also have fricatives involving a glottalic egressive airstream mechanism, indicated in transcription by an apostrophe, e.g. Tlingit (Alaska) voiceless alveolar [s'], voiceless velar [x'].

It is worth noting that English has a relatively large number of fricatives; many languages do not have as many differentiated places of articulation for this sound type.

3.3.1 Distribution

The labio-dentals [f] and [v], the dentals [θ] and [ð], the alveolars [s] and [z] and the voiceless palato-alveolar [ʃ] occur in all positions in English (i.e. word-intially, word-medially and word-finally), although for [ð] word-initial position is restricted to a small set of 'function words' such as articles ('the', 'this', 'that', etc.) and adverbs ('then', 'there', 'thus', etc.). The distribution for each of the voiced palato-alveolar [ʒ], the glottal [h] and the velar [x] (in those varieties that have it) is in some way restricted in English. The sound [ʒ] occurs in only a few words, and never word-initially; so, 'trea[ʒ]ure' and 'bei[ʒ]', but no words beginning with [ʒ] (apart from in loan words such as 'genre' and 'gigolo'). The glottal fricative [h] on the other hand occurs only word-initially or word-medially at the beginning of a stressed syllable, but never word-finally; so English has '[h]appy' and 'be[h]ead', but no words ending in [h]. The velar fricative [x] never occurs word-initially in those varieties which have the sound; so in Scottish English we have word-medial 'lo[x]an' (a small loch) or word-final 'drei[x]' (dreary), but no words beginning in [x].

3.3.2 Voicing

As with the stops, English fricatives – with the exception of [h] and [x] – may be voiceless or voiced, giving oppositions such as 'saf̲e' vs. 'sav̲e', 'wreat̲h̲' vs. 'wreat̲h̲e', 's̲ue' vs. 'z̲oo', and (somewhat marginally) 'ruc̲h̲e' vs. 'roug̲e'.

Again as with stops, the voiced fricatives undergo devoicing word-intitially and word-finally, typically only being fully voiced between other voiced sounds. Compare the 'v' in '<u>v</u>ague' or 'sa<u>ve</u>' with that in 'sa<u>v</u>ing'; the initial and final 'v's will be (partially) devoiced [v̥] whereas the 'v' in 'sa<u>v</u>ing' is voiced all through its production [v].

The voicing of a fricative also affects the length of the preceding sonorant (nasal, liquid or vowel). Voiced fricatives lengthen the duration of any sonorant they follow; compare the highlighted sonorants in 'fe<u>n</u>ce' and 'fe<u>n</u>s', 'she<u>l</u>f' and 'she<u>l</u>ve', 'f<u>a</u>ce' and 'ph<u>a</u>se'.

3.3.3 Variation in fricatives

The labio-dental fricatives [f] and [v] do not show a great deal of assimilation, though [v] may often become voiceless word-finally preceding a voiceless obstruent, as in 'ha[f] to' ('have to'), 'mo[f]e slowly' ('move slowly'), 'o[f] course'. Indeed, in faster speech, the sound may be lost altogether in unstressed function words such as 'of' and 'have' as in 'piece of cake' or 'could have been', where 'of' and 'have' have the same pronunciation as the unstressed indefinite article 'a' (the symbol for this is [ə], known as **schwa**). This loss of a segment is known as *elision*.

The dental fricatives [θ] and [ð] are also subject to elision when they precede [s] or [z], as in 'clothes' (homophonous with the verb 'close') or 'months' (pronounced as 'mo[ns]', rhyming with 'dunce'). In a number of varieties of English [θ] and [ð] may be replaced (either entirely or intermittently) by [f] and [v] respectively; thus for a number of South Eastern English and Southern U.S. English accents, 'three' and 'free' may sound identical, that is be homophones. In some Scottish varieties, on the other hand, word-initial [θ] and [ð] may be replaced by [s] as in '<u>th</u>ousand' and [ɾ] as in '<u>the</u>' respectively. Southern Irish English also often has a dental-stop-like realisation of these sounds ([t̪] and [d̪] respectively). In English in general in fast speech, word-initial [ð] (which, as was pointed out above, is restricted to a small set of 'function words') often assimilates entirely to a preceding alveolar sound; 'i[n n]e pub' ('in the pub'), 'a[l l]e time' ('all the time'), 'i[z z]ere any beer?' ('is there any beer?').

The alveolars [s] and [z] are often assimilated to a following palatal glide [j] or palato-alveolar fricative [ʃ] by retracting the active articulator to a palato-alveolar position, being realised as [ʃ] and [ʒ] respectively, as in 'mi[ʃ j]ou' ('miss you'), 'it wa[ʒ j]ellow' ('it was yellow') or 'ki[ʃ ʃ]eila' ('kiss Sheila'). There is also variation among speakers of British English as to whether words such as 'issue', 'assure', 'seizure' have a sequence of [s j]/[z j] or [ʃ]/[ʒ], with the assimilated forms being the more common, even among RP speakers. Although these words have in common a high back round vowel [u] or [ʊ] (see Section 4.4.6) following the segment(s) in question, the same alternation is not found for all words; 'assume' for instance is more commonly [sj].

The palato-alveolars [ʃ] and [ʒ] show little variation, though many of the (few) words which end with [ʒ] may variably have pronunciations ending in the affricate [ʤ] (see Section 3.2.1), e.g. 'garage', 'beige', etc. The sounds [ʃ] and [ʒ] often also involve some degree of lip-rounding, particularly after round vowels (see Section 4.1), again variable among speakers.

The glottal fricative [h], as we have seen, has no contrastive voiced counterpart, does not occur word-finally and is more or less absent in many non-standard English Englishes (though this is stigmatised). The sound [h] is also 'dropped' by all speakers in unstressed pronouns and auxiliaries such as 'her', 'him', 'have', etc.; the normal pronunciation of 'I could have liked him' does not include any instances of [h]. The sound [h] is also not present for some speakers in the words 'hotel' and 'historic(al)', and for most American English speakers in 'herb'. In words where the 'h' precedes the glide [j] (see Section 3.6) – such words typically involve an orthographic 'hu' sequence – such as 'human' or 'huge', the initial sound may well be the palatal fricative [ç] in many varieties. In North American Englishes there may be no [h] at all in these words, which thus begin with the glide [j].

3.4 Nasals

As was mentioned in Section 3.1, nasals are a variety of stop; they are formed with complete closure in the oral tract. The difference between nasal and oral stops is that for nasals the velum is lowered, allowing air into (and out through) the nasal cavity. Nasals are sonorants (unlike oral stops), and are thus typically voiced only – though a few languages (e.g. Burmese) do contrast voiced and voiceless nasals. English has nasal stops in the same places of articulation as it has oral stops: bilabial [m] (as in 'moth'), alveolar [n] (as in 'nuthatch') and velar [ŋ] (as in 'wing'). Other languages have nasal stops in other places of articulation, e.g. dental [n̪], as in Yanyuwa (Australia) [wun̪un̪u] 'cooked', palatal [ɲ], as in French *agneau* [aɲo] ('lamb').

3.4.1 Distribution and variation

The bilabial and alveolar nasals [m] and [n] occur word-intially, word-medially and word-finally in English: e.g. '[m]ill', 'tu[m]our', 'ra[m]', '[n]il', 'tu[n]a', 'ra[n]'. The velar [ŋ], on the other hand, cannot occur word-initially in English; 'si[ŋ]er' ('singer') and 'ra[ŋ]' ('rang'), but there are no words beginning with [ŋ]. Note that this is true of English but not for all languages with [ŋ], e.g. Burmese [ŋâ] 'fish' (the circumflex over the vowel indicates a falling tone, which does not concern us here; see Section 6.3). In some varieties of English, such as North West or West Midland English English, and Long Island American English, [ŋ] is always followed by an oral velar stop, either [k] 'thi[ŋk]' or [g] 'thi[ŋg]' (vs. 'thi[ŋ]' elsewhere), 'si[ŋg]er' (vs. 'si[ŋ]er').

Positionally, [ŋ] shows no important assimilation; there is, however, some socio-linguistically governed alternation between [ŋ] and [n] for the inflection '-ing', which may be (variably) either [ɪŋ] or [ɪn]. The bilabial

[m] may be labio-dental [ɱ] before the labio-dental fricatives [f] and [v] ('so[ɱ f]un'). As with the oral stops, it is the alveolar [n] that exhibits most assimilation, agreeing in place of articulation with the following segment. When the alveolar nasal is next to a bilabial segment, the result is typically [m], not [n]; so 'ri[bm̩]', 'i[m p]aris'. When it precedes labio-dentals, we get [ɱ]; 'i[ɱ v]ain'. Before dentals, a dental nasal [n̪] occurs; 'o[n̪ θ]ursday'. Before velars, we get the velar nasal [ŋ]; 'te[ŋ k]ups'.

3.5 Liquids

Liquid is a cover term given to many 'l' and 'r' sounds (or *laterals* and *rhotics* respectively) in the languages of the world. In a broad sense, what liquids have in common is that they are produced with unhindered airflow (which distinguishes them from obstruents) but nonetheless involve some kind of obstruction in the oral tract (unlike glides and vowels, which are articulated with open approximation). However, the exact nature of the obstruction, particularly in the case of those sounds grouped together as rhotics, is a complicated matter cross-linguistically which we will not deal with in any detail here.

Liquids are sonorants and, as such, are typically voiced. Voiceless liquids do occur (Scottish Gaelic has [ɾ̥], for example), but often voicelessness in 'l' and 'r' sounds also involves friction, as in the Welsh voiceless alveolar lateral [ɬ] in *llan* 'church' and, as such, these sounds are obstruents rather than liquids proper.

3.5.1 Laterals

With laterals there is contact between the active articulator (the tongue) and the passive articulator (the roof of the mouth), but only the central part of the tongue is involved in this contact (this is known as **mid-sagittal** contact); there is no contact for (at least one of) the sides of the tongue. The air is thus free to exit along the channels down the sides of the oral tract, hence the name lateral.

English has the lateral [l], as in 'lion'. For this sound, the mid-sagittal contact is between the tongue blade and the alveolar ridge; [l] is an alveolar lateral. Laterals at other places are also found: certain varieties of Spanish have a palatal lateral [ʎ] as in *calle* 'street', Mid-Waghi (Australia) has a velar lateral [ʟ] as in [aʟaʟe] 'dizzy'.

3.5.1.1 Distribution and variation

The English alveolar lateral can appear word-initially, word-medially and word-finally, as in 'louse', 'bullock' and 'gull' respectively. For many accents of English there is considerable variation in the articulation of [l] according to position. For most speakers, as we have seen in Section 3.1.3, following a voiceless obstruent the lateral devoices, so 'p[l̥]ay' vs. '[l]ay', etc.

There is also a noticeable difference for many speakers between the lateral in 'loot' compared to that in 'tool' or 'milk'. The 'l' in initial position has alveolar contact and nothing more; that in 'tool' and 'milk' has the same alveolar contact and in addition a simultaneous raising of the back of the tongue towards the velum (similar to the position for the vowel in RP or GenAm '<u>boo</u>k'). This latter sound thus has a secondary velar articulation, and is known as velarised or **dark 'l'**, for which the symbol is [ɫ]. The non-velarised version is known as **clear 'l'**. Clear 'l' occurs word-initially ('[l]uck') including before [j] for those speakers with pronunciations like '[lj]ute' (the musical instrument) and word-medially before a vowel ('pi[l]ow', 'hem[l]ock'). Dark 'l' occurs elsewhere, i.e. word-finally ('fi[ɫ]'), before a consonant ('fi[ɫ]m') and syllabically ('bott[ɫ]'). In some accents such as Cockney and other South East English varieties, and American varieties like that of Philadelphia, the dark 'l' may have little or no alveolar contact, resulting in a vowel-like realisation; [fɪo] 'fill', where [o] is a high mid back vowel (see Section 4.4.5).

Not all varieties of English have this clear vs. dark 'l'; in many North West English English, Lowland Scottish or American accents, laterals are fairly dark irrespective of position; in Highland Scottish, Southern Irish and North East English varieties, on the other hand, laterals tend to be clear in all positions.

3.5.2 Rhotics

A wide variety of articulations are subsumed under the general heading of rhotic, even within English. Rhotics include:

- ❑ the alveolar trill [r], in which the tongue blade vibrates repeatedly against the alveolar ridge (this is sometimes heard in Scottish accents)
- ❑ the alveolar tap [ɾ], a single tap of the tongue blade against the alveolar ridge (heard more commonly in Scotland)
- ❑ the alveolar continuant [ɹ], produced with the tongue blade raised towards the alveolar ridge and the sides of the tongue in contact with the molars, forming a narrow channel down the middle of the tongue (heard in many kinds of English English, including RP)
- ❑ the retroflex [ɻ], produced in a way similar to [ɹ] but with the tongue blade curled back to a post-alveolar position (heard in many North American and South West English Englishes)
- ❑ the uvular roll [ʀ] or fricative [ʁ], respectively produced with the back of the tongue vibrating against or in close approximation to the velum (heard in rural Northumberland and parts of Scotland; this is also the kind of rhotic often heard in French and High German)

In terms of articulatory phonetics these sounds do not have much in common; taps and trills involve contact between active and passive articulators, fricative rhotics involve close approximation and continuants involve neither contact nor friction. Grouping them together as a class has more to do with their behaviour in the language, that is, with phonology. As far as English is concerned, they are the sounds represented orthographically by 'r' (or 'rr', etc.); whatever kind of 'r' sound they may have, all English speakers have their particular variant, or one of their variants, at the beginning of a word like 'rat'.

3.5.2.1 Distribution

One of the major dialect divisions in the English-speaking world concerns the distribution of the rhotic; all varieties have pre-vocalic 'r', as in 'raccoon' or 'carrot', but not all have a rhotic in words like 'bear' or 'cart'. Accents which have some kind of 'r' in all these words are known as *rhotic accents*; those with only prevocalic 'r' (that is, no 'r' in the last two words above) are known as *non-rhotic accents*. Non-rhotic accents of English include most varieties of English English, Welsh English, Australasian Englishes, South African English, some West Indian Englishes and North American varieties such as Southern states, New England and African-American Vernacular English. Rhotic accents include most North American English, Scottish and Irish English, some West Indian Englishes, and English English varieties such as the South West and (parts of) Lancashire. As English orthography suggests, this difference is due to a historical sound change; the rhotic was lost post-vocalically (i.e. word-finally or before a consonant) in the precursors to those accents which are now non-rhotic, but retained in the others.

In fact, even in non-rhotic accents the 'r' at the end of words like 'bear' is not always absent; compare non-rhotic 'bear' pronounced in isolation or in the phrase 'bear pit' with the same word in 'bear attack'. In the first two instances, there is no rhotic, as expected; but in 'bear attack' there is an 'r' sound at the end of 'bear'. Whenever a word-final orthographic 'r' precedes a vowel sound, the 'ɪ' is pronounced; this phenomenon is known as *linking 'r'*. This occurs not only across word boundaries, as in the example just given or 'far away', 'major attraction', etc., but also within (morphologically complex) words; compare 'soar' in isolation with 'soaring', 'beer' with 'beery', or 'meteor' with 'meteoric', in which the first member of each pair has no 'r' sound, but the rhotic is present when a vowel-initial ending is added. For reasons to do with the history of English sounds, this word-final linking 'r' is limited to following the vowels [uː], [ɔː], [ɜː], as in 'car', 'bore', 'fur' respectively, and [ə] as in 'water', 'beer', etc.

Related to linking 'r' is the phenomenon known as *intrusive 'r'*. This is the occurrence in non-rhotic accents of a 'word-final' rhotic which is not there in the spelling; compare 'tuna' pronounced in isolation with the same word in 'tuna alert'. In the second instance an 'r' has been inserted between the two vowels, just as if 'tuna' ended in orthographic 'r', 'tuna [ɪ] alert'. Intrusive 'r' can be seen as the analogical extension of linking 'r', since it too only occurs following the vowels [ɑː], [ɔː], and [ə] as in 'Shah of Iran', 'paw or hoof', 'America in spring'. There are no words in English which end in [ɜː] which do not have historical (orthographic) 'r'. It is particularly prevalent after [ə]; some speakers may make a conscious effort to avoid intrusive 'r' after the other vowels. It is also variably heard word-internally for some speakers, so 'soaring' and 'saw[ɪ]ing' may be homophones, both with 'r'.

3.5.2.2 Variation

As well as the regional differences outlined above, rhotics are subject to considerable positional variation. As with the lateral, following an aspirated voiceless stop a rhotic is devoiced, so '[pr̥ay', '[tr̥ee', '[kr̥ab'. Following [t] and [d] the rhotic will typically become fricativised, though there is no separate symbol for this, as in 'tree' and 'dream'. In a number of English English accents which typically have the continuant [ɹ], this may become a tap [ɾ] between vowels, as in 've[ɾ]y', and after [θ] and [ð], as in 'th[ɾ]ee' and 'with [ɾ]ats'. For some speakers, there may also be a degree of lip-rounding associated with the rhotic, even when there is no following round vowel; indeed, the tongue articulation may be lost altogether, leaving just lip-rounding, resulting in a segment that sounds not unlike a [w]. This is often considered affected, and was typically a feature of upper-class (or would-be upper-class) English English. However, it is now also heard in working-class and lower-middle-class speech in South Eastern England (often called Estuary English).

3.6 Glides

In articulatory terms, glides are rather more like vowels (see Chapter 4) than consonants, since there is no contact of any kind between the articulators; indeed, an alternative term for such sounds is *semi-vowel*. They behave like consonants, however, in that they do not form syllabic nuclei; rather, they appear at the edge of syllables, as in the first sound of 'yes'. They are included here then for reasons more to do with their phonology than their phonetics; that is, their behaviour with respect to the other sounds of the language, rather than the details of their articulation (although it does also seem to be true that a typical glide articulation involves the articulators being somewhat closer together than for an equivalent vowel articulation).

English has two glides: the palatal [j] as in 'yes' and the labial-velar [w] as in 'weigh'. The palatal [j] involves an articulation similar to that for the vowel [i] (where [i] is a vowel sound like that in 'beat'), with the front of the tongue close to the palate; the labial-velar [w] is similar to [u] (where [u] is a vowel sound like that in 'shoe'), with rounded lips and the back of the tongue raised toward the velum. These two glides are by far the most common cross-linguistically, though other glides are occasionally found; French, for example, has a labial-palatal [ɥ] (similar to the front round vowel [y]) in words like *lui* [lɥi] 'him'.

3.6.1 Distribution

English [j] appears freely in word-initial position before a vowel; '[j]ield', '[j]es', '[j]ak', '[j]acht', '[j]awn', '[j]ou', etc. In a word-initial cluster, [j] is restricted to appearing before the vowels [uː] and [ʊə] (or some variant of [ʊə] such as English English [ɔː]; see Section 4.4.6 for further details), as in 'm[j]ute' and 'p[j]ure', except for many speakers in East Anglia, who have no [j] at all in these words. In non-word-initial clusters, [j] may also appear before [ə], as in 'fail[j]ure'. The exact range of consonants [j] may follow will depend on the variety of English in question; many forms of North American English have a more restricted set than British English varieties in that [j] cannot follow the alveolars [t], [d], [s], [z], [n] and [l], and the dental [θ] in words like 'tutor', 'dune', 'assume', 'resume', 'newt', 'lute' and 'enthuse' (though it is found after [n] and [l] in unaccented syllables; 'ten[j]ure', 'val[j]ue'). Even in British English, many words like 'lute' or 'suit' typically no longer have [j] for large numbers of speakers, and in some English varieties (e.g. Cockney, parts of the West Midlands and the North West), [j] may have a distribution similar to that found in North America.

The labial-velar [w] appears freely word-initially; '[w]e', '[w]est', '[w]ag', '[w]atch', '[w]ar' '[w]oo', etc. As part of a cluster, there are no restrictions on the following vowel ('t[w]it', 't[w]enty', 'q[w]arter', etc.), but English does not allow [w] after consonants other than [t], [d], [k], [s], [θ] and the sequence [sk]; 't[w]in', 'd[w]arf', 'q[w]it', 's[w]ay', 'th[w]art', 'sq[w]at'. The sound [w] may also follow [g], but only in loanwords like the proper name 'G[w]ynneth'.

The question of whether glides appear following vowels is to some extent again a phonological question. The word 'my' contains a vowel sequence, known as a diphthong, which may be represented either as a sequence of two vowels [aɪ] or as a vowel + glide [aj]. For some speakers, words such as 'here' or 'lower' may involve an intervocalic glide; [hijə] and [lowə] (as opposed to RP [hɪə] and [ləʊə], for example).

3.6.2 Variation

The articulation of [j] varies according to the following vowel; the front of the tongue is higher before high vowels (as in '[j]east'), lower before low vowels (as in '[j]ak').

Following voiceless obstruents, [j], as with other sonorants, is subject to devoicing; 'p[j]ewter'. Particularly following voiceless stops in stressed syllables, this may lead to friction, resulting in the palatal fricative [ç] rather than a devoiced glide. As was noted in Section 3.3.3, this is especially noticeable with the sequence [h] + [j], which may well coalesce, giving rise to pronunciations like '[ç]uman' ('human').

One possibility for sequences of [t] or [d] + [j] is that the two segments combine to form a palato-alveolar affricate, [ʧ] or [ʤ] respectively, as in '[ʧ]une' ('tune') or '[ʤ]une' ('dune'). This may also happen across word boundaries, as in 'hit you' [hɪʧə] or 'did you' [dɪʤə]. In a similar way, sequences of [s] or [z] + [j] may combine to form the palato-alveolar fricatives [ʃ] and [ʒ], both word-internally as in 'a[ʃ]ume' ('assume'), 're[ʒ]ume' ('resume') and across word boundaries as in 'mi[ʃ] you' ('miss you'), 'wa[ʒ] young' ('was young').

As with [j], the articulation of the labial-velar [w] will vary according to the height of the following vowel; the tongue is higher before high vowels ('[w]e'), lower before low vowels ('[w]as'). Furthermore, the degree of lip rounding will also vary according to the following vowel; the lips are more rounded before round vowels ('[w]oo'), less rounded before unround vowels ('[w]ept').

Following voiceless obstruents [w] devoices, and as with [j], this may result in friction being audible, especially after voiceless stops; 't[w̥]it' (devoicing) or 't[ʍ]it' (voiceless labial-velar fricative).

In some varieties, particulary Scottish, Irish and North American Englishes, the voiceless labial-velar fricative [ʍ] occurs as a speech sound in its own right, since these varieties have contrasts between words such as 'witch' and 'which', 'Wales' and 'whales', 'weather' and 'whether', etc., with the first member of each pair having the glide [w] and the second member having the fricative [ʍ]. For other speakers, these words are homophones, both having the glide.

3.7 An inventory of English consonants

Table 3.3 illustrates the range of consonants typically found in (varieties of) English.

Table 3.3 Typical English consonants

I *Obstruents*			
Ii *Stops*		Symbol	Examples
bilabial	voiceless unaspirated	[p]	happy, tap
	voiceless aspirated	[pʰ]	pit
	voiced	[b]	bit, rubber, lob
alveolar	voiceless unaspirated	[t]	writer, hit
	voiceless aspirated	[tʰ]	tip
	voiced	[d]	dip, rider, bid
	voiced flap	[ɾ]	writer, rider (North American English)
velar	voiceless unaspirated	[k]	looking, tick
	voiceless aspirated	[kʰ]	kit
	voiced	[g]	game, muggy, dog
glottal	voiceless	[ʔ]	writer, hit (many British English varieties)
Iii *Affricates*			
palato-alveolar	voiceless	[tʃ] ([č])	chuck, butcher, catch
	voiced	[dʒ] ([ǰ])	jug, lodger, fudge
Iiii *Fricatives*			
labio-dental	voiceless	[f]	fun, loafer, stuff
	voiced	[v]	very, liver, dive
dental	voiceless	[θ]	thin, frothing, death
	voiced	[ð]	then, loathing, bathe
alveolar	voiceless	[s]	sin, icing, fuss
	voiced	[z]	zoo, rising, booze
palato-alveolar	voiceless	[ʃ] ([š])	ship, rasher, lush
	voiced	[ʒ] ([ž])	treasure, rouge

| glottal | voiceless | | [h] | hop |
| velar | voiceless | | [x] | loch (Irish Eng, Sc Eng, Welsh Eng) |

II Sonorants
IIi Nasals

bilabial		[m]	man, tummy, rum
alveolar		[n]	nod, runner, gin
velar		[ŋ]	drinker, thing

IIii Liquids

alveolar	'clear'	[l]	long, mellow
lateral	'dark' (velarised)	[ɫ]	dull
alveolar		[ɹ]	run, very (also car, cart in rhotic
rhotic			varieties – e.g. Scottish English,
			North American English)

IIiii Glides

| palatal | | [j] | yes |
| labial-velar | | [w] | with |

Further reading

Ladefoged (2005) is an accessible textbook for greater detail on the production of consonants and vowels (see also the further readings for Chapter 2). For a reference book on the articulatory and acoustic detail of the sounds of a large number of languages, see Ladefoged and Maddieson (1996) and Ladefoged (2001). For English there is Gimson (2008). Works referring to a wide variety of Englishes include Trudgill and Hannah (2008) and Wells (1982).

Exercises

1   Describe the articulation of the following sounds. Be sure to include information about the path of the airflow, the state of the vocal cords, the position of the velum and any obstruction in the oral cavity.

  a. [b]   b. [ŋ]   c. [tʃ]
  d. [s]   e. [θ]

2   Assuming the consonants of English, indicate the symbol representing the sound described by each of the following:

  a. voiceless alveolar stop
  b. voiced dental fricative
  c. voiced labial-velar glide
  d. voiceless velar stop
  e. voiced alveolar nasal (stop)

3   Describe each of the following symbols in words. Example: [d] = voiced alveolar stop.

  a. [b]   b. [m]   c. [v]
  d. [dʒ]   e. [ɹ]

4   Identify the difference in articulation between the following groups of
    sounds. For example, [p b t g] differ from [f s ʃ θ] in that the sounds in
    the first set are all stops and the sounds in the second set are fricatives.

    a. [p t s k]   vs.   [b d z g]
    b. [b d g]   vs.   [m n ŋ]
    c. [n l ɹ]   vs.   [t d s]
    d. [p b f v m]   vs.   [t d s z n]
    e. [w j]   vs.   [l ɹ]

4

Vowels

Where the last chapter examined the articulation of consonants, this chapter focuses on vowels. After establishing their articulation and general classification and considering the vowel space, we turn specifically to the vowels of English. These (along with occasional illustrations from other languages) we discuss relative to the areas of the vowel space in which they appear, taking in turn the high front, mid front, low front, low back, mid back, high back and central areas. Following this broad overview of English vowels, we describe several specific vowel systems, including Received Pronunciation, General American, Northern English English and Lowland Scottish English.

4.1 Vowel classification

Vowels are articulated in a manner different to that of consonants: the articulators are far enough apart to allow the airflow to exit unhindered, that is, with open approximation. Given this, the manner of articulation classifications used for consonants are inappropriate for vowels. Moreover, vowels are produced in a smaller area of the vocal tract – the palatal and velar regions – which means that the consonantal place specifications are also inappropriate. Further, given that vowels are sonorants, they are typically voiced, hence the voiced/voiceless distinction important for consonants is generally unnecessary. (Having said that, voiceless vowels are found in some languages, such as Japanese, Ik (Uganda) and a number of Native American languages of the North West. The status of these vowels is not always clear: more often than not, as in Japanese, voiceless vowels are positional variants of voiced counterparts.) A small number of languages have vowels produced with other glottal states, such as the breathy voiced or murmured vowels of Gujarati (India).

There is nonetheless an established three-term classification system for vowels similar to that for consonants. Rather than manner as such, we talk of *vowel height*, determined, like consonantal manner, by the distance between the articulators: the higher the tongue, the higher the vowel, with the classifications being **high**, **mid** and **low**, with intermediate terms **high-mid** and **low-mid** being available if necessary. (The alternative terms 'close' and 'open', for high and low respectively, are sometimes used.) The vowels in English 'see', 'set' and 'car' are high, mid and low respectively.

Parallel to consonantal place, vowels are also classified horizontally, as **front**, **central** and **back**, referring to which part of the tongue is highest, with front being equivalent to palatal and back equivalent to velar. The vowels in most varieties of English 'sit', 'sir' and 'soon' are front, central and back respectively.

The third classification has to do with the attitude of the lips, which are either **rounded** or **unrounded** when making vowel sounds. If you look in a mirror, you should be able to see that when you produce the vowel in English 'see' your lips are unrounded (or spread), while for the vowel in 'sue' your lips are rounded.

Lip rounding is the only aspect of vowel articulation that is relatively easy to see or feel for yourself; unlike consonantal manner and place, vowel height and the front/back distinctions are much harder to judge without the aid of special equipment. Indeed, when techniques such as X-ray photography are used, it can be seen that the dimensions we have been discussing here are not necessarily entirely accurate. This is particularly true of vowel height; the highest point of the tongue for a 'mid' vowel like [ɔ] (as in 'sort') may well be lower than that for a 'low' vowel like [a] (as in 'sat') (see Figure 4.1). Despite this, the term vowel height is retained as a 'convenient fiction'.

Vowel sounds can thus be referred to in terms of **height**, **backness** and *rounding*. The vowel in 'fish' is classified as a high front unround vowel. That in 'horse' is a low-mid back round vowel.

There are a number of other distinctions which are relevant to the description of vowels, such as how long the vowel lasts (*vowel length*), whether the velum is raised or lowered (*nasality*), whether or not the tongue remains in the same position during the production of the vowel (*monophthong* vs. *diphthong*); these distinctions will be dealt with in the following sections.

4.2 The vowel space and Cardinal Vowels

For the moment, we will concentrate on the major classifications just outlined. The dimensions of high vs. low and front vs. back allow us to establish a limit to vowel articulation, known as the vowel space, outside which we are no longer talking about vowels. If the tongue is any higher than for the highest high vowel, or further back than for the furthest back back vowel, the articulation isn't a vowel, but a consonant, since there will no longer be open approximation.

To illustrate the vowel space, produce the vowel sound in English 'see' or 'we', then gradually lower and retract the tongue while still producing sound. You should move from the vowel in 'see' through a series of other vowels sounds, including ones something like those in English 'say', 'set' and 'sat' for example, finally reaching the vowel sound in 'car'. What you have done is started with a high front unround vowel [i] and moved gradually through high-mid, low-mid and low front vowels like [e], [ɛ] and [a] respectively, ending up at a low back unround vowel [ɑ]. If you now start with the 'car' vowel and raise the tongue while gradually rounding the lips, you should move through another series of vowels including

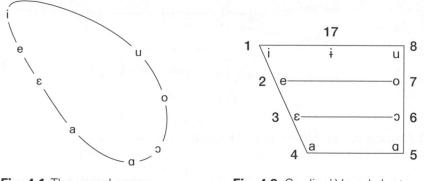

Fig. 4.1 The vowel space   Fig. 4.2 Cardinal Vowel chart

something like the low-mid back round vowel of 'sort' [ɔ], to the high back round vowel of 'sue' [u].

If we plotted a graph showing the highest points of the tongue along these two trajectories, we would come up with a visual representation of the vowel space like that in Figure 4.1, and we could indicate the positions of any other vowel within the space.

The most common way of representing the vowel space, however, is rather more stylised, being in terms of a quadrilateral, shown in Figure 4.2. This figure, known as the *Cardinal Vowel* chart, was first proposed by the linguist Daniel Jones in the 1920s, and has been the basis for vowel classification ever since. It shows the tongue position for the highest, furthest forward vowel [i] and the lowest, furthest back vowel [ɑ], with six other approximately equidistant divisions indicated, giving a series of 'cardinal' vowels, numbered one to eight moving anti-clockwise round the chart: 1[i] 2[e] 3[ɛ] 4[a] 5[ɑ] 6[ɔ] 7[o] 8[u]. Cardinals (C) 1–5 are all unround vowels; C6–8 are round. The consideration of lip rounding allows for a further eight 'secondary cardinals' which have the same height and degree of backness as C1–C8, but the opposite rounding value to the first eight: 9[y] 10[ø] 11[œ] 12[ɶ] 13[ɒ] 14[ʌ] 15[ɤ] 16[ɯ]. Cardinals 9–13 are round, C14–16 are unround. A further pair of vowels – the high central unround 17[ɨ] and the high central round 18[ʉ] – give a total of eighteen cardinal vowels.

Secondary cardinals 9–16 and 18 are at the same place of articulation as 1–8 and 17 respectively, with the opposite lip rounding.

It should be recalled that this chart does not represent an accurate anatomical diagram of the vowel space, but an idealised version of it, based more on perceptual than actual articulatory distances between vowels. The picture it presents is rather more accurate in acoustic phonetic terms; see Chapter 5 for some discussion of this issue.

It should also be noted that the positions on the chart are not necessarily those for the vowels for any particular language; rather they indicate the limits of vowelness, hence the term 'cardinal'. They give reference points against which specific vowels in specific languages can be indicated; thus

Fig. 4.3 Positions of [i] in German and English

English [i] in 's<u>ee</u>' is somewhat lower and more retracted than cardinal [i], whereas German [i] in s<u>i</u>e 'she' is closer to C1, as shown in Figure 4.3.

4.3 Further classifications

As was suggested in Section 4.2, factors other than the classifications given so far are relevant to a full description of vowel sounds. Consider the English words 'sit' and 'seat'; you should be able to hear that the vowel in 's<u>ea</u>t' [iː] is considerably longer lasting than that in 's<u>i</u>t' [ɪ]. While there are other differences between the vowels ([ɪ] is also lower and more central than [iː]), one of the most obvious differences is their length: [ɪ] is a short vowel, [iː] is long (the colon indicates a long vowel). Long vowels are typically 50–100 per cent longer than short vowels, and are sometimes represented by doubling the symbol (rather than using a colon) to indicate this; thus, [ii] for the vowel in 'see'. This notation also represents long vowels as being in some ways similar to diphthongs (discussed later in this section).

So as well as differing in terms of 'quality' (height, backness, etc.) vowels can also differ in terms of 'quantity'. While length in most kinds of English is never the sole factor distinguishing between vowels (as in 'sit' vs. 'seat'), this is not always the case for all languages. For example, Danish læsse 'to load' is distinguished from læse 'to read' purely by the length of the first vowel; [lɛsə] vs. [lɛːsə] (the [ə] represents a vowel sound like that at the beginning of '<u>a</u>bout'). Similarly, in a number of Scottish and Northern Irish varieties, length may be the only factor distinguishing between pairs of words like 'road' [rod] and 'rowed' [roːd], or 'daze' [dez] and 'days' [deːz] (for most English speakers, these words will be homophones).

A further important distinction between vowel types is seen in pairs like 'see' vs. 'sigh'. For the duration of the vowel in 's<u>ee</u>' the tongue stays in (pretty much) the same position, but for 'sigh' the highest point of the tongue shifts its position during the articulation of the vowel, starting low then raising. Try saying 'see' then 'sigh' with a lollipop stick in your mouth; the stick should remain relatively still for 'see' but should move for 'sigh'. Vowels which are relatively steady are known as monophthongs and are represented by a single vowel symbol, like [i] (or [iː]/[ii] for long monophthongs as in 'see'). Those which involve tongue movement are known as diphthongs and are represented by two symbols, the first showing the approximate starting position of the tongue, the second its approximate finishing position; thus, the vowel in 'sigh' might be transcribed as [aɪ], since the highest point of the tongue starts in a low front position as for [a], then is raised towards high front [ɪ]. Diphthongs are typically similar in duration to long vowels, though some languages, such as Icelandic, have short diphthongs. Diphthongs are sometimes represented as a 'vowel + glide' sequence, thus [aj] rather than [aɪ] for the vowel in 'sigh'. The choice between such representations depends on phonological rather than phonetic arguments, which we will not go into here. We will continue to represent diphthongs with a sequence of two vowel symbols.

Finally, as with consonants, it is possible to distinguish between vowels by considering the state of the velum; vowels produced with a lowered velum are known as **nasal vowels** and those produced with raised velum are known as oral vowels. French contrasts the two types in pairs such as *banc* [bɑ̃] 'bench' vs. *bas* [bɑ] 'low', where a diacritic '~' (tilde) indicates a nasal vowel. English doesn't make contrasts of this sort, but does have **nasalised vowels**; a vowel preceding a nasal stop will be produced with the velum lowered in anticipation of the following consonant, as in 'bean' [bĩːn]. That is, the vowel assimilates to the nasality of the following stop.

4.4 The vowels of English

One of the difficulties with describing 'the vowels of English' is that English speakers don't all have the same ones. We have already pointed out considerable variation with respect to consonants in different types of English, but there is much more variation when it comes to vowels. As with the consonants, such variation is in part to do with the regional origins of the speaker, and in part to do with sociolinguistic factors like social class and age.

For instance, not all speakers have the same vowel in any particular word. Take a word like 'book'; if you look this up in a pronunciation dictionary, it will give the vowel as the high back round [ʊ]; this is the RP (Received Pronunciation) and GenAm (General American) version: [bʊk]. But by no means all English speakers pronounce 'book' in this way. For many speakers in parts of Northern England, it has a longer, higher vowel [uː]; in Scotland, it may well have a high central [ʉ]; many younger Southern English speakers have a high-mid back unround vowel [ɤ]; a number of North American varieties also have an unround vowel.

Similarly, different types of English may well have different numbers of vowels in their inventories; RP is usually considered to have 19 or 21 distinct vowel sounds, but many varieties of Scottish English have only 10–14 – for example, Scottish English typically does not distinguish between 'pool' and 'pull', both having [ʉ] (as opposed to RP and other varieties with [uː] in 'pool' and [ʊ] in 'pull'). See Section 4.5.4.

The distribution of vowels among word sets also differs from one variety to another; so while both Northern and Southern English English have [ɑː] in 'car' or 'father', and both have a low front vowel (Northern [a]), Southern [æ]) in words like 'c<u>a</u>t' and 'l<u>a</u>dder', Northern varieties (in common with most other kinds of English) have [a] in words like 'p<u>a</u>ss', 'l<u>au</u>gh' and 'd<u>a</u>nce', while Southern varieties have [ɑː].

In the following sections we will look at the various 'cells' or divisions of the Cardinal Vowel chart, and discuss the vowels found in a number of the major varieties of English. Diphthongs will be treated under their starting point; so RP [eɪ], as in 'd<u>ay</u>' will be found under mid front vowels, [ɔɪ] as in 'b<u>oy</u>' under mid back vowels.

4.4.1 High front vowels

Most Englishes have two high front vowels: the long monophthong [iː], as in 'see' and the short monophthong [ɪ] as in 'sit'. As well as differing in length, the two vowels are also different in quality, with [ɪ] being somewhat lower and more centralised than [iː]. This distinction is often referred to as **tense** [iː] versus **lax** [ɪ]. Although [iː] is classified as a long vowel, it is in fact often not a pure monophthong; the highest point of the tongue may well start lower and more centralised, raising and fronting during the articulation, giving something like [ɪi]. Many kinds of Southern English English, as well as Australian English, Welsh English and Northern English varieties like Liverpool (Scouse) and Geordie have a short [i] in unstressed word-final position in words like 'city' [sɪti]; in North American varieties, this will often be long [iː]. Other Northern English English varieties (like Manchester or Leeds) and RP have [ɪ] here: [sɪtɪ]. In many Scottish and Northern Irish varieties the unstressed vowel in words like 'city' may be lower yet, being the high mid [e]; [sɪte].

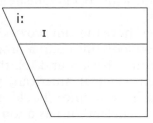

Fig. 4.4 High front vowels of English

Many non-rhotic Englishes also have a diphthong [ɪə] in words like 'beer' and 'fear', where the schwa is a remnant of the original 'r' sound. Rhotic accents have [ɪ] or [i] plus some kind of rhotic in these words; e.g. Scottish English [bɪɹ] 'beer'.

English has no high front round vowels (indeed, most English varieties have no front round vowels of any height); while such vowels are rare in the languages of the world, they do occur in a number of European languages; French, German, Swedish, Norwegian and Danish, for example, have high front round [y]: e.g. French *tu* [ty] 'you', Danish *sy* [sy] 'to sew'.

4.4.2 Mid front vowels

All varieties of English have a short mid front unround [ɛ] (sometimes transcribed [e]), as in 'bed'. The actual quality of the vowel varies – many English English varieties have a vowel midway between cardinals 2 and 3, but in North American varieties the vowel tends to be lower, while Southern Hemisphere Englishes (South African, Australian, New Zealand) typically have a higher vowel, closer to [ɪ].

Many varieties, such as Scottish, Irish and Northern English Englishes, have a mid or high-mid front vowel [eː] in words such as 'day'; this vowel is long in all varieties except Scottish English (and some Northern Irish English), where length varies according to context. For other varieties, including RP and Southern English English, words like 'day' have a diphthong [eɪ]. In most forms of North American English, the distinction between [eɪ] and [ɛ] is lost before a rhotic; 'Mary' and 'merry' are thus homophones, [mɛɹiː]. See Section 4.4.3 for further discussion.

Fig. 4.5 Mid front vowels of English

Some forms of non-rhotic varieties of English, such as Australian English, Cockney or RP, have the diphthong [eə] in words like 'chair', where the schwa is the remnant of the historical 'r'; but for many English English varieties this is no longer a diphthong, but rather a long low-mid vowel [ɛː], so that the difference between 'bed' and 'bared' in these varieties is largely only in terms of vowel length. In some Northern English English varieties (e.g. Liverpool, Manchester) the vowel may be a mid central [ɜː]. In rhotic accents, of course, words like 'chair' have a short front mid vowel followed by some kind of 'r'; so GenAm [tʃɛ˞] (where '˞' following a vowel symbol indicates rhoticisation, or 'r-colouring').

Again, as with the high front vowels, English does not usually have mid front round vowels, though the rounded equivalent of [e] – [ø] – is found in some broad Scots accents in words like 'boot'. Both [ø] and [œ] occur in French, German and the Scandinavian languages; French *bleu* [blø] 'blue', *peur* [pœʁ] 'fear', Danish *høns* [høns] 'hen', *øre* [œʁə] 'ear'.

4.4.3 Low front vowels

English has one short low front vowel, found in words like 'rat'; the RP and GenAm vowel is represented as [æ], midway between cardinals 3 and

4 (C3 and C4). Many other kinds of British English, including Welsh, Scottish and Northern English varieties, have a lower vowel, closer to C4, transcribed as [a]: [ɹat]. This lower vowel is also heard in some New England varieties of US English (e.g. Boston). On the other hand, Cockney, some RP and Southern Hemisphere varieties have a noticeably higher vowel which might be transcribed like C3, [ɹɛt]. In the South West of England and Northern Ireland the vowel is often rather longer than in other varieties: [ɹaːt]. It may also be further back, closer to [ɑ]: [ɹɑːt]. Low vowels are typically longer anyway than other vowels (compare 'rat' with 'writ'), and in some varieties (Southern US, Northern Irish) there may well be diphthongisation, especially before voiced consonants: [baəd] 'bad'. In many North American varieties the [æ] vowel is realised as [ɛ] before 'r' sounds (i.e. the opposition found elsewhere in North American English between [æ] and [ɛ] is neutralised; 'marry' and 'merry' are homophones [mɛɹiː]). Taken with the neutralisation mentioned in the preceding section between [eɪ] and [ɛ] before a rhotic, this gives a three-way neutralisation: 'Mary', 'marry' and 'merry' are all pronounced [mɛɹiː].

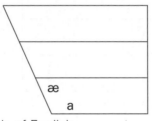

Fig. 4.6 Low front vowels of English

Most kinds of English have a diphthong which starts at a low front position and raises toward [ɪ]; RP and GenAm [aɪ], as in 'buy', 'die', 'cry', etc. The starting position for this diphthong varies somewhat, from near C3 [ɛ] in Geordie, low central [ʌ] in East Anglia and Scotland, low back unround [ɑ] in London to low back and round [ɒ] in the English West Midlands (where 'pint' may sound something like the 'point' of other varieties). In some varieties of Southern US English, the sound in these words is a monophthong [æː].

Similarly, most varieties have a diphthong which starts low but moves back and up towards [ʊ]; RP and GenAm [aʊ] as in 'now', 'mouth'. The starting position again varies; in RP and GenAm it is somewhat retracted compared to that for [aɪ], but may be in roughly the same place for Northern English English [aʊ], higher [æ] in London and other Southern English English [æʊ], or higher and centralised [ə] in Welsh English [əʊ] or Scottish English [ʌʊ]. In broader London accents, the realisation may well be monophthongal [æː]. A monophthong is also heard in broader Scottish and Geordie accents, though here the vowel is high and round: Scottish English high central round [ʉ], Geordie high back round [uː].

Although it is possible to produce a low front round vowel – C12 – and there is a symbol for this, [œ], no language is known to employ it.

4.4.4 Low back vowels

There are two common low back vowels in English: long low back unround [ɑː] as in the stressed vowel in RP and GenAm 'father', and short low back round [ɒ], as in many British varieties (though only rarely in North America outside Canada) in the vowel in 'dog'.

For most kinds of English, words like 'father', 'farm' and 'calm' have the low back [ɑ] vowel, either long for all these (in non-rhotic accents) or followed by a rhotic (as in GenAm) for words like 'farm'. However, a number of varieties have a very much fronted variant in these words, which may or may not contrast with the low front vowel in 'rat' in terms of quality and/or quantity. So, Australian English has [æ] (or [ɛ]) in 'rat' but [aː] in 'father'; a similar situation holds in South Western English English, though here the distinction may not hold for all members of the lexical sets, or may be one of length alone: 'Pam' [pam] vs. 'palm' [paːm] (though here the situation is further complicated by the possibility of the 'l' in words like 'palm' still being present, as it is in many kinds of American English). In many Scottish and Irish varieties, however, there is no front-back distinction at all with the low vowels, with a single vowel [a] being found in all these words. 'rat' and 'rather' have the same vowel, and 'Pam' and 'palm' are homophones (all with |a|).

Fig. 4.7 Low back vowels of English

In South Eastern English English varieties, and in RP, the [ɑː] vowel also has a somewhat wider distribution than in most other kinds of English, in that it appears in roughly 150 words which elsewhere have a short low front vowel [a]/[æ]. Typically, these words involve a following voiceless fricative [f], [θ], [s] ('laugh', 'after', 'staff ', 'path', 'bath', 'pass', 'grass', 'mask', etc., but not 'gaffe', 'maths', 'gas', etc.), or a nasal plus some other consonant ('plant', 'aunt', 'glance', 'dance', 'sample', but not 'ant', 'romance', 'ample'). For the majority of English speakers, however, all these words have some kind of short low front vowel, not a long back one.

For most kinds of British English and Southern Hemisphere English, words like 'top' and 'cough' have the low back round vowel [ɒ]: [tɒp], [kɒf]. In many North American, Irish and South Western English English accents, however, this vowel is not found; the words which have the vowel in other varieties are split between [ɑ] and [ɔ], so [tɑp] and [kɔf]. The details of the split are complex and vary between accents, depending partly on geography and partly on phonetic context.

In many Scottish and some North American (particularly Canadian) varieties, there is no contrast between [ɒ] and the low mid back round vowel [ɔ] (see Section 4.4.5), so that 'cot' and 'caught' are homophones, often with a vowel somewhere between the two (e.g. a lowered [ɔ] in Scottish varieties, or a raised and unrounded [ɑ] in Canadian accents).

4.4.5 Mid back vowels

Most kinds of English have a low mid back round vowel [ɔ] in words like 'bought', 'cause', 'paw' or (with or without a following rhotic) 'horse'. In many varieties of English English this is a long vowel [ɔː], though in North American varieties it is usually shorter. The vowel [ɔː] is also increasingly common in non-rhotic accents for earlier [ɔə] in words like 'door', 'shore', 'four' (though the older form is still heard in many accents in e.g. London or Northern England). It is also heard for [ʊə] in words like 'poor', 'moor', 'your'. So while some speakers may distinguish between 'paw' [pɔː], 'pour' [pɔə] and 'poor' [pʊə], for others they may be homophones: [pɔː].

As was mentioned in Section 4.4.4, for many Scottish and Canadian speakers, [ɔ] and [ɒ] are not distinguished. However, many Scottish and North American varieties do distinguish between pairs like 'horse' vs. 'hoarse' or 'morning' vs. 'mourning'; 'horse' and 'morning' have [ɔ] while 'hoarse' and 'mourning' have the higher [o].

Many varieties, such as Scottish, Irish, and broader Northern English Englishes, or North American varieties like Minnesota and Northern Plains English, have a mid or high-mid back round vowel [oː] in words such as 'goat'; this vowel is long in all varieties except Scottish English (and some Northern Irish English), where length varies according to context. In other varieties, including RP and other Southern English English, as well as most North American accents, words like 'goat' have a diphthong, though the starting point varies considerably; e.g. [əʊ] (RP), [ʌʊ] (London) or [oʊ] (many Northern English and North American accents). Increasingly, for younger RP and other younger Southern English speakers, the second part of the

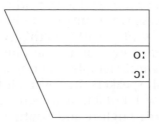

Fig. 4.8 Mid back vowels of English

diphthong is unrounded, giving [əɤ] or with a fronted starting position even [ɛɤ], so that words like 'coke' sound not unlike other varieties' 'cake'. Geordie sometimes has a round mid central vowel [ɵː] or a diphthong [ɵə].

English has a diphthong starting at a mid back round position then moving forward and up, and unrounding; [ɔɪ], as in 'boy', 'join', 'voice'. Again the starting point may vary, typically being higher [oɪ] in e.g. East Anglia and the South West of England, and lower in the English Midlands and Scotland [ɒɪ]. For some Irish and Scottish varieties there may be little distinction between words that elsewhere have [ɔɪ] vs. [aɪ], like 'boil' vs. 'bile' or 'voice' vs. 'vice', all with [ʌɪ] or [ae] in e.g. Glasgow English.

Non-low back unround vowels are typologically rare, though mid back unround vowels do occur in languages like Vietnamese. Some forms of English have high mid unround [ɤ] where varieties like RP and GenAm have [ʊ] – see the next section. For [ʌ] see Section 4.4.7.

4.4.6 High back vowels

Most kinds of English have two high back vowels: long [uː] as in 'shoe' and short [ʊ] as in 'put'. As with [iː] and [ɪ], the difference is in quality and quantity: [ʊ] is lower and more central, as well as shorter, than [uː]. Again parallel to the high front vowel [iː], [uː] is often diphthongised, starting out lower and more central; [ʊu]. For some varieties, such as London and East Anglia, as well as Scottish English (see below), the articulation of this vowel is central: [ʉː]. As mentioned above, [uː]/[ʉ] is found in some Geordie and Scottish English for RP [aʊ] in 'down', 'mouth', etc. The sound [uː] is also found in Northern English varieties in words ending in 'ook'; such as 'book', 'cook', 'look', etc.

For an increasing number of RP and Southern English English speakers, the short high back round [ʊ] is unrounding and centralising to [ɤ] or even [ə] in an increasing number of words, such as 'good', 'book', 'could', 'look', etc. For many Northern English English speakers (and for some Southern Irish speakers) [ʊ] is found in words that in other Englishes have [ʌ], like 'cup', 'bus', 'mud', etc. (see Section 4.4.7).

Older RP and many other non-rhotic accents (Welsh English, Cockney, Northern English English) have a diphthong [ʊə] in words which historically ended in a rhotic, like 'cure', 'pure', 'poor', 'tour', etc., though, as mentioned above, these are increasingly becoming [ɔː] in many varieties

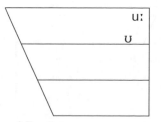

Fig. 4.9 High back vowels of English

of English English. Rhotic accents retain [u] or [ʊ] followed by some kind of 'r' in these words.

High back unround vowels are not found in English, but high back unround [ɯ] does occur in Japanese.

4.4.7 Central vowels

For most speakers of English, words like 'cup', 'luck', 'fuss', etc. have a vowel usually represented by the symbol [ʌ]. Although this represents a low mid unround back vowel in the cardinal vowel system, its articulation is typically further forward than back, being at least central for most speakers, and forward of central for many. Older RP speakers may still use a centralised back vowel, however; North American versions tend to be fairly central, and many British English varieties (including most RP) have a forward of centre vowel. In some Southern English English (e.g. London) and Southern Hemisphere English the vowel in these words is a front vowel [a]. In Welsh English, the vowel in these words is central but higher, being best represented by [ə].

For many Northern English English speakers, on the other hand, there is no distinct [ʌ]-type vowel at all. Many Northerners still have the historically earlier high back round vowel [ʊ] in these words, so that 'put' and 'putt', 'could' and 'cud' are homophones, all with [ʊ]. Other Northerners, with accents tending more toward the standard, may make a distinction between these words, but use [ə] (or something similar) rather than [ʌ].

Words like 'nurse', 'fir', 'her' and 'worse' typically have a mid central unround vowel [ɜː] in non-rhotic accents of English, though there is some variation of realisation; many West Midland and some North West English English accents (notably Birmingham and Liverpool) have a higher and/or further forward articulation (Scouse [nɛːs] 'nurse'). Similar articulations can also be found in Southern Hemisphere English. In many Northern accents there is no distinction between words which elsewhere have [ɜː] vs. [eə]/[ɛː], so that 'cur' and 'care' may be homophones: Liverpool [kɛː], Manchester [kɜː]. In broader Geordie accents, on the other hand, there is no distinction between what in RP would be words with [ɜː] vs. [ɔː], so that 'first' and 'forced', 'shirt' and 'short' may be homophones, all with a low mid back round vowel [ɔː]: [fɔːst], [ʃɔːt].

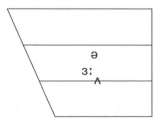

Fig. 4.10 Central vowels of English

The position with regard to the 'nurse', 'fir', 'her', 'worse' words in rhotic accents varies somewhat: in North American Englishes, and in rhotic English Englishes like the South West and central/northern Lancashire, there is a sequence of [ɜ] plus rhotic (usually realised as an r-coloured vowel [ɝ]). This is sometimes represented as [ɚ], an r-coloured schwa (especially with respect to North American Englishes), since there is little difference articulatorily. In many Scottish and Irish accents, however, the earlier vowel distinctions (suggested by the different orthographic vowels in the word set) have been retained, so that 'fir', 'fur' and 'fern' all have different vowels ([ɪ], [ʌ] and [ɛ] respectively). Other Scottish and Irish varieties may have [ɜ] followed by a rhotic for some of these words.

The remaining central vowel is schwa [ə]. This is typically found as the first vowel in 'about' or the last vowel in 'puma'. That is, it is the commonest vowel in syllables which do not carry stress. Indeed, in accents like RP and GenAm it does not occur at all in stressed syllables (unless words like 'nurse' in GenAm are considered to have an r-coloured schwa). Word-final schwa is typically somewhat lower (low mid) than non-final schwa (mid/high mid). In London English and Australian English, these vowels, when they occur word-finally, are often lower and further forward: [ɐ]; in Geordie they are often retracted and lowered to something close to [ɑ].

In Scottish English, the final vowels of words like 'miner' and 'minah (bird)', unlike most other Englishes, will often not be identical, with 'miner' having [ɪ] (followed by a rhotic), 'minah' having [ʌ]; for many Scottish English speakers, there is no [ə] at all.

For a number of non-rhotic accents of English, [ə] can appear after any of the (non-schwa final) diphthongs when these would be followed by a rhotic in rhotic varieties; thus (RP) 'tower' [taʊə], 'layer' [leɪə], 'mire' [maɪə], 'lawyer' [lɔɪə] and 'lower' [ləʊə]. These 'triphthongs' are often subject to reduction however, especially in RP and Southern English English varieties. This 'simplification' typically involves the loss of the middle vocalic element (often with concomitant lengthening of the first element): 'tower' [taːə], 'layer' [leːə], 'mire' [maːə], 'lawyer' [lɔːə]; for 'lower' the result is a long central mid vowel [lɜː], leading to 'slower' and 'slur' being potential homophones. Since [aʊə] and [aɪə] both reduce to [aːə], words like 'tower' and 'tyre' are also possible homophones. Further reduction is also possible, involving the loss of the final [ə] for [aːə], giving a long low vowel which may well not be distinguished from [ɑː], making 'tower', 'tyre' and 'tar' all [tɑː]. For the 'layer' words, the [eːə] reduces further to [ɛː], making 'layer' and 'lair' potentially homophonous.

4.4.8 Distribution

Vowels in English have few restrictions in terms of which consonants may precede or follow them. The major restriction concerns short monophthongs vs. long monophthongs and diphthongs: short vowels may not occur finally in stressed monosyllabic words, while long vowels and diphthongs may. So, while [biː] and [bɔɪ] are well-formed in English, *[bɪ] or *[bɒ] are not (the asterisk indicates a form not found in the language under discussion). Short vowels can only occur in stressed monosyllables when these are consonant final, like [bɪt] or [bɒg]. That is, short vowels are restricted to closed syllables in stressed monosyllabic words, while long vowels and diphthongs may occur in both open (as above) and closed syllables ([biːt], [bɔɪt]).

4.5 Some vowel systems of English

Pulling some of this welter of information together, we can now look at the vowel inventories, or vowel systems, of a number of major English varieties. As should be clear from the previous sections, the number of vowels in the system, and their distribution among the lexical items of English, is not the same for all varieties.

4.5.1 RP (Conservative)

Monophthongs are shown in Figure 4.11.

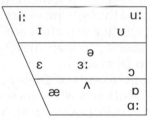

Fig. 4.11 RP (conservative) monophthongs

Diphthongs are as follows:

[eɪ, aɪ, aʊ, ɔɪ, əʊ, ɪə, eə, ɔə, ʊə]

Example words and their RP pronunciations are:

bee [biː], bit [bɪt], bet [bɛt], bat [bæt]
cart [kɑːt], bath [bɑːθ], cot [kɒt], caught [kɔːt], cook [kʊk], shoe [ʃuː]
cut [kʌt], curt [kɜːt], <u>a</u>bout [əbaʊt], butt<u>er</u> [bʌtə]
bay [beɪ], bite [baɪt], now [naʊ], boy [bɔɪ], go [gəʊ]
beer [bɪə], bear [beə], bore [bɔə], poor [pʊə]

This gives a total of 21 different vowels sounds for conservative RP; more recent, less conservative forms may not have [ʊə], [ɔə] or [eə], having [ɔː] for the first two and [ɛː] for the last, giving a total of 19 different vowels.

4.5.2 North American English (General American)

Monophthongs are shown in Figure 4.12.

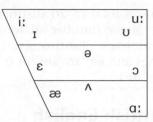

Fig. 4.12 North American English (General American) monophthongs

Diphthongs are as follows:

[eɪ, aɪ, aʊ, ɔɪ, oʊ]

Example words and their GenAm pronunciations are:

bee [biː], bit [bɪt], bet [bɛt], bat [bæt]
cart [kɑɾt], bath [bæθ], cot [kɑt], caught [kɔːt], cook [kʊk], shoe [ʃuː]
cut [kʌt], curt [kɚt], about [əbaʊt], butter [bʌɾɚ]
bay [beɪ], bite [baɪt], now [naʊ], boy [bɔɪ], go [goʊ]
beer [bɪɹ], bear [bɛɹ], bore [bɔɹ], poor [pɔɹ]

The main differences here compared to RP are the lack of the monophthong [ɒ] and of the three schwa final diphthongs (due to GenAm being rhotic; these are sequences of vowel plus 'r', realised as rhoticised, or r-coloured, vowels). This gives a total of 16 distinct vowels.

4.5.3 Northern English English

Monophthongs are shown in Figure 4.13.

Fig. 4.13 Northern English English monophthongs

Diphthongs are as follows:

[aɪ, aʊ, ɔɪ, ɪə, ɔə, ʊə]

Example words and their Northern English English pronunciations are:

bee [biː], bit [bɪt], bet [bɛt], bat [bat]
cart [kɑːt], bath [baθ], cot [kɒt], caught [kɔːt], cook [kuːk], shoe [ʃuː]
cut [kʊt], curt [kɜːt], about [əbaʊt], butter [bʊtə]
bay [beː], bite [baɪt], now [naʊ], boy [bɔɪ], go [goː]
beer [bɪə], bear [bɛː], bore [bɔə], poor [pʊə]

This variety of English has a total of 20 distinct vowels. Here the main differences rest with the larger number of long monophthongs (three extra mid long vowels which are diphthongs in RP) and the lack of [ʌ]. The schwa final diphthongs and [ɛː] are absent in rhotic Northern English accents, reducing the total to 16.

4.5.4 Lowland Scottish English

Monophthongs are shown in Figure 4.14.

Fig. 4.14 Lowland Scottish English monophthongs

Diphthongs are as follows:

[ae, (ʌʊ), (ɒɪ)]

Example words and their Lowland Scottish English pronunciations are:

bee [biː], bit [bɪt], bet [bɛt], bat [bat]
cart [kaɾt] ([kɑɾt]), bath [baθ], cot [kɔt] ([kɒt]), caught [kɔt],
cook [kʉk], shoe [ʃʉː]
cut [kʌt], curt [kʌɾt] ([kɜɾt]), <u>a</u>bout [əbʉt], butt<u>er</u> [bʌtʌɾ] ([bʌtəɾ])
bay [beː], bite [baet], now [nʉː] ([nʌʊ]), boy [bae] ([bɒɪ]), go [goː]
beer [bɪɾ], bear [bɛɾ], bore [bɔːɾ], poor [pʉːɾ]

Forms in parentheses are those found in Scottish English varieties closer to RP. This system is clearly rather different to those looked at so far, with possibly as few as 10 distinctive vowels, and with vowel length behaving in a way not found elsewhere, being determined by phonetic (and morphological) context; certain vowels are long before voiced fricatives and rhotics, as well as word-finally and before a morpheme boundary. Most of the differences have to do with lack of contrast between words that in other forms of English are distinct. Thus, for most Scots 'fool' and 'full' may be homophonous [fʉɫ]; for broader accents 'fool', 'full' and 'foul' may be homophonous [fʉɫ] – no distinction between (RP) [uː], [ʊ] and [aʊ]; 'don' and 'dawn' are both [dɔn] – no [ɒ] vs. [ɔː]; 'Sam' and 'psalm' are both [sam] – no [a] vs. [ɑː]. Other differences include fewer diphthongs: as in Northern English English, words like 'day' and 'go' have long monophthongs and there are no schwa final diphthongs, since Scottish English is rhotic.

Further reading

Given that the subject matter for this chapter and the previous one are closely related, see the further reading section in Chapter 3.

Exercises

1 How do the following sets of vowels differ from each other?

    a. [i y ɪ]   vs.   [u ʊ]
    b. [ʊ i ɛ]   vs.   [æ ɑ ɒ]
    c. [ɪ ɛ ʊ]   vs.   [i e u]
    d. [y u ʊ ɔ]   vs.   [i ɛ æ ə]
    e. [ə ʌ ɜ]   vs.   [e ɛ o ɔ]

2 Assuming the vowels of English, indicate the symbol representing the sound described by each of the following:

    a. high front short vowel
    b. mid central unstressed vowel
    c. high back long vowel
    d. low back unrounded vowel
    e. mid back to front diphthong

3 Place the members of the following vowel inventory in an appropriate place on a vowel quadrilateral: [i ɪ e æ ə ɑ o u]

4 Give the orthographic forms for the following transcriptions.

    a. [tʃiˑp]   d. [ɪnʤəɹiz]   g. [ɹʌʃl̩]
    b. [pʰaɪnɪŋ]   e. [ælfəbɛt]   h. [kɹuːzd]
    c. [ɹeɪnboʊ]   f. [θʌɹə]   i. [jənaɪtɪd]

5 Transcribe the following words in your own accent.

    a. think   e. chipmunk   i. gerbil
    b. shape   f. thrush   j. though
    c. queue   g. salamander k. yellow
    d. elephant   h. leisure   l. circus

Acoustic phonetics

We saw in the last chapters that speech sounds can be discussed in terms of their articulation – the physical processes involved in speech production. The focus of this chapter is another area of phonetics which deals with the physical properties of speech sounds. When sounds are produced in the mouth they have specific, measurable effects on the air involved. Acoustic phonetics is the study of these effects. Just as speech sounds can be distinguished by their manner of articulation, say stops vs. fricatives, they can also be distinguished by specific physical properties, for example the acoustic correlates typically associated with obstruents vs. sonorants.

While acoustics constitutes a broad area of scientific enquiry, we will be looking only at the basics of acoustic phonetics. After looking at some of the fundamental concepts involved in dealing with the acoustic properties of sounds, we will look more specifically at how speech sounds can be characterised in terms of these physical properties.

5.1 Fundamentals

Acoustic phonetics focuses not just on the physical properties of speech sounds, but on the linguistically relevant acoustic properties of speech sounds. That is to say that not all of the properties of speech sounds are relevant to language. As mentioned in Chapter 2, not all sounds produced by the human vocal apparatus are linguistic, e.g. burps, coughs, hiccups. Even when speaking specifically about speech sounds not all acoustic aspects are linguistically relevant. Among those that are, in this chapter we discuss periodic and aperiodic waves, frequency, amplitude and formants.

5.1.1 Waves

Much like the waves on the surface of a pond when a pebble is dropped into the water, sound moves through air in waves. Imagine dropping the pebble and freezing the water instantly while the waves are moving across the surface. Then cut a slice to view the waves from the side. In Figure 5.1 the line labelled B would represent the surface of the water at rest, C would represent the highest point, the peak of the wave, and A the lowest point, the trough of the wave.

For our purposes the two important characteristics of waves are their **frequency**, that is how close together the waves are, and their *amplitude*,

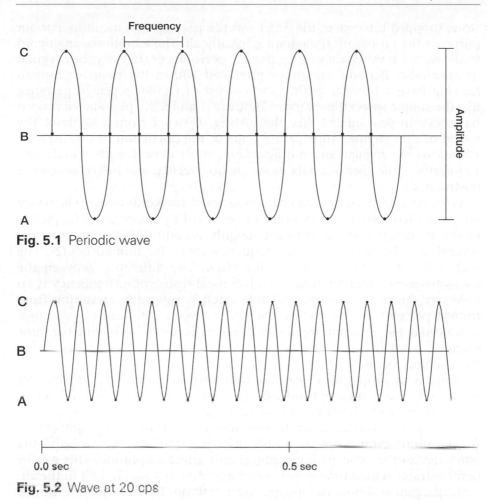

Fig. 5.1 Periodic wave

Fig. 5.2 Wave at 20 cps

the maximum distance the wave moves from the starting point, that is, between the point of rest, B, and either the peak, C, or the trough, A (i.e. B–C, or B–A). Frequency is measured in cycles per second (cps), also called Hertz (Hz). Movement from B to C to B to A to B is one cycle, so from rest, through the peak and trough of the wave and back to rest would be one cycle. Adding a time line to the wave represented in Figure 5.2, we can see that there are 10 cycles over the half second. Therefore, this particular wave has a frequency of 20 cycles per second or 20 Hz.

As we discuss below, understanding the behaviour of waves is fundamental to an understanding of acoustic phonetics.

5.1.2 Sound

Soundwaves are produced by **vibration** carried by a **propagation medium**, the substance through which sound travels. In the discussion above of a

57

stone dropped into water, the water was the propagation medium. For our purposes the propagation medium is usually air. The vibrations, analogous to the waves in water, may be regular, i.e. **periodic**, or they may be irregular or **aperiodic**. Periodic vibrations produced within the range of human hearing have a musical quality and consist of regular repeated patterns, like the simple waves illustrated in Figures 5.1 and 5.2. Aperiodic vibrations have less musical quality, like the hissing of steam from a kettle or the sound of a jet engine. Anticipating some of the discussion below, periodic vibrations are regular and are associated most closely with vowels and sonorants, while aperiodic vibrations are non-regular and help characterise obstruents.

As we have seen, one of the characteristics of the kinds of periodic waves above is their frequency. In order to be heard by people, the frequency of the vibration must be between roughly 20 and 20000 vibrations per second, i.e. the normal audible frequency range for human beings. The higher the frequency the higher the *pitch*. The difference between the terms frequency and pitch lies in a technical distinction: frequency is an objective, measurable property, while pitch is subjective, resulting from human perception. This means that under specific conditions two sounds produced at two different frequencies may be perceived as having the same pitch. It is for this reason that we talk about objective frequency rather than subjective pitch.

Along with propagation medium and frequency, the size or intensity of the vibration, its *amplitude*, is also important. Amplitude relates to loudness in much the same way as frequency relates to pitch – amplitude is an objective quantity, while loudness is (at least partly) subjective. As amplitude diminishes sound becomes less audible. Distance and the efficiency of the propagating medium also affect amplitude. This can be demonstrated with a tuning fork: strike a tuning fork and hold it in the air; strike it again and hold its base against a desktop. The second time will be louder, since wood (or formica!) is a more efficient propagating medium than air. As to distance, a tuning fork held near the ear will sound louder than one held at arm's length.

Another basic aspect of sound and our perception of sound is **quality**. Even when two sounds are at the same frequency and amplitude they can differ in quality or colouring. It is quality that allows us to tell the difference, for example, between a flute and a violin playing the same note at the same loudness. Differences in quality arise from the differences in the shape of the propagation medium and the material enclosing that medium, in this case the shape of the violin and the flute as well as the material the instrument is made of, here either wood or metal. The differing shapes and materials tend to emphasise different **harmonics**, i.e. vibrations at whole number multiples of the basic frequency of the note being played. Thus a note produced at 120 Hz will produce harmonics at 240, 360, 480 Hz and so on, some of which will be emphasised by the shape and material of whatever is producing that note.

5.1.3 Machine analysis

5.1.3.1 Spectrograms

In order to see and analyse the kinds of properties of sounds we have been talking about, phoneticians most often use a machine called a *spectrograph*, which allows measurement and analysis of frequency, duration, transitions between speech sounds, and the like. The output of a spectrograph is a *spectrogram*, either printed on paper or displayed on a computer screen. Figure 5.3 is a spectrogram of the sentence 'This is a spectrogram' in General American, spoken by a male speaker. We discuss the details of spectrograms in the following sections.

The scale on the left hand side shows the frequencies in KHz, while along the bottom is a time line in milliseconds. We can see that certain frequencies are emphasised in the spectrogram, indicated by dark marks. These patterns are called *formants* (labelled 1 in Figure 5.3). We can also see that certain parts of the spectrogram show patterns of regular vertical lines. These correspond to the periodic vibrations of the vocal cords. Other parts of the spectrogram show irregular striations, with emphasis in the higher frequencies (2 in Figure 5.3). These correspond to aperiodic vibrations. We can also see lack of acoustic activity, such as during stop closure (3 in Figure 5.3).

Fig. 5.3 Spectrogram for [ðɪsɪzəspɛktɹəgɹæm]

Notes:
1. Vowel formants
2. Aperiodic vibration in the higher frequencies, associated with fricatives
3. Absence of spectrographic activity, associated with voiceless stops

5.1.3.2 Waveforms

In addition to spectrograms, a *waveform* (Figure 5.4) can be a useful tool in analysing speech sounds. Waveforms show the pulses corresponding to each vibration of the vocal cords. So, along with other patterns visible on a spectrogram, the corresponding waveform records the variations in air pressure associated with speech sounds. Consequently, voiced sounds show up on the waveform as larger patterns than voiceless sounds. Consonants and vowels are also distinct from one another, thus allowing fairly precise measurements of various segments.

With voiceless stops there's an absence of vibration, characterised by a straight line. The release corresponds to either aspiration, also visible on the waveform, or the voicing of the following consonant. Voiced stops show up as subdued wiggly lines. Again the stop closure and release can be clearly seen contrasted with the surrounding vowels (or silence).

Different places of articulation cannot be distinguished on a waveform, that is, [p] looks like [t] looks like [k]; [b] looks like [d] looks like [g]; [s] and [ʃ] are similarly indistinguishable. However, waveforms do allow us to see differences in voicing and in manner of articulation and can be useful when used in conjunction with spectrograms.

5.2 Speech sounds

Let us turn now to how these physical properties relate to specific speech sounds. As we said earlier, speech includes periodic components and aperiodic components. Vowels and sonorants such as [ɑ] and [n], for

Fig. 5.4 Waveform of [ðɪsɪzəspɛktɹəɡɹæm]

example, are associated with regular waves while fricatives like [f] and [s] are associated with irregular waves. These correspond to the periodic and aperiodic vibrations we saw in the spectrogram above. There are also speech sounds which are associated with both regular and irregular waves, e.g. voiced fricatives like [v] and [z]: with [v] and [z] the fricative part of the sound is aperiodic while the voicing part is periodic. Quality also plays a role in distinguishing speech sounds. Differences in vowels have to do in large part with differences in quality: [i] and [u] differ because of differences in the shape of the oral tract. The position of the tongue changes the shape of the air in the oral cavity, thus [u] and [i] have a different quality.

5.2.1 Vowels and sonorants

For voiced speech sounds we distinguish the *fundamental frequency* (symbol: F0), the frequency at which the vocal cords are vibrating. Given the differences in the size of the vocal apparatus, men, women and children tend to have different fundamental frequencies: roughly speaking, the human voice produces speech sounds at fundamental frequencies of about 80–200 Hz for adult males, 150–300 Hz for adult females and 200–500 Hz for children. In addition to the fundamental frequency the production of a voiced sound causes the vocal tract to resonate in specific ways depending on the shape of the tract. Thus, apart from the fundamental frequency, this resonating emphasises certain frequencies above the fundamental frequency, as with the harmonics associated with musical instruments. With a particular vowel, for example, these emphasised harmonics are multiples of the fundamental frequency and correspond to the resonances of the vocal tract shape that accompany a particular vowel. In dealing with speech, resonances that are above F0 are called *formants* or **formant frequencies** (Figure 5.5). To take a concrete example, consider the vowel sound in the word 'sad'. During the production of [æ] the vocal cords may be vibrating at about 100 Hz and the first formant (F1) is about 500 Hz. This indicates that for that vowel the fifth harmonic, i.e. five times the frequency of the fundamental frequency, is emphasised, and it therefore appears darker on a spectrogram. The next emphasised frequency, F2, is at about the 11th harmonic, i.e. 1 100 Hz.

Of particular interest are the first, second and third formants (F1, F2 and F3), in other words, the first three sets of emphasised frequencies above the fundamental frequency. The reason these are important is because these formants pattern in ways which are characteristic for the speech sounds associated with them. For example, the formant pattern associated with [ɑ] is typical across speakers for that vowel, while being different from [ɪ], which has a formant pattern associated with it that is also typical across speakers. Despite the differences in fundamental frequency mentioned above, the formant patterns are still distinct. This means that the *patterns* are consistent from speaker to speaker, although the actual frequencies may differ. This is true also of voice quality; while voice quality may differ from speaker to speaker (and is often associated with changes in F4) the formant

Fig. 5.5 Vowel formant frequencies (American English)

patterns (of F1, F2 and F3) associated with particular speech sounds in a given language are consistent.

The spectrogram in Figure 5.6 illustrates the General American English vowels [i], [ɪ], [ɛ], [æ], [ɑ], [ɔ], [ʊ] and [u]. The formants of these vowels are seen on spectrograms as dark horizontal bars, representing the increased energy at these frequencies.

At this point it is important to mention the difference between articulatory and acoustic phonetics. As we saw in Chapter 4, it can be difficult to pin down vowel articulations since the articulators do not make contact in the production of vowel sounds. With acoustic analyses of vowels, however, precise statements can be made in distinguishing one vowel from another in terms of formant patterns. Thus distinctions between vowels are often more easily expressed in acoustic terms than in articulatory terms.

The relative positions of the first and second formants (F1 and F2) are characteristic of specific vowels. As we can see, F1 and F2 are farthest apart for [i], at about 280 Hz and 2 300 Hz respectively for this particular speaker. For [ɪ] F1 is higher and F2 lower than for [i]. For [ɛ] F1 is higher still and F2 lower still. For [æ] the trend continues with F1 higher and F2 lower than for [ɛ]. F1 and F2 are close together for [ɑ], at about 640 Hz and 1 020 Hz respectively. F1 and F2 both drop for [ɔ]. For [ʊ] and [u] F1 and F2 continue to drop.

Fig. 5.6 Spectrogram of vowel formants

Looking at these patterns in more general terms, we can see that the frequency of F1 correlates inversely with the height of the vowel – the F1 values for the high vowels [i] and [u] are the lowest while the F1 values for the low vowels [æ] and [ɑ] are the highest and the values for the mid vowels [ɪ], [ɛ], [ɔ] and [ʊ] are intermediate. At the same time, backness correlates with the difference between the frequencies of F1 and F2 – F1 and F2 are furthest apart for the front vowels [i], [ɪ], [ɛ], [æ] and closest together for the back vowels [ɑ], [ɔ], [ʊ], [u].

Note that the vowels we have been considering have been simple monophthongs. As we know, there are other types of vowels, i.e. diphthongs, and these also have characteristics which can be identified spectrographically. Consider what a diphthong is: a (functionally) single vowel which starts out in the position of one monophthong and ends up in the position of another. For example, the [aɪ] in 'high' starts at the position of a low [a] and moves towards the high front [ɪ]. Spectrographically, it is not surprising to find that diphthongs exhibit roughly the formant patterns associated with the related monophthongs. Taking 'high' again as an example, the first part of the diphthong is like [a] while the end of the diphthong is like [ɪ]. Along with the diphthongs in Figure 5.7 note the differing patterns of the fricatives [ʃ], [s] and [h] (about which more in Section 5.2.4.2).

Fig. 5.7 Spectrogram of diphthongs

5.2.2 Nasalisation, nasal vowels and rhoticisation

Along with the vowels themselves – monophthongs and diphthongs – there are other characteristics associated with vowels that affect their acoustic properties and which can be seen spectrographically. Two of these are nasalisation and rhoticisation.

5.2.2.1 Nasalisation and nasal vowels

Like nasal stops, vowels can also be pronounced with airflow through the nasal cavity. The vowel in the word 'man', for example, is often nasalised.

In English vowels nasalisation is typically the result of the influence of nasal stops on surrounding vowels. ('Typically' because some varieties of English tend to be fairly heavily nasalised even in the absence of nasal stops, resulting for instance in the perception of American speech as very nasal.) Given this sort of nasal assimilation, a distinction is frequently drawn between **nasalised vowels** and **nasal vowels**. The first, as in the English case, are vowels which are affected by the nasal characteristics of surrounding nasal stops. In other words, the vowels assimilate to the nasal properties of the adjacent stops. In other languages, e.g. French, Polish and Navajo (American southwest), however, there are nasal (as opposed to nasalised) vowels which are nasal regardless of surrounding consonants. In other words, the nasality of the vowels is not due to nasalisation. Taking French as an example, nasal vowels are part of its inventory. Compare for example *lin* [lɛ̃] 'flax' vs. *laine* [lɛn] 'wool' vs. *lait* [lɛ] 'milk' or *bon* [bɔ̃] 'good, masculine' vs. *bonne* [bɔn] 'good, feminine'. (This is true of the modern language; it could be argued that French nasal vowels arose historically through assimilation to right-adjacent nasal stops.) Nasal vowels look essentially like their oral counterparts, but also exhibit a typical 'nasal formant' at around 250 Hz and two linguistically significant formants above that. The French nasal vowels have the typical formant values for an average male voice shown in Table 5.1.

Table 5.1 Typical formant values of French nasal vowels

F2	750	950	1 350	1 750
F1	600	600	600	600
Nasal formant	(250)	(250)	(250)	(250)
	[ɔ̃] *bon* 'good'	[ɑ̃] *banc* 'bench'	[œ̃] *brun* 'brown'	[ɛ̃] *brin* 'mist'

Note: Formant frequencies given in Hz.
Source: Delattre 1965: 48.

5.2.2.2 Rhoticised vowels

Another characteristic that may be associated with vowels is rhoticisation or r-colouring – that is, the effect of an r-sound on an adjacent vowel. In varieties of English in which final r-sounds are pronounced, the vowel preceding the r-sound often has rhoticisation. In General American, for example, the vowels in 'law' and 'lord' differ in terms of rhoticisation. As we saw with nasalisation and nasal vowels, there are languages with rhotic vowels, i.e. vowels which exhibit rhoticisation even in the absence of a consonantal r-sound. While these are fairly rare in the world's languages, we find both varieties of English and Chinese which have rhoticised vowels. Spectrographically rhoticisation shows up as a lowering of the third formant.

5.2.3 Other sonorants

In addition to vowels, sonorants also have formant patterns. Laterals ('l-sounds'), nasals and rhotics ('r-sounds'), while looking rather like vowels, have additional characteristics. Laterals have additional formants at about 250, 1 200 and 2 400 Hz. Nasals have additional formants at about 250, 2 500 and 3 250 Hz. The postvocalic [ɹ] of many varieties of English is associated with a general lowering of the third and fourth formants, as seen in Figure 5.8a compared with Figure 5.8b, which show two versions of the sentence 'There's a bear here' in General American and in non-rhotic English English respectively (male speakers).

Fig. 5.8a Spectrogram of General American 'There's a bear here.'

Fig. 5.8b Spectrogram of non-rhotic English English 'There's a bear here.'

5.2.4 Non-sonorant consonants

Along with the highly visible formant patterns of vowels and sonorants, there are features associated with non-sonorant consonants that can also be seen on spectrograms. Stops are recognisable primarily by the absence of spectrographic information, while fricatives are associated with aperiodic noise seen as irregular vertical striations in the upper frequencies.

5.2.4.1 Stops

As the spectrogram in Figure 5.3 shows, stops are characterised by an absence of acoustic activity. Or to put it negatively, during the closure of the stop we see neither formants, as we would with a sonorant or vowel, nor striations in the upper part of the spectrogram, as we would with a fricative. A voiced stop differs from a voiceless stop only by the presence of voicing, indicated by a series of marks at the bottom of the spectrogram, known as a voice bar. Given the lack of information provided by stops themselves, the spectrographic stop information alone is not enough to identify them in terms of place of articulation. However, clues to their identity can be gleaned from surrounding spectrographic information. Note the differences between [pʰ], [p] and [b] in Figure 5.9. With [pʰ] we see frication associated with aspiration following the stop but before the onset of voicing in the vowel. With [p] we see vowel voicing beginning as soon as the stop is released. The [b] of 'buy' looks just like the [p] of 'spy' but with voicing showing at the bottom of the spectrogram.

Fig. 5.9 Stops [pʰ], [p] and [b] in 'pie', 'spy' and 'by'

5.2.4.2 Fricatives

While stops exhibit a relative lack of spectrographic activity, fricatives are accompanied by aperiodic vibrations in the higher frequencies. These show up on a spectrogram as irregular striations, dark vertical lines in the upper part of the spectrogram. The main resonant frequencies (i.e. the darkest part on a spectrogram) of fricatives rise as the size of the oral cavity decreases, that is, the further forward in the mouth the obstruction is. Thus, [h]'s strongest resonances are around 1 000 Hz, those of [ʃ] about 3 000 Hz, 4 000 Hz for [s], 5 000 Hz for [θ] and between 4 500 and 7 000 Hz for [f]. Figure 5.7 illustrates the fricatives [ʃ], [s] and [h].

5.2.4.3 Transitions

It was mentioned above that the spectrograms of stops themselves are fairly uninformative. However, transitions from the stop to neighbouring segments can give us more information about the place of articulation of a particular stop. Transitions can also give us useful information about the place of articulation of fricatives, which can help in identifying particular fricatives by reinforcing the information discussed above concerning the frequencies of the aperiodic vibrations associated with fricatives.

A transition is a movement in the formant pattern of a vowel/sonorant due to an adjacent consonant. For example, an alveolar consonant causes the F2 transition to rise before front vowels and lower before back vowels (compared with the vowel alone without a preceding alveolar), as does a labial consonant (again, compared with the vowel alone), as shown in Figure 5.10. Thus, in both cases the initial section of the second formant for the same vowel will be slightly different depending on what precedes it. When the consonant follows a vowel, the patterns are reversed. So, for a high front vowel preceding an alveolar, the F2 falls into the consonant articulation; for a back vowel before an alveolar, the F2 rises.

Transitions are usually stated with reference to a point known as the **locus**. The locus is the imaginary point at which the transition appears to originate. If the trajectories of the F2 formants for the vowels following [d] in Figure 5.10 are traced backwards, they would have a point of origin in the middle of the frequency range, at around 1 800 Hz, meaning that alveolar sounds have a locus for F2 at 1 800 Hz. The bilabial [b] has a lower F2 locus, at around 800 Hz. Velars are somewhat more complex for F2, with a locus of around 3 000 Hz adjacent to front vowels, and a second locus at c.1 200 Hz for back vowels, though this results in a falling F2 transition before all vowels.

In general terms obstruent transitions can be summarised as follows:

❑ Adjacent to labials the F2 transition rises for front vowels, lowers for back vowels, with a low locus.
❑ Adjacent to alveolars the F2 transition rises for front vowels, lowers for back vowels, with a mid locus.
❑ Adjacent to velars the F2 transition falls, with a high locus for front vowels, a mid locus for back vowels.

Fig. 5.10 Formant transitions

Source: adapted from O'Connor 1973.

5.2.4.4 Voice onset time

A further feature associated with stops (see also Section 3.1.3) that can be seen on spectrograms is *voice onset time* or VOT. After the release of the stop we can see spectrographic indications of the interplay between stop closure and voicing. With a fully voiced stop, the voicing continues during the closure of the stop. It is the difference in voice onset time that results in the difference between aspirated and unaspirated stops. In the case of an unaspirated stop like [p], voicing ceases with the closure of the articulators and begins again simultaneously with the release of the stop closure (see again Figure 5.9). In Figures 5.11–5.13 voicing is indicated by a thick black line (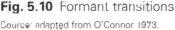), lack of voicing by a broken line (▥). The articulators are shown as closed by a straight line (—) and as open by parallel lines (⹀). A vertical line indicates the point at which the articulators open.

Thus, with a fully voiced stop we see that voicing continues from the first vowel [ɑ] through the closure and release of the [b] and into the second vowel [ɑ].

If there is a significant delay between the stop release and the subsequent onset of voicing, that is, if the stop is released before voicing begins, aspiration occurs. As we saw in Section 3.1.3, aspiration is a little puff of air accompanying the release of certain stops. In fact, it is the result of the timing sequence of stop release and voicing. An aspirated [pʰ] is shown in Figure 5.13.

Fig. 5.11 Fully voiced stop

Fig. 5.12 Voiceless unaspirated stop

Fig. 5.13 Voiceless aspirated stop

What is important to note here is that the voicelessness of the [p] has continued beyond the release of the stop. Voicing begins again only some time after the stop has been released. Coming back to spectrograms, aspiration of a voiceless stop can be seen clearly as aperiodic vibration in the higher frequencies.

Table 5.2 shows the main acoustic correlates of consonants. Note that these are broad indications only, since the actual acoustic correlates are strongly influenced by the combination of articulatory features in a sound.

Table 5.2 Acoustic correlates of consonant features

Place or manner of articulation	Main acoustic correlate
Voiced	Vertical striations corresponding to the vibrations of the vocal cords.
Bilabial	Locus of both second and third formants comparatively low.
Alveolar	Locus of second formant about 1 700–1 800 Hz.
Velar	Usually high locus of the second formant. Common origin of second and third formant transitions.
Retroflex	General lowering of the third and fourth formants.
Stop	Gap in pattern, followed by burst of noise for voiceless stops or sharp beginning of formant structure for voiced stops.
Fricative	Random noise pattern, especially in the higher frequency regions, but dependent on the place of articulation.
Nasal	Formant structure similar to that of vowels but with nasal formants at about 250, 2 500 and 3 250 Hz.
Lateral	Formant structure similar to that of vowels but with formants in the neighbourhood of 250, 1 200, and 2 400 Hz. The higher formants are considerably reduced in intensity.

Source: Ladefoged 2005.

5.3 Cross-linguistic values

Recall that in Section 4.2 we said English [i] and German [i] are not identical. The values we have been talking about here are typical for English. It is interesting to note that similar speech sounds in other languages may have different typical values. Not surprisingly, these differences account in part for a 'foreign accent'. As an example, a comparison of vowel formants in Table 5.3 indicates how similar vowels may have slightly different formant values. The values given are typical for a male voice; the formants for a female voice may be 10 to 15 per cent higher.

Table 5.3 Comparison of the first two formants of four vowels of English, French, German and Spanish. All values in Hertz.

Vowel		English	French	German	Spanish
[i]	F2	2 250	2 500	2 250	2 300
	F1	300	250	275	275
[ɛ]	F2	1 800	1 800	1 900	–
	F1	550	550	500	–
[ɑ]	F2	1 100	1 200	1 150	1 300
	F1	750	750	750	725
[u]	F2	900	750	850	800
	F1	300	250	275	275

Source: adapted from Delattre 1965: 49.

Further reading

Along with Ladefoged (1996) on acoustic phonetics other accessible works are the recent textbook by Johnson (2003) and Denes and Pinson (1963), which is old but quite clear.

A useful book on basic phonetic comparisons of English, French, German and Spanish is Delattre (1965).

Exercises

1 Plot the following American English vowels given in Table 5.4 on the grid in Figure 5.14. Plot the F1 frequency value on the vertical axis and the difference between the F1 and F2 frequencies on the horizontal axis. Discuss how the result does – or does not – match the kind of vowel quadrilateral seen in Chapter 4.

Table 5.4

F2	2 250	1 950	1 800	1 700	1 100	900	1 000	900
F1	300	350	550	750	750	550	375	300
Vowel	[i]	[ɪ]	[ɛ]	[æ]	[ɑ]	[ɔ]	[ʊ]	[u]

Fig. 5.14

2 Figure 5.15 shows a spectrogram of the phrase 'I should have picked a spade'. Transcribe the phrase underneath the spectrogram, placing the symbols to correspond to the spectrographic information. Discuss the differences between the *d* in 'should' and the two occurrences of *p* in 'picked' and 'spade'.

Fig. 5.15

3 Bearing in mind the various spectrograms you have seen in this chapter, discuss the reality of speech segmentation. In other words, can speech really be divided into discrete 'segments'? Address the question both from the perspective of speech spectrograms and from the perspective of needing to represent speech using typographic characters.

6

Above the segment

In the preceding chapters, we have in the main concentrated on the description and classification of individual speech sounds, or segments, with some discussion of how such segments interact with one another in terms of distribution and assimilation. In Section 2.3 we briefly introduced the notion of the syllable, a phonological unit larger than, and composed of, individual segments. In this chapter we will look in more detail at the nature of the syllable and other suprasegmental structures, and consider some of the phenomena that are relevant to them, such as stress and intonation.

6.1 The syllable

In this section we examine the notion of the syllable, beginning with a look at whether it can be said to have any physical, phonetic basis, then moving on to look at syllable structure and the principles governing it, and ending with an overview of possible syllable types.

6.1.1 The syllable as a phonetic entity

While it is relatively straightforward to come up with physical (i.e. phonetic) definitions or descriptions for individual speech sounds (as we have seen in the preceding three chapters), doing the same for the syllable is a much harder task. One such articulatorily-based attempt at definition involves the notion of a 'chest pulse' or 'initiator burst', that is, a muscular contraction in the chest (involving the lungs) which corresponds to the production of a syllable; each syllable, on this view, involves one burst of muscular energy. While such a proposal may have some validity for a language like French, in which each syllable lasts roughly the same length of time, it is far less successful for languages like English, in which syllables differ in duration depending on the degree of stress they bear (see below, Section 6.3, for more on stress); for example, the first syllable in 'pigeon' lasts considerably longer than the second, making it unlikely that each corresponds to a single contraction, since each contraction might reasonably be expected to be of the same duration.

While it may be true that there is no general consensus on a clear *phonetic* account of the syllable, this does not mean that the notion has no place in the *phonology* of natural language, since syllables are (in general) clearly identifiable by native speakers, and, as we shall see below (Section 6.3.3) and in Chapter 10, syllables play an important role in many phonological processes, and for this reason alone are worthy of our consideration. From now on, then, when we refer to the syllable we mean the phonological construct rather than some specific phonetic entity.

6.1.2 The internal structure of the syllable

At its most basic level, the typical syllable is made up of a vowel segment preceded and/or followed by zero or more consonantal segments; 'a', 'bee', 'up', 'seen', 'strength', etc. The vowel is known as the **nucleus** or peak of the syllable. Any consonants preceding the nucleus are said to be in the syllable **onset**, and those following the nucleus make up the syllable **coda**. Together, the nucleus and coda form a constituent known as the *rhyme*. So, in the English syllable 'crank', [kɹæŋk], the onset (O) is the sequence of consonants [kɹ], the nucleus (N) is the vowel [æ] and the coda (Co) is the sequence [ŋk], the latter two constituents comprising the rhyme (R) [æŋk]. We can represent this by means of labelled brackets, as $[_\sigma [_O kɹ]_O [_R [_N æ]_N [_{Co} ŋk]_{Co}]_R]_\sigma$, where the Greek letter *sigma*, σ, stands for 'syllable'. We can also represent the syllable as a tree structure, as in (6.1), which is visually somewhat easier to process:

(6.1)

A number of points need to be made about this structure. Firstly, the grouping together of nucleus and coda to form the rhyme is not an arbitrary combination; the rhyme forms a unit distinct from the onset in a number of ways. For example, for two words to rhyme, they must in fact share the same syllabic rhyme (nucleus + coda), whereas the nature of the onset (or even its presence) is irrelevant; so 'gold' rhymes with 'strolled' and with 'old'. In alliteration, on the other hand, it is the onset that is decisive, with the composition of the rhyme being unimportant; 'gold' alliterates with 'game' and with 'gaunt'. In a type of 'slip of the tongue' known as a spoonerism, it is typically onsets which are swapped between syllables, as in 'hog's dead' for 'dog's head' (see Section 10.4.1 for more on *spoonerisms*). More importantly, as we shall see below, a number of phonological processes crucially refer to such constituents, providing strong evidence for their existence.

A second point is that of the three lowest constituents, the onset, nucleus and coda, only the nucleus is always obligatory; both the onset and the coda are optional, as in English 'ape' (no onset), 'flea' (no coda) or 'eye' (neither onset nor coda) (in some languages, the onset is also obligatory, though the coda never is – see below, Section 6.1.3).

Thirdly, it is not always the case that the nucleus must be a vowel; many languages allow liquids and nasals as syllabic nuclei, as in the second syllables in the English words 'spittle' and 'mutton'. Some languages permit other segment types to fill the nucleus position as well; Berber, spoken across North Africa, has words like [.tf.tkt.] 'you suffered a strain', which allows a voiceless fricative and a voiceless stop (in bold) as syllabic nuclei (the dots indicate boundaries between syllables). See also Section 10.4.1 for more on syllable structure.

6.1.3 Sonority and syllables

The nature of the syllabic nucleus, and indeed the order of segments within the syllable as a whole, are in part governed by the notion of *sonority*. Every speech sound has a degree of sonority, which is determined by factors like its loudness in relation to other sounds, the extent to which it can be prolonged, and the degree of stricture in the vocal tract; the more sonorant a sound, the louder, more sustainable and more open it is. Voicing is also relevant here, in that voiced sounds are more sonorant than voiceless ones. In acoustic terms, sonority is related to formant patterns; the more sonorant a sound, the clearer, more distinct its formant structure. Based on these definitions, the most sonorant sounds are low vowels like [ɑ]; the least sonorant class is the voiceless stops, e.g. [t]. Speech sounds can be arranged on a scale of relative sonority, known as the *sonority hierarchy*, as shown below:

(6.4) Least sonorant   Voiceless stops
                         Voiced stops
                         Voiceless fricatives
                         Voiced fricatives
                         Nasals
                         Liquids
                         Glides
                         High vowels
        Most sonorant   Low vowels

This scale has an important role to play in determining the selection of the nucleus of a syllable and the order of segments within the onset and coda.

In general, the most sonorous sounds are selected as syllabic nuclei, with sonority increasing within the onset, and decreasing within the coda. This means that the nucleus forms a high point of sonority (hence the alternative term 'peak' for nucleus), with the margins (onset and coda) as slopes of sonority falling away on either side. So the English syllable 'crank' discussed above might be represented graphically as

75

(6.3)

k ɪ æ ŋ k

This idea of rising then falling sonority within the syllable helps explain certain cross-linguistic phonotactic restrictions. For instance, the reason that a sequence like [ɪkækŋ] is impossible as a *single* syllable in English (or any other language) is that what would be the onset shows falling sonority, [ɪ] being more sonorant than [k], and the coda shows increasing sonority, [k] being less sonorant than [ŋ]. The only way such a string is possible is as a sequence of three syllables, since it has three sonority peaks: [.ɪ.kæ.kŋ.].

It should be borne in mind, however, that not all phonotactic statements can be ascribed to sonority violations. For example, the ban on word-initial *[kn] in English has nothing to do with sonority, since the sequence adheres to the principle of rising sonority within the onset, and is perfectly acceptable in languages like Danish or German; its ungrammaticality is simply an arbitrary fact about English, unrelated to sonority.

On the other hand, it is clear that the sonority hierarchy is not always conformed to within syllables; it is possible in many languages to find acceptable syllables in which the segments in the onset or coda are in the 'wrong' order. So, for example, English has words like 'stoat' and 'skunk', with a fricative before a stop in the onset, i.e. *falling* sonority; and the codas in 'fox' and 'adze' exhibit *rising* sonority, with stop before fricative. Similarly, German allows words such as *Sprache* 'language' with initial [ʃp] or *Strauss* 'ostrich' with initial [ʃt]. While such forms are clearly counter to any generalisation based on sonority, they do appear to form a specific set of exceptions, in that they don't seem to involve just any random sequences of segments; the segment which is 'out of place' is typically a member of the class known as the *sibilant* fricatives [s, z, ʃ, ʒ].

6.1.4 Syllable boundaries

While the sonority hierarchy is useful in deciding the internal organisation of syllables, it is less helpful when it comes to deciding where one syllable ends and another begins. If we represent a polysyllabic word like 'parrot' in terms of a sonority graph, as we did with 'crank' in (6.3) above, we get the following:

(6.4)

p æ ɹ ə t

While this successfully identifies two sonority peaks at [æ] and [ə], and thus indicates that there are two syllables, it does not tell us where the boundary between them falls. We can surmise that the medial [ɹ] is on the boundary, since it constitutes a sonority trough, but we cannot tell whether it is in the coda of the first syllable or the onset of the second.

To determine the location of the boundary, we need to appeal to the principle of **onset maximisation**. As we noted above, Section 6.1.1, and as we shall illustrate further in the next section, some languages insist on the presence of an onset, and no languages require the presence of a coda. This can be interpreted as indicating that languages prefer onsets, that they are in some sense 'more important' than codas. What this means for syllable boundary placement (syllabification) is that where possible, consonants should be syllabified in onsets rather than codas. So, in the 'parrot' example in (6.4) the boundary comes *before* the [ɹ], which thus forms the onset of the second syllable. Interestingly, this division generally corresponds to native speakers' intuitions about where the boundary should lie (but see Section 10.4.1 for some further discussion).

Now consider the pair of words 'plastic' and 'frantic'; where is the boundary between the first and second syllables in these words? The word 'plastic' is straightforward; onset maximisation predicts that both the [s] and the [t] will be in the onset of the second syllable: 'pla.stic'. But with 'frantic' most speakers would agree that the boundary is between the two consonants: 'fran.tic'. This is because medial clusters can only be assigned to onsets to the extent that such sequences are possible word-initially in the language in question. In English, [st] is a possible word-initial cluster, as in 'stag', but *[nt] is not; there are no words beginning with [nt] in English. This means that the principle of onset maximisation does not apply blindly, assigning all medial consonants to onsets, but takes into account language-specific phonotactic restrictions on permitted onsets. Any medial consonants which cannot be part of a licit word-initial sequence are assigned to the coda of the preceding syllable, as with the [n] in 'frantic' above, or the [k] in 'extra' [ɛk.stɹə] (since while [stɹ] is a permitted initial sequence (as in 'string'), *[kstɹ] is not). It may be the case that more than one of the medial consonants must be assigned to the preceding coda, as in 'ant.ler', since English allows neither *[ntl] or *[tl] initially.

6.1.5 Syllable typology

Languages show considerable variation in what combinations of segments they allow as an acceptable syllable, from the highly restrictive Fijian (Fiji) or Senufo (West Africa), which require a single onset consonant followed by a single nucleus vowel, and never have coda segments, to languages such as Thargari (Western Australia), which allows a single segment in each of the three syllable positions, to rather more liberal languages like English or Polish, which allow three onset segments, long vowels or diphthongs in the nucleus and three or even four coda consonants.

Despite this variation, it is possible to make a number of cross-linguistic generalisations concerning what does or does not constitute a potential syllable in natural language; that is, to establish a typology of syllable structures.

The most basic pattern is that exhibited by Fijian and Senufo, a single onset segment followed by a single nucleus segment, with no coda; a CV syllable. All languages have this structure as a possible syllable type (though as we have mentioned, the nucleus of a syllable is not always necessarily a vowel, making the widely-used CV notation potentially misleading).

In some languages, such as Cayuvava (Bolivia), the onset may be optional, giving two possible syllable shapes, CV and V. This is schematically represented as (C)V, where the brackets around the onset C indicate its optionality. A third possibility is that the language has the basic CV pattern, but also allows optional codas, a situation found in e.g. Thargari, allowing CV and CVC shapes, represented as CV(C). Finally, the language may allow both onsets and codas to be optional, i.e. (C)V(C), giving the syllables CV, V, CVC, VC, as in Mokilese (Micronesia). Note that certain facts emerge from this range of possibilities; i) all languages require the syllable to have a nucleus, ii) no language prohibits onsets (though they may be optional) and iii) no language requires codas (though again they may be optional). So there are no languages in which e.g. *V or *VC are the only possible syllable shapes (the asterisk * indicates an ungrammatical form); any language with V or VC syllables must also permit CV syllables.

This account of syllable patterns obviously needs to be extended somewhat, since many languages, including English, allow more than one segment to occupy syllabic positions; that is they allow complex onsets, nuclei and codas. As an example, consider English 'grind', which has an onset consisting of two consonants, a diphthongal nucleus and a two consonant coda. So, for each of the patterns above, there are further sub-options allowing complex onsets and/or codas, as well as the possiblity of the nucleus being a long vowel or diphthong. The number of segments allowed in the onset and/or coda may be limited to two, as for Finnish or Totonac (Mexico), or the language may allow three or more segments in these positions, as in English or Dutch.

6.2 Stress

In a sequence of syllables making up a word, one syllable is always more prominent than the others. This syllable involves more muscular effort in its production; it is louder, longer and shows more pitch variation than the surrounding syllables (on pitch, see below, Section 6.3.1). This more prominent syllable is said to bear **stress**. So, in 'pa.rrot' the first syllable is more prominent than the second, i.e. is stressed (shown in bold); the second syllable is said to be 'unstressed'. In 'ra.ccoon', on the other hand, it is the last syllable which is louder and longer than the first, i.e. bears the stress.

The position of the stressed syllable is usually stated with respect to the right edge, i.e. the end, of the word, so '**pa**.rrot' is described not as having initial stress, but rather as having penultimate stress, just as 'ar.ma.**di**.llo' does; words such as '**e**.le.phant' and 'a.**spa**.ra.gus' are said to have antepenultimate stress. Words like 'ra.**ccoon**' and 'ba.**boon**', with stress on the last syllable, are said to have final stress.

In longer words like 'a.lli.ga.tor' or 'ar.ma.**di**.llo' it is not simply a matter of one syllable being stressed and the others unstressed, as was the case with '**pa**.rrot'. If you say these longer words, it should be clear that the syllables bear different amounts or degrees of stress; in '**a**.lli.ga.tor', while the initial syllable is clearly the most prominent, it is also the case that 'ga' is more prominent than 'tor'. The same holds for 'ar' with respect to 'ma' in 'ar.ma.**di**.llo'. Within a word it is useful to recognise three different degrees of stress; a syllable may bear the **primary** (or 'main') stress, it may bear **secondary** stress, or it may be unstressed; so in 'ar.ma.**di**.llo', 'di' bears the primary stress, 'ar' has secondary stress, and 'ma' and 'llo' are unstressed. In transcriptions, primary stress is indicated by a superscript ' at the beginning of the relevant syllable, secondary stress by a subscript ˌ and unstressed syllables are left unmarked; an RP transcription of 'ar.ma.**di**.llo' would thus be [ˌɑːməˈdɪləʊ].

This alternating pattern of a stressed syllable followed by an unstressed syllable is very common across languages. The effect is known as *eurhythmy*, and a crucial component of eurythmy is the *foot*. Just as syllables are made up of segments, so the foot is made up of syllables. The foot is a phonological structure consisting of a stressed syllable (often known as the *head*) plus any associated unstressed syllables, so both 'alligator' and 'armadillo' have two feet (phonologically). A foot which is made up of a stressed syllable followed by one or more unstressed ones, such as 'wa.lla.by', is known as a 'left-headed foot' or *trochee*. The opposite pattern, where the unstressed syllable(s) precede(s) the stressed syllable, as found in French cro.co.**dile**, is known as a right-headed foot or *iamb*. See below, and Section 10.4.3, for more discussion of feet.

To return to our discussion of stress, it should not be thought that secondary stress is only a feature of longer words in English (or other languages); consider the difference in the stress patterns of pairs of words like 'rabbit' and 'rabbi' or 'contain' and 'maintain'. In the first pair, the main stress is on 'ra', in the second pair on 'tain'; the difference lies in the degree of stress on the other (non main stress-bearing) syllable in each word. Compare the second syllables in the words in the first pair, 'bbit' versus 'bbi'. It should be apparent that they are not equal in terms of the degree of stress they bear; 'bbi' is more prominent than 'bbit'. This is because 'bbi' bears secondary stress, whereas 'bbit' is unstressed. The same is true of the syllables 'main' and 'con' in the second pair of words; 'main' bears secondary stress, 'con' is unstressed. This difference is in part the reason for the distinction in vowel quality between the non main stressed syllables in each pair; fully unstressed syllables show reduced vowels like [ɪ] and [ə], whereas syllables with secondary stress show much less vowel reduction, here the diphthongs [aɪ] and [eɪ] respectively. In terms of foot structure, we can say that 'rabbit' consists of a single trochaic foot, whereas 'rabbi' has two feet, each comprising a single (stressed) syllable. The same is true of 'maintain', which also has two monosyllabic stressed feet. The case of 'contain' is a little more complex; it might be thought that such words comprise an iambic foot, with an unstressed syllable preceding a stressed one. However, English is usually considered to have only trochaic feet, meaning that if the word is produced in isolation, the 'con' syllable is not part of any foot (a 'stray' syllable), or, in the more usual case, belongs to a *preceding* trochaic foot, as in '|**tins** con|**tain** it|', where 'tins' and 'tain' bear stress (foot boundaries are marked by |). Note that this means that word boundaries and phonological boundaries do not necessarily occur in the same places; a single word can be part of two different feet.

6.2.1 The functions of stress

All languages exhibit stress in some form or other, but the role it plays may vary. In some languages, stress always falls on the same syllable within a word; in Czech, for example, the first syllable of a word always bears main stress, irrespective of the word's length – *pivo* 'beer', *kocovina* 'hangover'. In French or Turkish, it is the final syllable of the word which bears main stress; in Polish, the penultimate. In such languages, stress may be said to have a 'delimiting' function, in that it identifies word boundaries; if you hear a stressed syllable in Czech, you know that you're at the beginning of a word, whereas if you hear a stressed syllable in Turkish, you know you're at the end of a word.

Stress in English, on the other hand, clearly does not behave in this way, since main stress can occur on any of the antepenultimate, penultimate or final syllables, as we saw above, and may vary within different forms of the same word; so 'photograph' has main stress on 'pho', but in 'photography' 'to' bears main stress, and in 'photographic' it's 'gra' which is most prominent (we consider what governs the placement of English stress in the next section). On occasion, the position of the main stress may even vary within the same word itself; so, in isolation, numbers like 'thirteen' are stressed on the final syllable ('thir**teen**'), but when they are followed by another stressed syllable, the stress on 'teen' shifts to the first syllable to preserve eurhythmy, as in '**thir**teen pints'. While it is true that each word in English only has one main stress, just as in Czech and French, we cannot tell where a word begins or ends simply by knowing the position of the stressed syllable.

One of the functions stress may have in English is to distinguish between words; it has a differentiating function. Consider the words 'insult', 'compound' and 'invalid'; each of these has two different readings depending on the position of the main stress. In the first two words, if the first syllable is stressed, we have nouns: 'an **in**sult', 'a **com**pound'; if the second syllable is stressed, we have a verb: 'to in**sult**', 'to com**pound**'. The third word is either a noun, '**in**valid' (with antepenultimate stress) or an adjective, 'in**val**id' (with penultimate stress). Such pairs of words, which are identical except for one component of their make-up, in this case stress, are known as **minimal pairs** (other examples of minimal pairs include '*k*in' vs. '*p*in' or 'do*g*' vs. 'di*g*', where the contrasting components are in italics; see Section 8.2.1 for a fuller discussion). Stress can also be used to mark contrast, as in 'I said a **big** farm, not a **pig** farm', or to indicate emphasis, as in 'He **ran** all the way to the pub'.

6.2.2 Stress placement

Given our discussion above concerning the variability of the position of stress in a language like English, it might reasonably be asked whether there are any rules which govern the placement of stress in a word. Clearly, for languages such as Czech or French, such rules are easily and simply stated; 'Place main stress on the initial syllable' (for Czech) or 'Place main stress on the final syllable' (for French). But for many languages, including English, this approach is clearly not going to work, as we have seen; the rules will need to be rather more complex to allow for the wider range of possible sites for stress. But it is important to be aware that there are nonetheless rules governing stress placement in English. It is not a case of having to learn the position of stress for each individual word. That stress placement *is* usually predictable can be shown quite easily; consider the words 'hariolate' and 'oblavity'. The chances are that you will not be familiar with either, yet if you are a native speaker of English (and probably even if you're not), you will be likely to pronounce the first (which means 'to tell the future with beans') with main stress on the initial syllable and secondary stress on the final, and the second word (which doesn't mean anything at all – we made it up) with stress on the antepenultimate syllable. That (most) speakers agree on this suggests that there must be some principles or rules determining where stress is placed.

So what does determine where stress falls in an English word? There are a number of factors involved, including the word class (noun, verb, adjective, etc.) and the nature of any suffixes that may form part of the word (-ate, -ic, -ity, etc.). A full account of stress placement in English is far beyond the scope of this book, but we will look at some of the more obvious generalisations in this section.

One of the most important factors in locating stress within the word is syllable structure. Consider the stress placement in the nouns listed below, where syllable boundaries are again indicated by dots.

(6.5) a. e.le.phant   b. hy.e.na   c. ve.ran.da
          wa.lla.by   com.pu.ter   u.ten.sil
          al.ge.bra   po.ta.to   con.vic.tion
          oc.to.pus   ko.a.la   pen.tath.lon

In (6.5a), the words have antepenultimate stress, whereas those in (6.5 b & c) have stress on the penultimate syllable. For the majority of nouns in English, stress is determined by the nature of the penultimate syllable, or more specifically the nature of the *rhyme* of the penultimate syllable, since what (if anything) is in the onset is irrelevant to stress placement. In (6.5a) the penultimate rhyme is just a short vowel nucleus, whereas in (6.5b) the penultimate rhyme has a long vowel or a diphthong in the nucleus and in (6.5c) the penultimate rhyme is a short vowel nucleus followed by a consonant in the coda. So there is more 'phonological material' in the rhymes of the penultimate syllables in the words in columns b) and c).

81

Syllables (or rhymes) consisting of long vowels, diphthongs or those with codas, such as those exemplified by the penults in (6.5 b and c) are known as **heavy**; syllables with rhymes consisting only of a short vowel are known as **light** (for more on syllable weight, see Section 10.4.2). For the majority of English nouns of more than two syllables, if the penultimate syllable is heavy, it takes stress; if the penultimate syllable is light, stress is placed one syllable to the left, on the antepenult (even if this is also light, as in 'elephant'). In two syllable words, the penultimate typically bears the stress irrespective of its weight, as in '**musk**rat', '**tur**nip', '**par**rot', '**co**bra'.

These generalisations hold true for large numbers of nouns in English, though there is a relatively small set of exceptions, such as 'kangaroo', 'chimpanzee', 'balloon', 'monsoon', 'abyss', which all have stress on the final syllable. One generalisation we can make about such exceptions is that in each case the final stressed syllable is heavy, but it is not true that all nouns with final heavy syllables have final stress, as words from (6.5) like 'elephant', 'octopus', 'utensil' indicate.

So stress placement in English is dependent in part on syllable **weight** – whether a particular syllable is heavy or light, with heavy syllables attracting stress. Languages for which syllable weight is important in determining stress are said to be **quantity sensitive**, and include Russian, Arabic and many others. Those languages for which syllable weight is irrelevant (i.e. where stress falls on a particular syllable irrespective of its internal structure) are known as **quantity insensitive**, and include French, Czech and Hungarian.

For verbs in English we can make a statement similar to that for nouns, except that the key syllable is not the penultimate, but the final syllable:

(6.6)　a. con.si.der　b. a.ppeal　　c. in.tend
　　　　　a.sto.nish　　en.ter.tain　　co.llapse
　　　　　i.ma.gine　　con.fuse　　　re.pre.sent
　　　　　pro.mise　　　de.ny　　　　su.ggest

In (6.6), the columns parallel those in (6.5) in that (6.6 b and c) have heavy final syllables, and so attract stress. The words in (6.6a), however, appear to have final syllables which aren't the same structure as the equivalent penults in the nouns. In (6.5a) the penults are light, consisting only of a short vowel, but in (6.6a) there is a coda consonant in the final syllable in all four verbs for rhotic varieties, and in all but 'consider' for non-rhotic Englishes. To get around this, and to maintain the generalisation about stress placement and syllable weight, we have to ignore the final consonant in English verbs, if there is one. That is, the stress rules of English act as though the final [ʃ] of 'astonish' or the final [n] of 'imagine' simply aren't there; the final syllables of these two verbs behave as if they were [nɪ] and [dʒɪ] respectively. As such, they are light, and push stress one syllable to the left, onto the penult. Note that this is not just an arbitrary sleight of hand applied to the verbs in (6.6a); it also applies to the verbs in (6.6 b and c), which remain heavy even without the final consonant, having either a long vowel or diphthong, or a short vowel followed by (one) consonant, in their rhymes.

When some element of phonological structure is invisible to a rule in this way, it is said to be **extrametrical**; that is, outside the domain to which the rule applies. As a further example of this idea, returning to the noun stress patterns, we can combine the generalisation regarding nouns with that for verbs by saying that for nouns, the whole of the final syllable is extrametrical, that is, invisible to the stress rules. The rules then apply in the same manner to the final *visible* syllable for both nouns and verbs.

As was the case with nouns, not all verbs adhere to the pattern outlined above; there are many sets of exceptions to the general rules. Verbs like 'permit', 'express', 'begin', 'discuss', for instance, all have final stress even though they have the same final syllable structure as the verbs in (6.6a). As we said above, this is not the place for a complete account of English stress placement; the point to be made is that it is possible to state some generalisations, and that syllable weight is an important conditioning factor in these generalisations.

Adjectives in English are even more complex, typically behaving either like nouns, as in

(6.7) a. won.der.ful   b. en.thra.lling   c. a.ttrac.tive
          in.cre.di.ble   u.ni.ted   tri.um.phant
          con.fi.dent   a.ma.zing   a.ttack.ing

or like verbs, as in

(6.8) a. so.lid   b. in.sane   c. co.rrupt
          sim.ple   com.plete   un.kempt
          ur.gent   ob.tuse   in.tact

The distinction is in part dependent on the morphological structure of the adjectives; those with suffixes, as in (6.7), often behave like nouns, those without suffixes, as in (6.8), mainly behave like verbs. Further, the nature of the suffix may well influence the stress placement; the adjective-forming suffix '-ic', for example, attracts stress onto the immediately preceding syllable, as in '**pho**tograph' but 'photo**gra**phic'. This is true not just for adjectival suffixes, but also for other word classes; the noun-forming suffix '-ity' behaves like '-ic' in attracting stress to the immediately preceding syllable, as in '**per**sonal' but 'perso**na**lity', and '-ation' always takes main stress on the first syllable of the suffix, so 'con**si**der' but 'conside**ra**tion'. Suffixes such as '-ic', '-ity' and '-ation' are known as **stress-shifting** suffixes, and contrast with suffixes like '-ly', '-al' and '-ness' which are **stress-neutral**, in that they have no effect on stress placement: '**per**sonal(ly)', 'in**flec**tion(al)', '**squa**lid(ness)'.

6.2.3 Stress above the level of the word

Just as one syllable in each word is more prominent than the others, so in longer stretches of syllables like phrases and sentences, one syllable will always be most prominent. In the following English sentences, spoken with normal delivery, the most prominent syllable of all is the head syllable of the final foot:

(6.9)   he likes watching **foot**ball
        United were **win**ning
        she was out last **night**
        the group all left to**get**her

However, in these larger structures, the position of stress is much less fixed than for individual words. The most prominent syllable may be in some other position in the sentence, to indicate contrast, for example, as in 'he likes **watch**ing football (but not playing it)' or 'U**ni**ted were winning (but City were losing)'. Similarly, stress may be moved for emphasis; 'she **was** out last night (definitely)' or 'the group **all** left together (every last one of them)'.

6.3 Tone and intonation

In this section, we look at two further phonolological phenomena which affect syllables and larger units: tone and intonation. In a sense, these are really the same thing, in that they are both fundamentally based on pitch (see Section 5.1.2 and the next section below). The distinction between tone and intonation has to do in part with the size of the unit to which they apply, tone being essentially a property of individual syllables or words, while intonation can apply to much longer stretches, such as phrases or sentences. The other major difference between tone and intonation has to do with the role they play in a language; tone is typically used as a way of distinguishing between items at word level (such as minimal pairs, words which are identical except for one component), whereas intonation is used for a variety of functions including distinguishing between clause types (e.g. statements vs. questions) or signalling speaker attitude.

6.3.1 Pitch

The physical basis for tone and intonation is the rate of vibration of the vocal cords. To recap from Chapter 5, the number of times the vocal cords vibrate (as when producing a voiced sound) in one second is known as the fundamental frequency, measured in 'cycles per second' (cps) or Hertz (Hz), and our perception of this rate of vibration is known as *pitch*. The greater the fundamental frequency, the higher pitched we perceive the sound to be; hence women typically have higher voices than men, because the vocal cords in human females vibrate more quickly than those of males, with average fundamental frequencies of c. 220 Hz for women, but only c. 120 Hz for men.

When we speak, we vary the rate of vocal cord vibration, making our voices sound higher or lower, either deliberately for some specific effect (like imitating someone else) or unconsciously in the same way we raise or lower the velum for oral vs. nasal sounds, or use the front or back of the tongue for different vowels. As was mentioned in Section 6.2 above, this kind of (unconscious) variation in pitch is one of the properties of a stressed syllable.

6.3.2 Tone

In many languages, pitch variation is used to distinguish one word from another, just as English uses voicing ('pit' vs. 'bit') or place of articulation ('pit' vs. 'kit'). For example, in Nupe (Nigeria), the sequence [ba] has three completely different meanings, depending on the pitch with which it is produced; if the pitch is high, it means 'to be sour', if the pitch is low, it means 'to count' and if the pitch level is between the two, [ba] means 'to cut'. Languages which use pitch in this way are known as **tone languages**, and the individual pitch patterns associated with words or syllables are known as **tones**. So the Nupe syllable [ba] can have three different tones associated with it, high, low and mid, and the choice of tone determines which Nupe word is pronounced. Terms like 'high', 'mid' and 'low' pitch are, of course, relative rather than absolute; a 'high' tone is high only in relation to other tones, and the actual value in Hertz will vary from speaker to speaker, and from language to language. Recall that men typically have lower-pitched voices than women, so a male high tone might have lower pitch than a female low tone for speakers of the same language.

In the case of the Nupe syllable [ba], each tone stays the same throughout the syllable – that is, the pitch is maintained at the same rate for the duration of the syllable; such tones are known as **level tones**. In other instances, the pitch may vary during the production of the syllable, for example starting high and ending low, i.e. a falling tone, or starting low and ending high, a rising tone. Further, the starting point of the rise or fall can vary, giving for example a high-rise or a low-rise, a high-fall or a low-fall. Even more complex combinations are encountered, such as high-low-high (a fall-rise), or low-high-low (a rise-fall); tones exhibiting pitch variation during their production are known as **contour tones**. Cantonese, for example, has six different tones, four level and two contour; so the syllable [jau] can be any one of six different words depending on the tone. With a high level tone, [jau] means 'worry', with a mid tone it means 'thin', with a low tone it means 'again', with a very low tone 'oil'; with a high rise contour tone [jau] means 'paint' and with low rise contour it means 'have'.

Other languages use tone to distinguish between groups of words which have a tone, and those which don't, rather than distinguishing minimal pairs as such; these languages are known as pitch-accent, or accentual, languages, and include Japanese and Punjabi. In Japanese, for example, one class of words, known as *accented*, has a fall from the stressed syllable to the following syllable, as in *ongaku* 'music', where the first syllable has high pitch and the second low pitch, or *tamanegi* 'onion', with high pitch on the penultimate and low pitch on the final syllable. This class is distinguished from words like *sakana* 'fish', known as *unaccented*, which show a standard tonal pattern of low pitch for the first syllable and high pitch for any following syllables, irrespective of the position of the stressed syllable.

Although tone languages may seem exotic to speakers of European languages, it is estimated that at least 50 per cent of the world's languages employ tone to some extent; the figure may even be as high as 70 per cent. Many languages in East and South-east Asia, the Pacific, Africa, as well as North and South America, are tonal; only in Europe, the Middle East and Australasia are tone languages rare. Yet even in Europe there are languages which are tonal to some degree, including Swedish, Norwegian, Serbo-Croat and Lithuanian, along with some varieties of Dutch and Basque. Lithuanian and Serbo-Croat are accentual languages, like Japanese, but in Swedish, for example, there are some 350 bisyllabic minimal pairs which are distinguished by tone, such as *anden* which with a falling tone means 'the duck' and with a fall-rise means 'the spirit', or *tanken* which means 'the tank' with a falling tone but 'the thought' with a fall-rise. While Swedish could not be said to be a fully-fledged tone language like Cantonese, in that only a small proportion of the vocabulary employs tonal distinctions, it is nonetheless clear that tone does have a role in the phonology of Swedish.

6.3.3 Intonation

The majority of European languages do not use pitch variation to make distinctions at word level, as we have seen above. Nonetheless, pitch variation *is* used in languages like English, Danish, Italian or Romanian; such languages use pitch variation over larger structures like phrases or sentences, when it is known as **intonation** (and the languages as **intonation languages**).

Consider the pattern of pitch variation, or the 'tune', of an English sentence like 'He went to the pub' spoken with an umarked, neutral delivery. Here, the pitch is low on 'he', jumps sharply for 'went', lowers slightly for 'to' and for 'the' and then falls on 'pub', the most prominent syllable in the sentence. This syllable is known as the **tonic** syllable, and in English is typically the stressed syllable of the final foot. We can show this pattern, or **intonation contour**, as in

(6.10)

He   went   to   the   pub

where a dot indicates a syllable's pitch level, a larger dot being a more prominent syllable (i.e. showing some degree of stress), and a line indicates a pitch contour on the tonic syllable. Compare this pattern with the same sequence when pronounced as a question, as in (6.11).

(6.11)

     - • - - ♩

He went to the pub

In this case all the syllables have relatively high pitch, and the final syllable shows a rise rather than a fall.

These two contours are typical of the intonational distinction in English between statements, as in (6.10), which have a fall on the tonic syllable, and yes/no questions (i.e. those which can be answered by either 'yes' or 'no'), which have a rise on the tonic syllable. Questions like 'When are we going?' (known as wh- questions because they begin with words beginning 'wh-'), which can't be answered with 'yes' or 'no', typically have a fall on the tonic (in this case, 'go'), similar to statements. Other common patterns in English include a series of rises terminated by a fall, used for enumerations or lists, as in 'We've got bitter, mild, stout and porter' which has rises on 'bitter', on 'mild' and on 'stout', but a fall on 'porter'. Imperatives are characterised by a fall on the tonic syllable, as in 'Leave it!', with a fall on 'leave' and low pitch on 'it'; greetings or salutations by a rise on the tonic, as in 'congratulations', with a rise in pitch on 'la'. As we shall see below, however, intonation patterns are not fixed with respect to clause type; those outlined above are simply the ones most commonly associated with the particular type of clause in unmarked situations.

Intonation contours are organised into units known as **intonation groups** (or 'tone groups'). An intonation group is characterised by the presence of a tonic syllable plus any associated non-tonic syllables. The tonic syllable is the syllable which shows the most noticeable pitch variation, and, as mentioned above, in unmarked structures in English is typically the stressed syllable of the last foot. In the example sentences above, 'He went to the pub' (either as a statement or a question) constitutes a single intonation group, as does 'When are we going?' In the case of 'We've got bitter, mild, stout and porter', on the other hand, there are four intonation groups: 'We've got bitter' (tonic on 'bi'), 'mild' and 'stout' (both consisting solely of a tonic syllable), and 'and porter' (tonic on 'por'). We can represent this as in (6.12), where the vertical lines indicate the intonation group boundaries.

(6.12)

         -    -

-      •   ♩   ♩ - ↘ -

We've got bitter | mild | stout | and porter

It might be thought that intonation group boundaries necessarily coincide with pauses, since it would not be unlikely, for instance, to hear the above sentence with small pauses corresponding to the vertical lines. However, it is equally likely that the sentence would be produced with no pauses at all, but it would still have four intonation groups. It is also possible to pause in places that are not intonation group boundaries, for instance between 'and' and 'porter' in the above example, in order perhaps to keep someone waiting, or to create suspense (or because of a poor memory). So although pauses and group boundaries *may* coincide, there is no necessary link between them.

Intonation can also be used to signal information regarding the syntactic structure of an utterance. Consider a sentence like 'the team which was knocked out of the competition was found guilty of match-fixing' (deliberately written without punctuation). This sentence can be read in two ways, depending on where the intonation group boundaries are located. If there are only two groups, with a boundary between 'competition' and 'was', as in (6.13), with tonics on 'ti' and 'match', then the relative clause 'which was knocked out of the competition' serves to identify the particular team that is being discussed (it's a *restrictive* relative clause).

(6.13) | the team which was knocked out of the compe**ti**tion | was found guilty of **match**-fixing |

If there are three intonation groups, with a boundary between 'team' and 'which' as well as between 'competition' and 'was', as in (6.14), with a tonic on 'team' as well as on 'ti' and 'match', then the identity of the team is already known.

(6.14) | the **team** | which was knocked out of the compe**ti**tion | was found guilty of **match**-fixing |

In this case, the relative clause simply gives extra, incidental information concerning the team (it's a *non-restrictive* relative clause, which would be enclosed by commas in written English).

Perhaps the most obvious use of intonation, however, is to indicate **attitude**. This is an immensely complex area, and one that we can hardly scratch the surface of here. There is considerable variation, both across languages and across varieties of a single language, and there are many other non-linguistic factors which play a role. In very broad terms, however, in English a falling contour often indicates notions like certainty or completion (cf. its use in statements discussed above), whereas a rising contour often indicates uncertainty and continuation (as in questions). In the same way, falling contours often indicate negative attitude, especially in instances where a rising pattern might be expected. So a yes/no question with a fall on the tonic syllable might indicate a lack of interest, or dismissiveness, or unfriendliness, on the part of the speaker, as might a list like that in (6.12) with a series of falls replacing the rising tonic syllables. Rising patterns, on the other hand, typically indicate positive attitudes, especially if the unmarked pattern for the utterance would be a fall. So a wh- question like 'When are we going?' with a rise on the tonic 'go' might indicate things like enthusiasm or friendliness on the speaker's part. Combinations like fall-rise and rise-fall on the tonic syllable also fit this general pattern, with a fall-rise often indicating some degree of uncertainty, or a need for reassurance, as in 'I think I want to go', with a fall-rise on 'think'. A rise-fall, on the other hand, may indicate that the speaker is impressed, or strongly agrees with what is being said, as in 'I definitely want to go', with a rise-fall on 'go'.

The overall level of pitch, and the size of the falls or rises, also contribute to an indication of attitude; a low general level of pitch often indicates a lack of interest or boredom, whereas high pitch, or marked movement between pitch levels, typically indicates enthusiasm and commitment. This is also seen in the size of pitch variations; a low fall often indicates a reserve, or seriousness, or coldness on the part of the speaker, whereas a high fall might indicate more interest, or be used for emphasis. A low rise might indicate some degree of criticism or contradiction or puzzlement, whereas a high rise often indicates surprise or incredulity.

It must be remembered that these general associations of intonation contours to attitude are exactly that: general. The specific interpretation of an intonation pattern in any particular case is obviously dependent on many contextual factors, most of which will be non-linguistic (including facial and manual gestures, the topic of conversation, the setting, and so on).

It must also be remembered that the comments above apply only to some varieties of English. Just as languages and varieties have different vowels or consonants, so too they have different intonation patterns. For example, a number of British English varieties, including Birmingham, Geordie and Welsh Englishes, seem to show a greater number of rises on tonic syllables than the general discussion above might suggest. Final rising pitch where one might expect a fall is also a feature of the speech of many younger Australians and Californians (as well as becoming increasingly common among younger British speakers, though this is stigmatised by older speakers). However, unlike other aspects of regional variation, intonational differences are much less well understood and documented.

Languages also differ in intonation patterns and usages. If we compare the contours in English with those in, say, Danish, we might find that in statements, Danish often has a low rise where English has a fall: so *det regner* 'it's raining' has low pitch on the tonic 'reg' and a slightly higher pitch on the unstressed 'ner', whereas the English equivalent has a fall on the tonic 'rain' and low pitch on unstressed 'ing'. A further difference is that the overall pitch level in Danish tends to be at the lower end of the spectrum, and shows less overall movement in height than English. Again, however, there is unfortunately a paucity of clear information on cross-linguistic aspects of intonation.

Further reading

There is an accessible treatment of the syllable and English stress in Carr (1999), with more detailed discussions in Giegerich (1992). Ewen and van der Hulst (2001) covers suprasegmental structure from a wider perspective than just English. On tone, see Yip (2004) and on intonation, see Cruttenden (1997) and Ladd (1997).

Exercises

1 Mark the syllable boundaries in the following words. It may be helpful to transcribe the words first, since orthographic representations are often misleading with respect to the number of segments present.

    a. petrol
    b. hippopotamus
    c. ethnicity

    d. unknown
    e. construction
    f. reputable

2 Draw labelled syllable trees for the following words

    a. central   b. attraction   c. bottle   d. complexity

3 Indicate whether the location of the primary stress in the following words is on the antepenult, the penult or the final syllable and say whether the stress placement is regular or irregular (that is, whether or not stress placement is governed by the various generalisations given in Section 6.2.2). If the stress placement is regular, what factor or factors are responsible for its location?

    a. implement (noun)
    b. implement (verb)
    c. cockatoo

    d. athletic
    e. construct (verb)
    f. mahogany

    g. wolverine
    h. indentation
    i. delinquent

4 Given the rules of English stress placement outlined in Section 6.2.2, which syllable would you expect to bear the primary stress in the following, and why?

    a. displactable b. intertracolomy c. bilamic d. golarda e. compandity

5 Identify the tone groups and the tonic syllables in the following, and give the pitch contour for the tonic in each case.

    a. Yesterday I saw him in the pub twice.
    b. Did he have a lot to drink?
    c. I'm not absolutely sure, to be honest.
    d. He seemed to spend most of the time slumped in a corner with a packet of nuts.

Features

In Chapters 2, 3 and 4 we discussed the articulatory description of speech sounds, and saw that each speech sound is not a 'single whole', but is rather composed of a number of separate but simultaneous physical events. In this chapter we look at proposals for treating segments as composed of properties or features.

7.1 Segmental composition

Consider the production of a sound like [t]. A number of independent things have to happen at the same time in order to produce the sound: there must be a flow of air out from the lungs, the vocal cords must be wide apart for voicelessness, the velum must be raised for an oral sound and the blade of the tongue (the active articulator) must be in contact with the alveolar ridge (the passive articulator). If any of these factors is changed, a different sound will result: were the vocal cords to be closer together, causing vibration, the voiced [d] would be produced; if the blade of the tongue were lowered to close approximation with the alveolar ridge, the fricative [s] would result; lowering the velum would result in a nasal, and so on.

From this, we see that speech sounds can be decomposed into a number of articulatory components or properties, each largely independent of the others. Combining these properties in different ways produces different speech sounds. Reference to these properties, or **features**, allows us among other things to show what sounds have in common with each other and how they are related or not related.

Thus [t] and [d] differ from each other by virtue of just one of the articulatory features outlined above (the state of the vocal cords): all the other features are the same for these two sounds. The two sounds can be said to constitute a **natural class** (of alveolar stops), in that no other sounds share this particular set of co-occurring features. In the same way, the set [p, t, k] may be said to constitute a natural class (of voiceless stops), since they differ only in terms of the active and passive articulators involved. On the other hand, [t] and [v] differ in a number of ways: the state of the vocal cords, the active articulator (tongue blade vs. lower lip), the passive articulator (alveolar ridge vs. upper teeth) and the distance between the articulators. The only features [t] and [v] share from those outlined above are direction of airflow and a raised velum, and since many other sounds also have these properties (e.g. [f, d, s, z, k, g]), [t] and [v] do not by themselves constitute a natural class. Being able to refer to natural classes directly and formally in this way is useful for phonologists, since phonological processes typically refer to recurring groupings. Given the phonologist's goal of understanding the system underlying the speech sounds of language, such recurring groupings typically constitute the type of natural class we are interested in discussing. Non-recurring groups of sounds typically do not constitute a class. For instance, nasalisation in English (see Section 3.4) affects only vowels (not a group like [i, r, t, z, u, g]) and is triggered only by nasals (not a group like [w, o, v, k]). Unlike the random sets of sounds in square brackets in the previous sentence, vowels and nasals are each easily identifiable as a natural class. Natural classes may consist of any number of sounds, from two, as in [t, d], to many, as in the class of all vowels. Typically, the smaller the class, the more features will be shared.

7.2 Phonetic vs. phonological features

To characterise segments (and classes) adequately we clearly need a rather more sophisticated and formalised set of features than the loose parameters outlined in the previous section. So what exactly should these features be? If we consider the features necessary to characterise place of articulation, one possible approach might be to translate the physical articulatory terms of Chapter 2 directly into features such as [bilabial], [dental], [alveolar], [palatal], [velar], [uvular], etc. and to classify speech sounds accordingly, specifying for any segment a value of '+' (if the feature is part of the classification of the sound) or '–' (if it is not) for each of the features. A feature which has just two values (+ or –) is known as a **binary** feature. Thus [p], [t] and [k] could be represented in terms of matrices of such binary features, each feature specified as '+' or '–' as in (7.1).

$$
(7.1) \quad [p] \begin{bmatrix} + \text{bilabial} \\ - \text{labiodental} \\ - \text{dental} \\ - \text{alveolar} \\ - \text{palatal} \\ - \text{velar} \\ - \text{uvular} \end{bmatrix} \quad [t] \begin{bmatrix} - \text{bilabial} \\ - \text{labiodental} \\ - \text{dental} \\ + \text{alveolar} \\ - \text{palatal} \\ - \text{velar} \\ - \text{uvular} \end{bmatrix} \quad [k] \begin{bmatrix} - \text{bilabial} \\ - \text{labiodental} \\ - \text{dental} \\ - \text{alveolar} \\ - \text{palatal} \\ + \text{velar} \\ - \text{uvular} \end{bmatrix}
$$

These matrices, each of which lists all of the place of articulation features, imply, however, that each place of articulation is entirely separate from all others. One disadvantage of this is that the majority of 'natural classes' can only be defined negatively; many of the possible classes are those sets of segments not classified as '+' for some feature, e.g. all segments except [p, b, m] are [– bilabial] and would thus form a putative natural class. The problem with this is that while the positively defined classes (such as [+ alveolar] or [+ bilabial]) are the kind of sets of segments we want to be able to refer to in phonology, the negatively defined sets (such as

[– velar] or [– palatal]) typically do not need to be referred to when doing phonological analysis. Furthermore, there is no way of referring to some of the groups we often do need, such as those consisting of more than one place of articulation. Bilabials and labiodentals ([p, b, f, v]), for example, may be classed as 'labials' but cannot be referred to, since there are no combinations of articulatory feature specifications which isolate just these sounds. Conversely, if we replaced 'bilabial' and 'labiodental' with 'labial', we would then be unable to deal with [p, b] separately from [f, v].

A further problem with this approach is that it makes possible many combinations of feature values which are not needed by languages or, worse still, simply cannot be articulated, since if each feature is potentially '+' or '–' nothing in the system will prevent matrices such as those in (7.2), which are nonsensical because they would require the active articulator to be in more than one position (or none) at once. Our goal as phonologists is to express true generalisations about phonological structure as economically as possible and in doing so not leaving open the possibility of making wild and unwanted claims at the same time.

(7.2)

$$
\begin{bmatrix}
+ \text{ bilabial} \\
- \text{ labiodental} \\
+ \text{ dental} \\
- \text{ alveolar} \\
+ \text{ palatal} \\
- \text{ velar} \\
+ \text{ uvular}
\end{bmatrix}
\begin{bmatrix}
- \text{ bilabial} \\
- \text{ labiodental} \\
- \text{ dental} \\
- \text{ alveolar} \\
- \text{ palatal} \\
- \text{ velar} \\
- \text{ uvular}
\end{bmatrix}
\begin{bmatrix}
+ \text{ bilabial} \\
+ \text{ labiodental} \\
+ \text{ dental} \\
+ \text{ alveolar} \\
+ \text{ palatal} \\
+ \text{ velar} \\
+ \text{ uvular}
\end{bmatrix}
$$

This discussion suggests that concrete features like those above are inadequate for our purposes. We therefore need a different set of features. The set we require must allow us as far as possible to make the claims and generalisations we want about how sounds behave in languages, that is, generalisations about sound systems, without having the excessive power of a set like those illustrated in (7.1) and (7.2). That is, we need a less 'concrete', less phonetic, more abstract set of **phonological features**. To illustrate this (and anticipating the discussion below), let us look at the way many phonologists deal with representing the major places of articulation. This is typically done using just two binary features, [anterior] ([+ anterior] sounds are produced no further back in the oral tract than the alveolar ridge) and [coronal] ([+ coronal] sounds are produced in the area bounded by the teeth and hard palate). These two features give four possible combinations, each of which represents a group of sounds as in (7.3).

(7.3)

$$
\begin{bmatrix} + \text{anterior} \\ - \text{coronal} \end{bmatrix}
\begin{bmatrix} + \text{anterior} \\ + \text{coronal} \end{bmatrix}
\begin{bmatrix} - \text{anterior} \\ + \text{coronal} \end{bmatrix}
\begin{bmatrix} - \text{anterior} \\ - \text{coronal} \end{bmatrix}
$$

LABIALS	ALVEOLARS DENTALS	PALATALS	VELARS UVULARS
[p, b, f, v]	[t, d, s, z, θ, ð]	[j, ʃ, ʒ, ʧ, ʤ]	[k, g, x, ʀ]

Further features are necessary to make distinctions within these groups (see Section 7.3), but the problems encountered in the matrices in (7.1) and (7.2) have been resolved: larger groupings can be referred to (e.g. dentals, alveolars and palatals as [+ coronal]) and there are no unused combinations of features. That is, we can make the generalisations concerning the sound systems of languages we want to make without the formal possibility of reference to groups we do not want; a great deal of work is done by just two phonological features.

7.3 Charting the features

As we have just seen, a distinction can be made between phonetic features, that is, those that correspond to physical articulatory or acoustic events, and phonological features, those that allow us to look beyond individual segments at the sound system of language.

One of the goals of linguistics is to determine the universal properties of human language. In terms of phonological features, this means that we need to establish the set of features necessary to characterise the speech sounds found in the languages of the world. Let us assume that there is a universal set of features and that each specific language will require a subset of this universal set, but the set will be both finite and universally available.

To take a concrete example, consider the implosives [ɓ], [ɗ] and [ɠ]. A number of languages have implosives in their inventories of speech sounds, e.g. Sindhi (India), Uduk (Sudan), Swahili (Africa), Hausa (Nigeria), Ik (Nigeria and Uganda), Angas (Nigeria). English, however, does not. This means that universally we need some feature to characterise a segment associated with ingressive airflow, yet that feature is irrelevant to a description of English. Thus, the universal set of phonological features will include a feature for implosives which will either be present but unused in English, or will not be selected for English. While the focus of much of our discussion of features will be English, ideally a featural system must be able to account for all human phonologies. Thus, we will also refer to features that are of relevance to languages other than English.

We have seen that speech sounds can generally be divided into at least two major classes: consonants and vowels (which can be further subdivided into obstruents, sonorant consonants, vowels and glides). If our goal is to achieve the greatest generality, then, ideally, it would be desirable to have a single set of features used to characterise them all rather than, for example, two sets of features, one applicable to consonants and one applicable to vowels. As will be seen below, one way of doing this is to distinguish between obstruents, sonorants, vowels and glides on the basis of major features relevant to all speech sounds, while relying on subsets of features to characterise consonants and vowels further. That is, the phonological system makes available a single full set of features, but some of those features are relevant only for consonants while others are relevant only for vowels.

7.3.1 Major class features

The first set of distinctions we need to make is between the major classes of speech sounds: consonants and vowels, sonorants and obstruents. To do this, we use the features [syllabic], [consonantal] and [sonorant]. Note that the lists of segments and examples given throughout this section, unless otherwise stated, are for RP English. The examples are given in phonetic transcription only (to encourage the reader to become familiar with its use).

[+/− syllabic] allows us to distinguish vowels from other sound types (the symbol ' indicates that the following syllable is stressed):

[+ syll]   sounds are those which function as the nucleus of a syllable, such as the [æ] and [ɪ] in [ˈɹæbɪt];
[− syll]   sounds are those which do not function as syllabic nuclei, such as the [ɹ], [b] and [t] in [ˈɹæbɪt].

Note that under certain circumstances segments other than vowels may be [+ syllabic], for example the liquids and nasals mentioned in Sections 2.3, 3.4 and 3.5, e.g. the final sound in [ˈbʌtn̩].

[+/− consonantal] allows us to distinguish 'true' consonants (obstruents, liquids and nasals) from vowels and glides:

[+ cons]   sounds are those which involve oral stricture of at least close approximation, such as the [p], [l] and [t] in [ˈpælɪt];
[− cons]   sounds are those with stricture more open than close approximation, such as the [j] and [ɛ] in [jɛs].

[+/− sonorant] allows us to distinguish vowels, glides, liquids and nasals from oral stops, affricates and fricatives:

[+ son]   sounds are those which show a clear formant pattern, such as the [n], [j] and [uː] in [njuːts];
[− son]   sounds are those which have no clear formant pattern, such as the [t] and [s] in [njuːts].

Combining these three features gives us precisely the distinctions we need among the major classes of segments, namely the vowels, glides, sonorant consonants and obstruents. The figure in (7.4) shows the classification of the sounds of English in terms of these three major class features.

7.3.2 Consonantal features

Having established the major distinctions between vowels, glides, sonorant consonants and obstruents, we need further features to distinguish among the segments in each of these categories. Concentrating on features that are relevant to consonants, let us see how particular features can be used to characterise smaller and smaller groups of sounds, starting with the feature [voice].

(7.4)

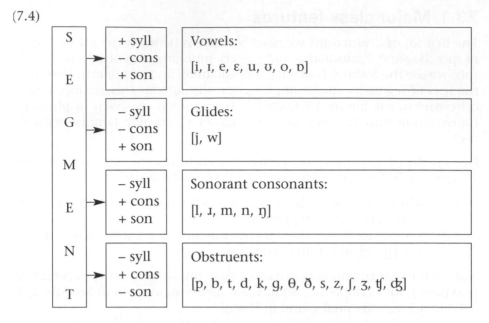

[+/− voice] distinguishes between those consonants that are associated with vibrating vocal cords and those which are not.

[+ voi]   sounds are produced with airflow through the glottis, in which the vocal cords are close enough together to vibrate. These include the glides, sonorants and voiced obstruents, such as the [l], [m], [n] and [d] of ['sælə,mændə] (' indicates primary stress; , indicates secondary stress);

[− voi]   sounds are those produced with the vocal cords at rest, and is relevant primarily to obstruents, such as the [s] and [p] of [æsp].

Note that although vowels and sonorants are typically considered to be [+ voi], we do find voiceless vowels, indicated with a subscript ring, such as the [i̥] in the Totonac (Mexico) word [ʃumpi̥] 'porcupine' and voiceless sonorants such as the [m̥] in the words [tam̥] 'bench' in the Nigerian language Angas, or even the [ɹ̥] in English [fɹ̥aɪ].

7.3.3 Place features

[+/− coronal] is used to distinguish segments involving the front of the tongue, that is, the dentals, alveolars and palatals, from other sounds.

[+ cor]   sounds are those articulated with the tongue tip or blade raised, such as the [t], [d] and [l] sounds in ['tæd,poʊl]. Note that there is some variation with respect to classifying palatal consonants as [+ coronal]. Some phonologists consider palatal sounds to be [− coronal];

[− cor]   sounds are those whose articulation does not involve the front of the tongue, such as the [p] in ['tæd,poʊl].

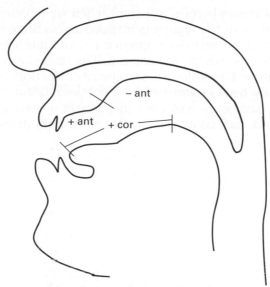

Fig. 7.1 Sagittal section showing [anterior] and [coronal]

[+ cor]: [j, l, ɹ, n, t, d, θ, ð, s, z, ʃ, ʒ, ʧ, ʤ]
[– cor]: [w, m, ŋ, k, g, h, f, v, p, b]

[+/– anterior] distinguishes between sounds produced in the front of the mouth – that is, the labials, dentals and alveolars – and other sounds

[+ ant] sounds are those produced at or in front of the alveolar ridge, such as the [s] and [n] in [sneɪk];

[– ant] sounds are those produced further back in the oral cavity than the alveolar ridge, such as the [k] and [ʤ] in [keɪʤ]. Note that [w] is classified as [– ant] despite its dual articulation.

[+ ant]: [l, ɹ, n, m, t, d, θ, ð, s, z, f, v, p, b]
[– ant]: [j, w, ŋ, ʃ, ʒ, ʧ, ʤ, k, g, h]

Using these two features together, we can define four natural classes of segments, namely

LABIALS:	[– cor, + ant]:	[m, f, v, p, b]
DENTALS/ALVEOLARS:	[+ cor, + ant]:	[l, ɹ, n, t, d, θ, ð, s, z]
PALATO-ALVEOLARS/PALATALS:	[+ cor, – ant]:	[j, ʃ, ʒ, ʧ, ʤ]
VELARS/GLOTTALS:	[– cor, – ant]:	[w, ŋ, k, g, h, ʔ]

Note that the last combination, [– cor, – ant], also includes uvular and pharyngeal segments such as the voiced uvular fricative [ʁ], as in French [ʁuʒ] 'red', and the voiced pharyngeal fricative [ʕ], as in Arabic [faʕala] 'he did'. Note also that while [ɹ] is clearly [+ cor, + ant], not all r-sounds are, for example the uvular trill [R] of German and the uvular fricative [ʁ] of French are neither [+ cor] nor [+ ant].

These natural classes become apparent when we represent the features as vertical columns, with the segments mapped across them from left to right. In the following chart, and in subsequent ones, a double line appears between feature values (+ or –) within the column. The shaded areas represent the + value for the feature. The dotted lines represent distinctions between segments that have already been established by a previous feature. Maintaining the convention of having the voiceless member of a voiceless/voiced pair of sounds on the left, each column is labelled at the bottom for voicing.

(7.5)

7.3.4 Manner features

The features presented in this section are: [continuant], [nasal], [strident], [lateral], [delayed release].

[+/– continuant] distinguishes between stops and other sounds:

[+ cont] sounds are those in which there is free airflow through the oral cavity, such as all the sounds in [fɪʃ];

[– cont] sounds are those in which the airflow is stopped in the oral cavity. This includes both oral and nasal stops, such as the [m] and [p] sounds in [mæp].

[+ cont]: [j, w, l, ɹ, θ, ð, s, z, ʃ, ʒ, h, f, v]
[– cont]: [n, m, ŋ, t, d, ʧ, ʤ, k, g, p, b]

Note that there is some difference of opinion about the status of [l] as [+ cont]; in some of the primary literature [l] is classified as [– cont]. It can be seen as [+ cont] due to the continued airflow but as [– cont] due to the mid-sagittal obstruction (see Section 3.5.1).

(7.6)

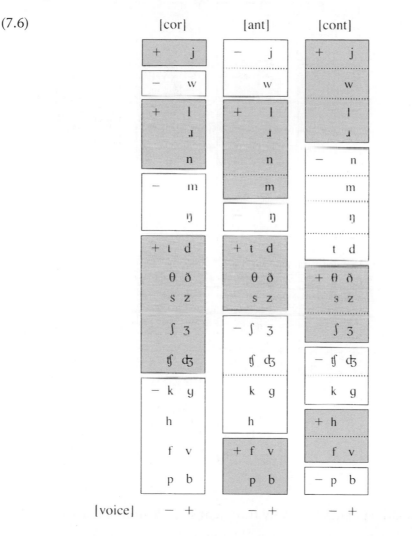

[+/– nasal] differentiates between nasal sounds and non-nasals:

[+ nas] sounds are produced with the velum lowered and consequent airflow through the nasal cavity, as the [m] sounds in ['mæməθ];

[– nas] sounds are produced without airflow through the nasal cavity, for example all the sounds in [θɪʌʃ].

[+ nas]: [n, m, ŋ]
[– nas]: [j, w, l, ɹ, t, d, θ, ð, s, z, ʃ, ʒ, ʧ, ʤ, k, g, h, f, v, p, b]

Note that the feature [nasal] may also be relevant for vowels in some languages, distinguishing, for example, between French *lait* [lɛ] 'milk' and *lin* [lɛ̃] 'flax'.

(7.7)

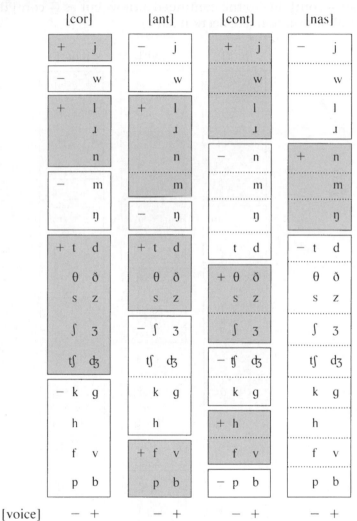

[+/– strident] separates relatively turbulent sounds from all others:

[+ strid] sounds involve a complex constriction which results in a noisy or hissing airflow, such as the [ʃ] in [ʃiːp];
[– strid] sounds are those without such constriction, as the [θ] and [n] in [θɪn].

100

[+ strid]: [s, z, ʃ, ʒ, tʃ, ʤ, f, v]
[− strid]: [j, w, l, ɹ, n, m, ŋ, t, d, θ, ð, k, g, h, p, b]

(7.8)

	[cor]	[ant]	[cont]	[nas]	[strid]
j	+	−	+	−	−
w	−		+		
l	+	+			
ɹ					
n			−	+	
m	−				
ŋ		−			
t d	+	+		−	
θ ð			+		
s z					+
ʃ ʒ		−			
tʃ ʤ			−		
k g	−				
h			+		
f v		+			+
p b			−		−

[voice]   − +   − +   − +   − +   − +

[+/− lateral] separates [l]-sounds from all others, thus distinguishing [l] from [ɹ], with which it shares all other features:

[+ lat] sounds are produced with central oral obstruction and airflow passing over one or both sides of the tongue;

[− lat] refers to all other sounds.

[+ lat]:   [l]
[− lat]:   [j, w, ɹ, n, m, ŋ, t, d, θ, ð, s, z, ʃ, ʒ, tʃ, ʤ, k, g, h, f, v, p, b]

Other languages may have different [l]-sounds, for example, the voiceless lateral fricative [ɬ] of Welsh as in *llyfr* [ɬɪvr] 'book' and the palatal lateral [ʎ] of Italian as in *gli* [ʎi] 'the, masculine plural'. These sounds are also [+ lat].

(7.9)

	[cor]	[ant]	[cont]	[nas]	[strid]	[lat]
j	+	−	+	−	−	−
w	−					
l	+	+				+
ɹ						−
n			−	+		
m	−					
ŋ		−				
t d	+	+		−		
θ ð			+			
s z					+	
ʃ ʒ		−				
ʧ ʤ			−			
k g	−				−	
h			+			
f v		+			+	
p b			−		−	
[voice]	− +	− +	− +	− +	− +	− +

[+/− delayed release] distinguishes affricates from other [− cont] segments:

[+ del rel] sounds are produced with stop closure in the oral cavity followed by frication at the same point of articulation, as is the [ʧ] in ['ʧɪp,mʌŋk];

[− del rel] sounds are produced without such an articulation.

[+ del rel]: [ʧ, ʤ]
[− del rel]: [j, w, l, ɹ, n, m, ŋ, t, d, θ, ð, s, z, ʃ, ʒ, k, g, h, f, v, p, b]

(7.10)

	[cor]	[ant]	[cont]	[nas]	[strid]	[lat]	[del rel]
j	+	−	+	−	−	−	−
w	−						
l	+	+				+	
ɹ						−	
n			−	+			
m	−						
ŋ		−					
t d	+	+		−			
θ ð			+				
s z					+		
ʃ ʒ		−					
tʃ dʒ			−				+
k g	−				−		−
h			+				
f v		+			+		
p b			−		−		

| [voice] | − + | − + | − + | − + | − + | − + | − + |

7.3.5 Vocalic features

The features dealt with in this section are primarily of relevance to distinctions between vowels, though some are also relevant to consonantal distinctions. Vowels need to be distinguished in terms of height, backness, roundness and length, and for these distinctions we use the features [high], [low], [back], [front], [round], [tense] and [Advanced Tongue Root].

7.3.5.1 *[high]*

[+/– high] distinguishes high sounds from other sounds:

[+ hi] sounds are those which involve the body of the tongue raised above what is often called the 'neutral' position (approximately that in [ə]), such as the [ɪ]s in ['wɪpɪt]; [+ hi] consonants include the [j] and [k] in [jæk];

[– hi] sounds are those where the body of the tongue is not so raised, such as the [ɛ] in ['fɛɹɪt]. [– hi] consonants include the [p, ɹ, t] in ['pæɹət].

7.3.5.2 *[low]*

[+/– low] distinguishes low sounds from other sounds:

[+ lo] sounds are those in which the body of the tongue is lowered with respect to the neutral position, such as the [æ] in [ænt]. The only [+ lo] consonants in English are the glottal stop [ʔ] and the glottal fricative [h], though pharyngeals (found in Arabic, for instance) are also [+ lo];

[– lo] sounds are those without such lowering, such as the [ɔː] in [hɔːs]. All English consonants except [h] and [ʔ] are [– lo].

Note that the specification [– hi, – lo] characterises mid vowels such as [ɛ] and [ɔ].

(7.11)

	[high]		[low]
+	iː	–	iː
	ɪ		ɪ
	ʊ		ʊ
	uː		uː
–	ɔ		ɔ
	oː		oː
	ɒ	+	ɒ
	ɑː		ɑː
	ʌ		ʌ
	æ		æ
	eː	–	eː
	ɛ		ɛ
	ə		ə
	ɜː		ɜː

7.3.5.3 [back]

[+/– back] distinguishes back sounds from other sounds:

[+ back] sounds are those in which the body of the tongue is retracted from the neutral position, such as the [uː] in [bəˈbuːn]: [+ back] consonants include the [k], [ŋ] and [g] in [ˌkæŋɡəˈɹuː];

[– back] sounds are those in which the tongue is not retracted, such as the [ɛ] in [wɛlk]. All English consonants except the velars are [– back].

7.3.5.4 [front]

[+/– front] distinguishes sounds produced at the front of the mouth from those produced at the back.

[+ front] sounds are those for which the body of the tongue is fronted from the neutral position. These include the vowels [iː] and [ɪ] as in [ˈiːɡɹɪt], the [ɛ] of [ɛft] and the [æ] of [æsp];

[– front] sounds are those for which the tongue is not fronted. [– front] includes both central and back vowels, e.g the [ə] and [uː] of [bəˈbuːn].

(7.12)

[high]	[low]	[back]	[front]
+ iː	− iː	iː	+ iː
ɪ	ɪ	ɪ	ɪ
ʊ	ʊ	+ ʊ	− ʊ
uː	uː	uː	uː
− ɔ	ɔ	ɔ	ɔ
oː	oː	oː	oː
ɒ	+ ɒ	ɒ	ɒ
ɑː	ɑː	ɑː	ɑː
ʌ	ʌ	− ʌ	ʌ
æ	æ	æ	+ æ
eː	− eː	eː	eː
ɛ	ɛ	ɛ	ɛ
ə	ə	ə	− ə
ɜː	ɜː	ɜː	ɜː

Note that the combination of the features [front] and [back] allows us to characterise *central* vowels, i.e. those that are neither front nor back, [– back, – front], e.g. [ə], [ʌ], [ɨ].

7.3.5.5 [round]

[+/– round] distinguishes rounded sounds from unrounded sounds:

[+ rnd]   sounds are those which are produced with rounded (protruding) lips, such as the [ɔː] in [hɔːs]: Only [w] among the consonants of English is [+ rnd];

[– rnd]   sounds are produced with neutral or spread lips, such as the [ɑː]s in ['ɑːdvɑːk]. All English consonants apart from [w] are [– rnd].

(7.13)

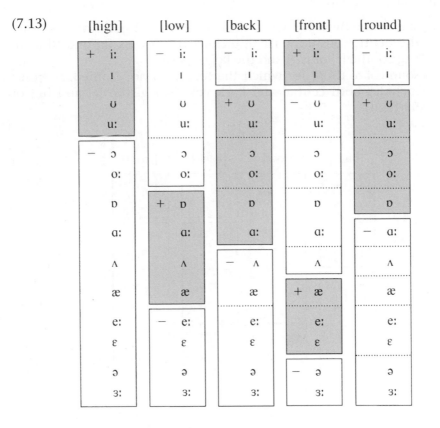

7.3.5.6 [tense]

[+/– tense] can be used to distinguish long vowels from short vowels; [tense] is not generally considered relevant for consonants:

[+ tns]   sounds involve considerable muscular constriction ('tensing') of the body of the tongue compared to its neutral state. This constriction results in a longer and more peripheral sound, such as the [iː] in [ʃiːp];

[– tns] sounds involve no such constriction, resulting in shorter and more centralised sounds, such as the [ɪ] in [dɪp].

(7.14)

	[high]	[low]	[back]	[front]	[round]	[tense]
iː	+	−	−	+	−	+
ɪ						−
ʊ			+	−	+	
uː						+
ɔ	−					−
oː						+
ɒ		+				−
ɑː					−	+
ʌ			−			−
æ				+		
eː		−		+		+
ɛ				+		−
ə				−		
ɜː						+

7.3.5.7 [Advanced Tongue Root]

One further feature often referred to in the characterisation of vowel sounds is [Advanced Tongue Root], a feature particularly useful for the description of a number of West African and other languages which show *vowel harmony* phenomena. In Akan (Ghana), for instance, words may have vowels either from the set [i, e, ɜ, o, u] or from the set [ɪ, ɛ, a, ɔ, ʊ], but not (typically) a mixture of vowels from both sets: e.g. [ebuo] 'nest' or [ɛbʊɔ] 'stone', but not *[ebʊɔ].

[+/– Advanced Tongue Root] distinguishes advanced vowels from others:

[+ ATR] sounds are produced with the root of the tongue pushed forward from its 'neutral' position, typically resulting in the tongue body being pushed upward, such as the Akan vowels [i, e, ɜ, o, u];

[– ATR] sounds are those in which the tongue root is not pushed forward, such as the Akan vowels [ɪ, ɛ, a, ɔ, ʊ].

107

It should be noted that [ATR] is sometimes used in the description of English for the distinctions referred to above under the feature [tense], since advancing the root of the tongue often involves a concomitant raising of the tongue body; thus [+ ATR] can be seen as similar to [+ tns].

7.3.6 Further considerations

While the set of features outlined in the preceding sections is much the same as that found in most textbooks, and indeed in many primary sources, it should be noted that it is by no means uncontroversial or unproblematic.

For instance, the features proposed for vowels in Section 7.3.5 involve a number of awkward compromises and omissions with respect to vowel systems encountered in the languages of the world. Vowel height is characterised above in terms of the features [high] and [low]. Formally, this gives us four possible feature combinations, since each feature is binary: [+ hi, − lo], [− hi, − lo], [− hi, + lo] and [+ hi, + lo]. The problem here is two-fold; firstly, although there are four combinations, the system can actually only characterise three vowel heights. The combination [+ hi, + lo] represents a physical impossibility, since the tongue cannot be simultaneously raised and lowered. This means that languages with more than three vowel heights, like Danish, with [i, e, ɛ, a] (high, high-mid, low-mid, low), are impossible to characterise using just these features. The second aspect to the problem is that the system overgenerates, in that it formally allows a combination, [+ hi, + lo], that represents a vowel-type that is not found in human languages (and, indeed, *could* never be found). The system is thus failing to model the facts of language, by having to allow a segment type that cannot exist.

Similarly, many accounts use a single feature, [back], to characterise the horizontal axis, but this creates difficulties for languages with central vowels (like English [ʌ] and [ə]), since only two horizontal positions, [+ back] and [− back], are possible. If we get around this by proposing *two* features, both [back] and [front], as we do above, then although this allows us to characterise central vowels as [− front, − back], it runs into the same problem of overgeneration that we have just encountered with vowel height, in that it allows the unwanted (and physically impossible) [+ front, + back].

This problem of overgeneration is in fact endemic in binary feature systems; given the eighteen binary features listed here, over 260 000 different feature combinations are possible, the vast majority of which will never be utilised to represent segments, and a large proportion of which are simply impossible as characterisations of actual speech sounds.

There are also problems with some of the individual features. The feature [tense] has sometimes been appealed to as a way of solving the problem of representing four vowel heights. So, for English [iː] vs. [ɪ], where [ɪ] might be seen as high-mid, the height distinction is dealt with by claiming that [iː] is [+ tense], and so higher than [ɪ], which is [− tense] (see Section 7.3.5.6). Whilst this approach might be considered adequate for English, where both the length and quality of the vowels are different, it does not deal with languages such as Danish, which have length contrasts without concomitant quality differences, as in [iː] vs. [i], while also having contrasts like [e] vs. [ɛ], where there is no length distinction, but purely one of height. But not only is the feature [tense] not able to solve the problem, it is also problematic in other ways; its articulatory definition is dubious at best, and to the extent it is relevant to consonants at all, it seems to do a completely different job, being largely concerned with voiceless ([+ tense]) vs. voiced ([– tense]) sounds.

A similar difficulty is encountered with a feature like [delayed release]; while this seems to be a feature like any other, in fact it only serves one, very specific, purpose; its sole role is to distinguish affricates, as [+ del rel], from other stops, which are [– del rel]. Furthermore, it fails to capture the nature of the difference between affricates and stops, which has to do with the extent of lowering of the active articulator, rather than the timing of the release (cf. Section 3.2).

A different kind of problem is encountered with the feature [voice]. This feature clearly allows for two glottal states, [– voice] i.e. voiceless and [+ voice] i.e. voiced, and we have used this to characterise the difference between /p, t, k/ and /b, d, g/ in English. However, we have also noted that there are other important differences between these two groups in English. We saw in Section 3.1.3 that the first group are often aspirated, whereas the second group never are, but none of the features we have discussed so far can be said to account for aspiration versus lack of it. It could be argued that since aspiration is not distinctive in English (i.e. it has only phonetic but not phonological significance), this lack of a phonological feature for aspiration is of no import. However, given that there are languages (such as Danish) for which it is aspiration, not voicing, that is the active distinguishing characteristic between the sets of stops, we need to be able to characterise the distinction. A possible solution is to introduce the feature [+/– spread glottis], where [+ spread glottis] involves a fully open glottis, as for aspirates; non-aspirated sounds (whether voiced or voiceless) are [– spread glottis]. Indeed, it can be, and has been, argued that this is the appropriate way of characterising the distinction between /p, t, k/ and /b, d, g/ in English, given that, along with the aspiration facts, voicing may be variable for the second group, but not for the first group (cf. Section 3.1.4). The [+/– voice] distinction would then be reserved for languages such as French in which the /b, d, g/ set are always fully voiced, and the /p, t, k/ set always unaspirated. The full characterisation of laryngeal states is rather more complex than outlined here (see Section 2.1.2), and may well involve yet more features; this is not the place for a full discussion.

Another problem for this characterisation of segments in terms of lists of distinctive features arises when we consider 'complex' sound types such as diphthongs and affricates. The features outlined in this chapter refer to *states*, in the sense that each value for a feature describes a particular setting of the vocal organs, such as 'velum lowered' for [+ nasal], or 'tongue raised' for [+ high]. The difficulty here is that diphthongs and affricates are

109

'dynamic', in the sense that the tongue starts in one position and moves to another (see Section 4.3). It might be possible to think of diphthongs as a sequence of two sets of features, i.e. as one vowel followed by another, but this would fail to indicate the 'single sound' aspect of a diphthong, which behaves in many ways like a long vowel and not as a sequence of two short vowels. The same is true for affricates; see again Section 3.2.

We shall return to some of the issues raised here in Chapters 10 and 13, where possible solutions to some of these problems will be outlined.

7.4 Conclusion

The focus of this chapter has been on features as the building blocks which make up segments. A segment can thus be seen as comprising a list – or matrix – of features; [p] might thus be as in (7.15).

(7.15)
$$
\begin{array}{l}
/p/ \\
\left[\begin{array}{l}
- \text{ syll} \\
+ \text{ cons} \\
- \text{ son} \\
- \text{ cor} \\
+ \text{ ant} \\
- \text{ cont} \\
- \text{ nas} \\
- \text{ stri} \\
- \text{ lat} \\
- \text{ del rel} \\
- \text{ high} \\
- \text{ low} \\
- \text{ back} \\
- \text{ round} \\
- \text{ voice}
\end{array}\right]
\end{array}
$$

Although, as we have seen in the preceding section, there are some difficulties with the mechanics of this view of segmental structure, the basic insight, that segments are made up of smaller phonological entities, remains valid. By referring to phonological features like those we have discussed in this chapter, phonologists are able to identify formally natural classes of sounds as those sharing a set of common feature specifications. So, the set of sounds [p, t, k, b, d, g] in English share the feature specifications [+ consonantal], [– sonorant], [– continuant] and [– delayed release]. No other sounds in English can be grouped together with these same feature specifications. Similarly, English [l, ɹ] can be singled out as [+ consonantal], [+ sonorant] and [– nasal]; again, this particular conjunction of feature specifications is unique to just these two sounds. On the other hand, the set [w, ɔː, t, h, ɒ, g] does not constitute a natural class, and cannot be identified on the basis of a set of shared feature specifications. There is no combination of feature values which will identify just this set of sounds as separate from all others in English, since there is no single feature specification shared by all members of this set.

By referring to natural classes in this way, generalisations can be made concerning the behaviour of sounds in a particular language or in human language in general. As we shall see more clearly in the following chapters, using features allows us to capture such generalisations in a more insightful way; rather than referring to natural classes in terms of the individual segments in the class, we can refer to the features which the segments share, allowing a more economical and elegant statement of our claims.

In the charts in Tables 7.1 and 7.2 we summarise the feature specifications for the consonants and vowels found in many kinds of English.

Further reading

There is an important discussion of features in Chomsky and Halle (1968), often referred to as SPE (SPE isn't, however, recommended for the beginner!). Most modern textbooks on phonological theory contain discussion of distinctive features. For some recent treatments see Gussenhoven and Jacobs (2005), Kenstowicz (1994), Carr (1993) and Durand (1990).

Table 7.1 Feature specifications for English consonants

	p	b	t	d	ɾ	k	g	ʔ	tʃ	dʒ	f	v	θ	ð	s	z	ʃ	ʒ	x	h	m	n	ŋ	ɹ	l	w	j
syll	-	-	-	-	-	-	-	-	-	-	-	-	-	-	-	-	-	-	-	-	-/+	-/+	-/+	-/+	-/+	-	-
cons	+	+	+	+	+	+	+	+	+	+	+	+	+	+	+	+	+	+	+	+	+	+	+	+	+	-	-
son	-	-	-	-	-	-	-	-	-	-	-	-	-	-	-	-	-	-	-	-	+	+	+	+	+	+	+
cor	-	-	+	+	+	-	-	-	+	+	-	-	+	+	+	+	+	+	-	-	-	+	-	+	+	-	-
ant	+	+	+	+	+	-	-	-	-	-	+	+	+	+	+	+	-	-	-	-	+	+	-	+	+	-	-
cont	-	-	-	-	-	-	-	-	-	-	+	+	+	+	+	+	+	+	+	+	-	-	-	+	+	+	+
nas	-	-	-	-	-	-	-	-	-	-	-	-	-	-	-	-	-	-	-	-	+	+	+	-	-	-	-
stri	-	-	-	-	-	-	-	-	+	+	+	+	-	-	+	+	+	+	-	-	-	-	-	-	-	-	-
lat	-	-	-	-	-	-	-	-	-	-	-	-	-	-	-	-	-	-	-	-	-	-	-	-	+	-	-
del rel	-	-	-	-	-	-	-	-	+	+	-	-	-	-	-	-	-	-	-	-	-	-	-	-	-	-	-
high	-	-	-	-	-	+	+	-	+	+	-	-	-	-	-	-	+	+	+	-	-	-	+	-	-	+	+
low	-	-	-	-	-	-	-	+	-	-	-	-	-	-	-	-	-	-	-	+	-	-	-	-	-	-	-
back	-	-	-	-	-	+	+	-	-	-	-	-	-	-	-	-	-	-	+	-	-	-	+	-	-	+	-
round	-	-	-	-	-	-	-	-	-	-	-	-	-	-	-	-	-	-	-	-	-	-	-	-	-	+	-
voice	-	+	-	+	+	-	+	-	-	+	-	+	-	+	-	+	-	+	-	-	+	+	+	+	+	+	+

Stops: p b t d ɾ k g ʔ — Affricates: tʃ dʒ — Fricatives: f v θ ð s z ʃ ʒ x h (Obstruents)

Nasals: m n ŋ — Liquids: ɹ l — Glides: w j (Sonorants)

Table 7.2 Feature specifications for English vowels

	iː	ɪ	uː	ʊ	ɔ	oː	ɒ	ɑː	ʌ	æ	eː	ɛ	ə	ɜː
high	+	+	+	+	−	−	−	−	−	−	−	−	−	−
low	−	−	−	−	−	−	+	+	+	+	−	−	−	−
back	−	−	+	+	+	+	+	+	−	−	−	−	−	−
front	+	+	−	−	−	−	−	−	−	+	+	+	−	−
round	−	−	+	+	+	+	+	−	−	−	−	−	−	−
tense	+	−	+	−	−	+	−	+	−	−	+	−	−	+

Exercises

1   From the vowel charts given below fill in matrices using features relevant to vowels to characterise each of the vowels shown.

   a. Japanese monophthongs

   b. Russian monophthongs

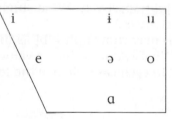

   Given the vowel chart for French monophthongs in (c), what further considerations are necessary that were not needed for either Japanese or Russian? Why?

   c. French monophthongs (Parisian; excluding nasal vowels)

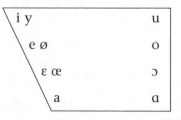

2. The following sets form natural classes. How can they be characterised in terms of features? Assume the sounds of English.

a. [t d n ɹ s z l θ ð]
b. [m n ŋ l ɹ]
c. [p v b f m]
d. [e ɛ ə ɔ o]

e. [f θ s ʃ]
f. [b d g ʤ]
g. [i ɪ ʊ u]
h. [k g ŋ]

3 Identify the English consonants represented by the following feature matrices.

a. $\begin{bmatrix} + \text{anterior} \\ - \text{coronal} \\ - \text{continuant} \end{bmatrix}$
b. $\begin{bmatrix} + \text{anterior} \\ + \text{coronal} \\ + \text{sonorant} \end{bmatrix}$
c. $\begin{bmatrix} - \text{anterior} \\ - \text{coronal} \\ - \text{sonorant} \end{bmatrix}$

d. $\begin{bmatrix} - \text{anterior} \\ + \text{del rel} \\ - \text{voice} \end{bmatrix}$
e. $\begin{bmatrix} - \text{continuant} \\ - \text{voice} \end{bmatrix}$

4 Answer the following questions using distinctive features:

a. Assume a language in which the voiceless stops [p, t, k] surface as the corresponding fricatives [f, θ, x] at the beginning of a word, yet the voiced stops [b, d, g] are unaffected in the same position. What feature of [p, t, k] needs to change for them to surface as fricatives? What feature(s) can be used to distinguish [p, t, k] from [b, d, g]? How can [p, t, k] be isolated from all other consonants?

b. Assume a language in which [i] and [u] at the end of a word show up as [e] and [o] respectively. What single feature can be changed to express both changes?

c. In English, [d] may show up as [b] as in 'ba[b] man' or as [g] as in 'ba[g] king'. What feature value or values of [d] need to change for this to occur? In each case, change the fewest features possible.

Phonemic analysis

8.1 Sounds that are the same but different

Recall that in Chapter 1 we saw that there is something about the t-sounds in 'tuck', 'stuck' and 'cut' that is the same, in the sense that speakers of English group these together as 't-sounds'. At the same time we recognise that phonetically these t-sounds are different. In the same way consider the t-sounds in 'tea', 'steam' and 'sit': the 't' in 'tea' is likely to be aspirated, the 't' in 'steam' unaspirated and the 't' in 'sit' may be unreleased (indicated by ⁿ).

(8.1)   t-sounds: tea [tʰiː]   steam [stiːm]   sit [sɪtˀ]

It is not difficult to find other groupings of sounds that are both the same and different in just the same way. In parallel with the t-sounds we find that English also has a set of p-sounds – those in 'pea', 'spin' and 'sip' – and a set of k-sounds – those in 'key', 'skin' and 'sick'

(8.2)   p-sounds: pea [pʰiː]   spin [spɪn]   sip [sɪpˀ]
         k-sounds: key [kʰiː]   skin [skɪn]   sick [sɪkˀ]

These sets of p-sounds and k-sounds also represent phonetically different speech sounds, yet can clearly be grouped together as p-sounds and k-sounds. The fact that native speakers of English often do not realise that [p], [pʰ] and [pˀ] differ also suggests that there may be some relationship between them. While it is not a crucial piece of evidence that the t-sounds, p-sounds and k-sounds *are* groups of related sounds, it does say something about how speakers of English feel about their relatedness. Compare this with the feelings of a Thai speaker towards these sounds. For Thai speakers [p] and [pʰ] are felt to be distinct sounds (see Section 3.1.3), as in [pàa] 'forest' vs. [pʰàa] 'to split' (the accent over the first [a] indicates low tone, which does not concern us here), and a speaker of Thai is no more likely to judge them to be 'same sounds' than a speaker of English is to judge [t] and [d] to be the same.

These groupings like English [t], [tʰ] and [tˀ], with respect to their simultaneous unity and diversity, have traditionally been dealt with in terms of two levels of representation. That is to say that at a concrete physical level the members of these groups of sounds *are* different phonetically – they have different phonetic properties – but that abstractly it is useful to group them together as being related. In fact, grouping them together this way reflects the intuition of the native speaker that these sounds are 'the same' in some sense. Taking this view we can say that abstractly English has a 't' and that concretely the pronunciation of this 't' depends on the context in which it occurs. That is, if the 't' of English appears at the beginning of a word it is pronounced as [tʰ], if it appears as part of a consonant cluster following [s] it is pronounced as [t], if it appears at the end of a word it may be pronounced as [tˀ] (or indeed as [ʔ] or [t]). In the same way, we can say that English 'p' has several concrete representatives: [p], [pʰ] and [pˀ].

In order to make it clear which level of representation we are dealing with, abstract or concrete, the convention is to use square brackets – [ ] – to enclose the symbol(s) for concrete speech sounds as they are pronounced – phonetic material – and to use slashes – / / – to enclose the symbols representing the abstract elements – underlying material. Taking again the p-sounds of English, we can say that the group is represented abstractly by /p/, which is pronounced concretely as [p], [pʰ] or [pˀ], depending on where it occurs in a word. In this same way, the k-sounds consist of /k/, representing the group which is pronounced [k], [kʰ] or [kˀ].

By using this approach we can distinguish between the surface sounds of a language – those that are spoken – and the underlying organising system. If we know, for instance, that we're talking about underlying /p/, we can predict for English which member of the group of phonetic p-sounds – [p], [pʰ] or [pˀ] – will occur in a particular position. The abstract underlying units are known as **phonemes** while the predictable surface elements are known as **allophones**. In these terms we can say that the phoneme /p/ is realised as the allophone [pʰ] word-initially, as the allophone [p] in an initial cluster following [s] and as the allophone [pˀ] at the end of a word. The relationship can be shown graphically as in (8.3).

(8.3)

Viewing speech sounds this way enables us to distinguish systematically between underlying representations and sounds actually occurring in a language. This, in turn, allows us to establish the relatively small inventory of underlying phonemes of a language and relate them to the greater number of sounds that speakers of that language actually produce. By looking at the speech sounds of a language in this way we start to see the underlying system. Coming back to a point made in Chapter 1, phonologists are interested in the patternings, or systematic relationships, of speech sounds in human languages. The phoneme/allophone distinction enables us to see patterns in the distribution of speech sounds in an insightful way, and in a way we could not see simply by listing all of the speech sounds of a given language.

Knowing, for instance, that English contains [b], [p], [pʰ] and [pˀ] – a list – tells us nothing about any possible phonological relationships between these sounds, that is that [p], [pʰ] and [pˀ] are allophones of a single phoneme, /p/, and that [b] is an allophone of a contrasting phoneme, /b/.

It is important to recognise that this kind of abstraction from the concrete to the underlying is not unique to linguistics and is, in fact, a familiar concept from the natural sciences. Consider water. We all know certain facts about water. First of all, we know that, abstractly, it is composed of two hydrogen molecules and an oxygen molecule, which we represent formally as H_2O. We also know that at a temperature below 0°C H_2O appears as ice; between 0°C and 100°C H_2O appears as liquid water and above 100°C H_2O appears as water vapour. Just as the p-sounds [p], [pʰ] and [pˀ] are underlyingly /p/, water, ice and water vapour are underlyingly H_2O.

(8.4)

What this means is that in both cases, the phonological and the physical, we have a single entity – i.e. /p/ and H_2O – that occurs in various forms in specific environments. If we chose not to view phonology in this way we would be forced to say that [p], [pʰ] and [pˀ] are not related to a single abstract entity, which would be analogous to saying that water, ice and water vapour are not related to H_2O.

What we are suggesting is that by representing groupings of speech sounds – allophones – as being related to some single abstract notion – the phoneme – we start to gain an insight into the organisation of speech sounds into systems. This raises the question of just what a phoneme is. As an abstract representation it is *not* something that can be pronounced; it is not a speech sound itself. What it is, however, is a symbolic representation which allows us to relate specific speech sounds to each other, recognising their phonological sameness despite their phonetic differences. Along with helping the phonologist determine the underlying system of the speech sounds of a language, this also ties in with why native speakers of English have difficulty in perceiving the phonetic difference between [t] and [tʰ]: although these two sounds are demonstrably different phonetically, that difference is obscured for the naïve native speaker by their underlying phonological sameness. In other words, as a speaker of English you have to learn to tell the difference between [t] and [tʰ], something which would strike the native speaker of Thai as perfectly self-evident. This is because the sound systems of English and Thai are organised differently. While both languages have both sounds, in English [t] and [tʰ] are associated with a single phoneme, /t/, whereas in Thai [t] and [tʰ] are allophones of two different phonemes, /t/ and /tʰ/.

8.2 Finding phonemes and allophones

Assuming that distinguishing between phonemes and allophones is the correct way of approaching the study of the sound system of language, we still need a way to clearly identify groups of related sounds and to distinguish these sounds from others belonging to other groups. In other words, we need first to be able to determine the phonemes then relate them to their allophones. Phonemes are most often established by finding a contrast between speech sounds. These contrasts can be most easily seen in minimal pairs.

8.2.1 Minimal pairs and contrastive distribution

The clearest sort of contrast is a ***minimal pair***, that is, a pair of words which differ by just one sound and which are different lexical items. By 'different lexical items' we mean distinct items of vocabulary, regardless of their meaning. In American English 'car' and 'automobile' are two lexical items, though they mean the same thing; in British English 'football' and 'soccer' are two lexical items, though again their meanings are the same. If we compare 'bat' and 'mat', for example, we know as speakers of English that they are two different lexical items and we can see that they differ from each other by precisely one sound, the initial [b] versus [m]. Therefore we can say that [b] and [m] **contrast**. On the basis of that contrast we can suggest that [b] and [m] are allophones of separate phonemes, /b/ and /m/ (remembering that allophones are the actual speech sounds appearing in square brackets). If we then compare the initial sound in 'fat' we see that there is a contrast with both [b] and [m], since 'fat', 'bat', and 'mat' are different lexical items and since each differs from the other by only one sound. Thus, [f] contrasts with [b] and [m]. Therefore we can say that [b], [m] and [f] are each allophones of separate phonemes, /b/, /m/ and /f/ respectively.

Minimal pairs rest on ***contrastive distribution***, as we have just seen with the initial consonants in 'fat', 'bat' and 'mat' which contrast with each other. We saw this contrast by means of a ***commutation test***, i.e. a substitution of one sound for another yielding a different lexical item. Contrastive distribution can show a contrast anywhere in the word, however, not just initially. This means that 'rub' and 'rum', or 'robed' and 'roamed' are just as much minimal pairs as 'bat' and 'mat' since in each case the sounds in question appear in identical phonetic environments and constitutes the only phonetic difference between the two lexical items. Compare (8.5), in which we see that except for the sounds in question, [b] and [m], the phonetic structures of the words are the same.

(8.5)　　　　　　[b]　　　　　　　　　　[m]
　　　　　rub　　[ɹʌ＿]　　　rum　　[ɹʌ＿]
　　　　　robed　[ɹoʊ＿d]　　roamed　[ɹoʊ＿d]

Sometimes in a given language there are no minimal pairs to contrast for a specific pair of sounds, yet we can still establish phonemes. Consider the [ʃ] of 'shoe' and the [ʒ] of 'leisure'. Word-initial position does not help us find a contrast since in English [ʒ] does not occur word-initially (apart from a very few loanwords). Word-finally the occurrence of [ʒ] is also limited, e.g. 'beige'. Word-medially both sounds occur: [ʃ] 'fissure', 'usher', [ʒ] 'measure', 'leisure' (see Section 3.3.1). But even in this position we do not find a true minimal pair, that is we do not find two lexical items differing by only one speech sound. What we can find, however, is a **near minimal pair**, such as 'mission' and 'vision'. Note that with this pair the immediate phonetic environment of the two sounds concerned, [ʃ] and [ʒ], is identical, i.e. between a stressed [ɪ] and a [ə]: ['mɪʃən] vs. ['vɪʒən]. (Superscript ' indicates stress.)

(8.6)   [ʃ]   [ʒ]
        mission 'ɪ___ə   vision 'ɪ___ə

So, even though this is not a true minimal pair (because the lexical items differ by more than one speech sound) it is convincing evidence of a contrast since the sounds we are comparing occur in identical phonetic environments.

8.2.2 Complementary distribution

Notice that a minimal pair or commutation test will not help us at all with the kinds of sound groups we discussed above, that is the p-sounds, the k-sounds, the t-sounds (see Section 8.1). This is because in the environment where we find one of the p-sounds we won't find any of the other p-sounds: we find [pʰ] at the beginnings of words but not in clusters following [s]; we find [p'] at the ends of words but not word-initially. This state of affairs, in which two sounds do not occur in the same environment, is referred to as *complementary distribution*. It is precisely because we cannot get the p-sounds to contrast with each other that we know they belong to the same phoneme, that is they are allophones of a single phoneme. Referring to the water analogy again, at a temperature at which we find water we do not find ice and at a temperature at which we find ice we do not find steam. The three related manifestations of H_2O, like the three related p-sounds, do not appear in the same environment. Note that we *do* find contrasts between members of different groups of sounds – [pʰ] and [kʰ] contrast, as do [p] and [k] and so on – but we find no contrasts among the members of a group.

Above we referred to allophones as being predictable sounds. We can now see what is meant by that. Taking the p-sounds again, we know that we find [pʰ] word-initially and [p] in clusters following [s]. Therefore, if we know that we are dealing with a p-sound, i.e. one of the set of allophones of /p/, we can predict *which* p-sound will be pronounced in which context. This is what we mean by allophones being predictable. As an example, take the following word of English which is missing the initial consonant:

(8.7)   [__ ɛt]

Without knowing what word it is supposed to be we cannot guess whether the initial consonant should be [m] or [b] or [pʰ] or [l] or [g] or a number of other consonants. However, if we are told that the blank must be filled in with a p-sound, we know which one it will be: [pʰ]. The phoneme is unpredictable but the allophone, once we know which phoneme is involved, *is* predictable.

8.2.3 Free variation

While the distinction between allophones and phonemes is quite clear cut, there are some phenomena which can obscure the identification of phonemes. One of these is so-called free variation. In our discussion of the t-sounds we have indicated in a number of places that a voiceless stop may be unreleased at the end of a word, e.g. [mætˀ]. But we have also indicated in passing that /t/ has other realisations at the end of a word, including unaspirated release [mæt] and glottal stop [mæʔ]. Given that these are three phonetically different speech sounds in the same position one might suggest that they are related to different phonemes. But note that these do not contrast: [mætˀ], [mæt] and [mæʔ] are three different pronunciations of the *same* lexical item. Since they involve the same lexical item, we can say that the three sounds are in free variation, since there are no minimal pairs. We can thus maintain that they are allophones of a single phoneme.

8.2.4 Overview

What we have seen so far in Section 8.2 is that by using the commutation test to identify positions in which speech sounds contrast and those in which they are in complementary distribution or free variation, we can start to see the systematic organisation of the phonological component of a grammar. In the preceding sections we have seen that when two phones are in contrastive distribution they are allophones of different phonemes; when they are in complementary distribution or free variation they are allophones of a single phoneme. However, the results of the commutation test are not always problem-free. Consider, for example, the word 'economic'. Many speakers of English have two pronunciations of this word, either with initial [iː] or initial [ɛ], that is [iː] and [ɛ] are in free variation in this word. If the commutation test were applied blindly, this would suggest that [iː] and [ɛ] were allophones of a single phoneme. But consideration of further environments shows that this cannot be the case, since [iː] and [ɛ] contrast in the vast majority of cases, e.g. 'bead' ~ 'bed', 'seed' ~ 'said', 'each' ~ 'etch', etc. See also the discussion of English [h] and [ŋ] in Section 8.4.2. So, even though the commutation test is an important tool for phonemic analysis, the results must be treated with caution and other considerations may need to be taken into account. Some of these will be discussed in the following sections.

By identifying the phonemes and determining how these phonemes are realised, we can go well beyond lists of speech sounds occurring in a language and say something about the relatedness of particular sounds to each other. It is here that we can truly start to see the difference between phonetics and phonology. While phonetics is concerned with the speech sounds themselves, phonology is concerned with the organisation of the system underlying the speech sounds. By abstracting away from the concrete we can gain an understanding of the system that holds it all together.

We can thus view the phonemic level as a way of representing native speakers' knowledge of the sound system of their language. In this sense, phonology is a cognitive study – that is concerned with the representation of knowledge in the mind – whereas phonetics is concerned with the physical properties of speech sounds.

Consider for a moment what this means for the voiceless stops we have been using for illustration. Many varieties of English have ten voiceless stop sounds, which we can list as [p], [pʰ], [pˀ], [k], [kʰ], [kˀ], [t], [tʰ], [tˀ] and [ʔ]. Yet by knowing something about where we find these different sounds we can relate this list to just three underlying phonemes: /p/, /t/ and /k/, which are realised concretely as ten different speech sounds.

(8.8)

We can now start to see why a speaker of English considers [t], [tʰ], [tˀ] and [ʔ] to be 'the same thing' despite the phonetic differences between them: at the mental level there is only one element /t/ and [t], [tʰ], [tˀ] and [ʔ] are simply the surface physical manifestations of this abstract element.

8.3 Linking levels: rules

In the preceding sections, we saw that we can establish two levels of representation: (1) the underlying (mental) phonemic level, which contains information concerning the set of contrasts in the phonology of a language, and (2) the surface phonetic level, which specifies the particular positional variants (allophones) which realise the underlying phonemes.

The information on the underlying phonemic level may be thought of as a set of underlying representations for the words of the language, so 'cat' might be represented as /kæt/, where each of these symbols, /k/, /æ/ and /t/, stands as an abbreviation for an entire feature matrix. These underlying representations are stored in the lexicon, which we can think of as similar to a dictionary (see Section 1.2). The stored items, referred to as lexical entries, include not only phonological information but also other grammatical information such as syntactic class (noun, verb, etc.), specification of meaning, and so forth.

We also need some way of linking these two levels, that is of representing our knowledge of when a particular allophone should show up on the surface. A common way of doing this is via a set of statements which detail the distribution of allophones; such statements are typically referred to as rules. The rule system can be said to mediate between the two levels, and the overall composition of the phonological component of a generative grammar (see Section 1.2) can be represented as in (8.9):

(8.9) Underlying forms   distribution statements   surface forms
       (phonemic level) ⟷ (rules)   ⟷ (phonetic level)

The double-headed arrow in (8.9) is intended to indicate the idea that the generative model is an attempt to represent passive knowledge, not an attempt to represent a process (see again Section 1.2, and further Chapter 11). The representation in (8.9) is thus not intended to be an outline of a computer program for the production or interpretation of speech sounds, but rather a model of how that part of our linguistic competence which has to do with the organisation of speech sounds might look.

The rules themselves can be expressed in a variety of ways, some of which will be dealt with in detail in the following chapters. However, whatever formal means we employ, rules essentially state that some item becomes some other item in some specific environment. That is, we need to specify the item or items affected, the change that takes place, and the environment in which the change occurs. The most common way of expressing such a statement formally involves a rule of the form:

(8.10) $A \rightarrow B / X\_\_Y$

The formula in (8.10) states that A becomes ($\rightarrow$) B in the environment of (/) being preceded by X and followed by Y, where X and Y are variables – the dash (__) represents the position of the item affected by the rule, i.e. A. That is, the rule in (8.10) takes an input string XAY and converts it to XBY.

As an illustration, in English vowel phonemes typically have a nasalised allophone before a nasal stop (see Section 4.3); thus underlying /fæn/ is realised as [fæ̃n], etc. So, to cast this nasalisation process in terms of the rule formalism in (8.10), we might write:

(8.11) $/æ/\rightarrow[æ̃]/$ __ $/n/$

That is, the phoneme /æ/ is realised as its allophone [æ̃] in the environment of being followed by /n/. Note that in this example /æ/ corresponds to A in the rule schema in (8.10), [æ̃] to B, and /n/ to Y. X is not represented in (8.11), i.e. it is an empty variable, since what precedes the vowel has no bearing on the process and thus need not be specified in the rule. Having a rule like (8.11) in the phonological component of the grammar is a way of representing the knowledge a speaker has that an underlying phonological sequence /æn/ will occur on the surface phonetic level as [æ̃n]. In other words, rule statements like (8.11) are a way of capturing our knowledge of how the different levels of phonological organisation are linked.

In this particular instance, our knowledge is in fact rather more general than (8.11) might suggest since, as we said above, all vowels in English are nasalised before any nasal stop, not just /æ/ before /n/, e.g. 'ram', 'rang', 'tin', 'dim', 'sing', 'oink', 'join', 'tame', 'seem', etc. Writing a separate rule for each vowel and nasal phoneme concerned might involve three rules for each of the twenty or so vowels of English (one rule for each of the three nasals in English), giving some sixty rules. It makes more sense in terms of capturing native-speaker intuitions and expressing generalisations to formulate the rule using distinctive features of the sort introduced in the preceding chapter. We might thus recast the nasalisation process more generally as in (8.12).

(8.12)   [+ syllabic] → [+ nasal] / ___ [+ nasal]

The rule in (8.12) will result in any [+ syllabic] segment (i.e. any vowel) being nasalised if it occurs before any [+ nasal] segment. We shall have more to say about rules and their formulation in Chapter 9.

8.4 Choosing the underlying form

Having established two different levels of representation – the phonemic and the phonetic – and proposed rule systems as a way of linking the levels, we now turn to the question of how we decide on the representations at the underlying phonemic level; that is, how we choose the phonemic representation for a particular allophone or set of allophones. While there is no formula we can apply to ensure that we always get the 'right answer' (since there isn't necessarily a single right answer anyway), there are nevertheless a number of heuristics, or rules of thumb, which we can use.

In Section 8.1 we spoke of [p], [pʰ] and [p̚] as being 'p-sounds'; i.e. of realising the underlying phoneme /p/. Why choose the symbol 'p' for this? We might equally use a number such as '3', or some other arbitrary label like 'Fred'; rules would simply have these elements to the left of the arrow instead of /p/. We thus might say that 'Fred becomes aspirated when stressed': Fred → [pʰ] /___ [V, + stress]. One obvious reason for not using things like '3' or 'Fred' is that reading the rules would be much harder, so using /p/ serves as a useful mnemonic to tell us what the rule is about. There is more to it than this, however; using /p/ tells us that the allophones associated with /p/ all share something, in that they all contain the same specifications for features like [voice], [continuant], [anterior], [coronal], etc. That is, they are phonetically similar to each other, and phonetically dissimilar to other sounds.

So a primary consideration when deciding on an underlying form is that our choice is 'phonetically natural', that the symbol we choose to represent the abstract entity (the phoneme) tells us something about the nature of the set of its physical instantiations (the allophones). This leads to a second consideration: that the underlying form should, unless there are very good reasons otherwise, be represented by a symbol which is the same as that representing one of the surface forms. Of course, if there is only one surface form, then there is no problem: [f] can be represented as /f/. But if there are

123

several surface forms, which do we choose? Again, there is no 'discovery procedure' which will lead to an unambiguous decision; each case must be decided on its merits. To take the case of /p/ again, we might have used /pʰ/ or /pˀ/ to represent the phoneme, since both are surface forms and both share a set of feature specifications. We choose /p/ in this instance because it is in some sense the 'simplest' of the three: the other two both have something 'added' to their common 'p-ness', being aspirated or being unreleased.

In general, too, it is usual to take the form which has the widest distribution (i.e. occurs in the largest number of environments) since in terms of rule writing it will typically be easier, and hopefully more revealing, to specify the distribution of the allophones which occur in the more constrained environments. For instance, in many kinds of English there is an alternation between voiced and voiceless liquids and glides. (See Sections 3.5.1.1, 3.5.2.2 and 3.6.2.)

(8.13)   a.   [kw̥ɪt], [fl̥eɪ], [tɹ̥ap], [pju̥ːɹaɪɫ], [sw̥aɪp]
         b.   [jes̬], [wɪʃ], [bɔːɫ], [skʌɹɪ], [bɹɪk], [glas], [fɪɫθ], [fɪɫm]

As can be seen from (8.13a), voiceless liquids and glides occur immediately following a voiceless consonant. Voiced liquids and glides occur word-initially, word-finally, between two vowels, following a voiced consonant or before any consonant, as in (8.13b). If the voiceless allophone were chosen as the phonemic representation then our rule or rules linking this to its surface voiced allophone would require specification of a number of environments: a voiceless oral sonorant becomes voiced when (1) word-initial, (2) word-final, (3) before a consonant, (4) between two vowels and (5) following a voiced consonant. This is shown more formally as the set of rules in (8.14a) to (8.14e).

Using the voiced member of the pair, the allophone with the widest distribution, we need specify only one environment in the rule, since a voiced oral sonorant becomes voiceless when following a voiceless segment. This is shown in (8.15).

Not only is (8.15) simpler but it also expresses the generalisation that non-nasal sonorants devoice following voiceless segments. The rule in (8.15) shows that we are dealing with an assimilation process, in that the voicelessness of the initial stop is spreading to the following sonorant (see also the discussion in Sections 3.5 and 3.6). There is no similar generalisation captured in (8.14). In other words, (8.15) provides some insight into the sound system of English while (8.14) does not. Further, choosing the voiced member fits well with the idea outlined above that the symbol for the phoneme should represent the 'simplest' of the allophones: since sonorants are typically voiced, devoicing requires the 'addition' of voicelessness.

(8.14)   a. $\begin{bmatrix} + \text{son} \\ - \text{syll} \\ - \text{nas} \end{bmatrix} \rightarrow [+ \text{voice}] \ / \ \# \ \_\_$

b. $\begin{bmatrix} + \text{son} \\ - \text{syll} \\ - \text{nas} \end{bmatrix} \rightarrow$ [+ voice] / __#

c. $\begin{bmatrix} + \text{son} \\ - \text{syll} \\ - \text{nas} \end{bmatrix} \rightarrow$ [+ voice] / __C

d. $\begin{bmatrix} + \text{son} \\ - \text{syll} \\ - \text{nas} \end{bmatrix} \rightarrow$ [+ voice] / V__V

e. $\begin{bmatrix} + \text{son} \\ - \text{syll} \\ - \text{nas} \end{bmatrix} \rightarrow$ [+ voice] / $\begin{bmatrix} + \text{cons} \\ + \text{voice} \end{bmatrix}$ __

(8.15) $\begin{bmatrix} + \text{son} \\ - \text{syll} \\ - \text{nas} \end{bmatrix} \rightarrow$ [– voice] / [– voice] __

8.4.1 Phonetic naturalness and phonological analysis

In the previous section we discussed that in choosing an underlying representation, naturalness may be a criterion. It is important to be clear about what is meant by 'natural'. Natural in this context means something like 'to be expected', or 'frequently found across languages', or 'phonetically similar' in ways that we shall shortly see. What natural here does *not* mean is necessarily 'English-like', that is, 'familiar to us as speakers of English'. Consider onset clusters. English has no words beginning with [ps] or [pn] or [pt], yet these are perfectly permissible clusters in many languages, e.g. German [psalm] *Psalm* 'psalm', French [pnœ] *pneu* 'tyre', Greek [pteron] 'wing'. Just being un-English does not mean that something is unnatural. Nor is something natural just because it occurs in English. Recall the discussion of the aspiration of voiceless stops. In English we know that [p] and [pʰ] are phonologically related (as two allophones of a single phoneme, /p/) and that native speakers regard these sounds as 'the same'. Another language, however, may use these same sounds differently, in that they are perceived by native speakers to be 'different sounds' and they exhibit a contrast, as shown by minimal pairs. Recall, for example, that Thai also has both [p] and [pʰ] (as mentioned in Section 3.1.3), but in this language they contrast [pàa] 'forest' and [pʰàa] 'to split'.

8.4.2 Phonetic similarity

In choosing an underlying representation we saw above that in terms of simplicity there were reasons to choose /p/ – over /pʰ/ and /pˀ/ – as the underlying representation of the p-sounds. A further argument for using this symbol has to do with the notion of phonetic similarity. As a logical possibility it could be argued that [pʰ] is in complementary distribution not only with [p] in the environment 's__', but also with both [t] and [k] as in 'sty' and 'sky'. It would thus be possible, though not particularly insightful, to associate [pʰ] with either /t/ or /k/. That we don't do so, but rather associate it with /p/, captures the fact that the *p*-allophones are phonetically similar to each other (and phonetically dissimilar to the t- and k-sounds). At the same time this also expresses the native speaker intuition that [pʰ] 'is a' p-sound, and not a t-sound or a k-sound.

As another instance in which phonetic similarity may play a role in deciding on the relatedness or otherwise of particular sounds, consider the distribution of [h] and [ŋ] in English. The sound [h] occurs only syllable-initially, never syllable-finally. The sound [ŋ] occurs only syllable-finally, never syllable-initially (the asterisk indicates a non-occurring form):

(8.16) h: syllable-initial   ŋ: syllable-final
        [hæm]   [bɹɪŋ]
        [hæt]   [bʌŋ]
        [hɛd]   [ˈɹiːdɪŋ]
        [ˈhɪkʌp]   [θɪŋ]
        [ʌpˈhiːvəɫ]   [ˈsɪŋɪŋ]
        [əˈhɛd]   [ˈθæŋkɪŋ]
  N.B.: *[iːh], *[uːh]   *[ŋiː], *[ŋuː]

On the basis of this distribution alone, one might suggest that [h] and [ŋ] are in complementary distribution and, therefore, allophones of the same phoneme. There is, however, a significant problem with this analysis.

The piece of evidence that is perhaps most significant in suggesting that [h] and [ŋ] are not allophones of a single phoneme is the lack of phonetic similarity between the two sounds. If we compare the features associated with the two we see that they have very little in common. Certainly the characteristic features of these sounds are different: [ŋ] is nasal, sonorant, non-continuant while [h] is non-nasal, obstruent, continuant – the only important feature they share is that they are both consonants, and this they share with all other non-vowels and non-glides. There is simply no feature shared by [h] and [ŋ] to the exclusion of other consonants that would allow us to refer to them as a class.

Given this dissimilarity, it is difficult to see what one might choose as an underlying representation, or more importantly why. Although one could certainly invent a fictitious symbol to represent the 'group' [h] and [ŋ], this grouping simply gives us no insight into a possible relationship between [h] and [ŋ] in the way that /p/ relates to [p], [pʰ] and [pʼ]. Interestingly, this also captures native-speaker intuition that [h] and [ŋ] aren't related in the way that, for instance, the 't-sounds' are felt to be related.

8.4.3 Process naturalness

A further consideration for determining the appropriate underlying representation is the nature of the process linking a phoneme to its allophones. Consider the following data of English which involve an alternation between [s] and [ʃ].

(8.17)　pass　[pæs]　pass you　[pæʃju]
　　　　this　[ðɪs]　this year　[ðɪʃjiə]

Clearly, the [s] and [ʃ] here are related since 'pass' is the same lexical item in 'pass you' and in other forms of the verb 'pass' such as 'pass' alone, 'passed', 'passing', 'passes'. If we accept that [s] and [ʃ] are related in these pairs of words, the question that arises is how to represent this relationship. Recalling the two levels of representation, which symbol should we use to represent the underlying phoneme? That is, do we derive [s] from /ʃ/ or [ʃ] from /s/? Either one is logically possible. There are, however, at least two linguistic reasons to derive [ʃ] from /s/. First consider the immediate phonetic environment of the two sounds in question. The [s] is in each instance preceded by [æ]; it is followed by a pause in 'pass', by [t] in 'passed', by [ɪ] in 'passing' and by [ə] (or [ɪ]) in 'passes'.

(8.18)　[s]
　　　　æ_#　in 'pass'
　　　　æ_t　in 'passed'
　　　　æ_ɪ　in 'passing'
　　　　æ_ə　in 'passes'

In the case of [ʃ] the sound is again preceded by [æ] but followed exclusively by [j], as in 'pass you' [pæʃju]. Thus, [s] appears in more environments than [ʃ]. This appearance of [s] in a wider range of environments is one reason to suppose that an underlying /s/ is more appropriate.

Given the current discussion of naturalness there is a yet more convincing reason to suggest that /s/ is underlying. Note the phonetic characteristics of the alternating sounds: [s] is an alveolar, [+ coronal, + anterior]; [ʃ] is palato-alveolar, [+ coronal, – anterior]. Consider now the [j], which is a palatal, [+ coronal, – anterior]. When we look at the cases of 'pass you' and 'this year', we see that what is elsewhere a [+ anterior] sound, [s], is surfacing as [– anterior] [ʃ]. Why should this be so? By assuming underlying /s/ we can rely on a simple, very common sort of assimilation process to explain why [ʃ] occurs where it does: the value of the feature [anterior] is assimilating to the [– anterior] specification of the following [j], therefore surfacing as [ʃ] rather than [s] (see Section 3.3.3). Consider the alternative: if we suggest that /ʃ/ → [s], what justification might there be for this process? There is no reason to expect a /ʃ/ to become a [s] word-finally, before [t], before [ɪ] or before [ə], since these have no features in common, i.e. they do not form a natural class.

Consider another set of English data, this time involving an alternation between [t] and [tʃ], and between [d] and [ʤ].

(8.19)　a. last　[læst]　last year　[læstʃjiə]
　　　　　let　[lɛt]　let you　[lɛtʃjə]
　　　　b. loud　[laʊd]　loud yell　[laʊʤjɛɫ]
　　　　　feed　[fiːd]　feed you　[fiːʤjə]

As with the data in (8.17), we see here that the same lexical items exhibit different sounds depending on where they appear with respect to other sounds/words. In absolute word-final position we find [t] and [d], while in word-final position followed by [j] we find [tʃ] and [dʒ]. The question which arises again is how we can represent this alternation in the most insightful, i.e. explanatory, way. What are the characteristics of the sounds involved? Again we find [+ anterior] sounds, [t] and [d], and [− anterior] sounds, [tʃ], [dʒ] and [j]. Again we find that in these data the [− anterior] affricates occur only when followed by the [− anterior] glide. As with the 'pass' vs. 'pass you' alternation we have a reason to suggest that in these data [t] and [tʃ] are underlyingly /t/, while [d] and [dʒ] are underlyingly /d/.

8.4.4 Pattern congruity

As we saw in Section 8.4.2 with [h] and [ŋ], simply using the commutation test does not always give us an appropriate analysis of our data, and we need to supplement our battery of tools by appealing to notions like phonetic similarity or dissimilarity. This, too, may not always allow us to make a decision concerning allophonic relationships, and we may need to employ further heuristics to deal with the data confronting us.

Consider again the distribution of aspirated and unaspirated stops in many varieties of English (see Section 3.1.3). Aspiration is found on voiceless stops which occur at the beginning of a stressed syllable except when the stop is preceded by [s], so 'pin' has an initial aspirated stop, [pʰ], but the oral stop in 'spin' is unaspirated, [p]. When we look at the phonetic characteristics of the oral stop in 'spin', which we have hitherto described as 'voiceless unaspirated', we see that in fact [p] shares as much with [b] as it does with [pʰ]: there is no delay in voicing onset, and the articulation is 'lax'. These are both characteristics which we associate with voiced stops in English. On the other hand, like voiceless segments, the stop does not have concomitant vocal cord vibration. In terms of phonetic transcription, then, either [p] or [b̥] (a 'devoiced' /b/) would be appropriate; phonologically, we might thus equally well associate the oral stop in 'spin' with either the phoneme /b/ or /p/, since it is in complementary distribution with all other positional variants of these phonemes, and phonetically indeterminate between the two.

How, then, do we make the choice? In this instance, it helps to look at the phonological consequences of choosing one phoneme over the other. That is, we must consider the wider effects of our choice on the analysis of the sound system as a whole, and appeal to the notion of pattern congruity, i.e. the systematic organisation of the set of phonemes and their distribution. In English, word-final obstruent sequences like those in (8.20a) and (8.20b) are well-formed, whereas those in (8.20c) are not:

(8.20)   a. /-ft, -pt, -ps, -kst, -sp/, e.g. 'daft', 'apt', 'apse', 'next', 'asp'
         b. /-bd, -dz, -zd, -vz/, e.g. 'robbed', 'adze', 'phased', 'leaves'
         c. */-fd, -bt, -pz, -ds/

There is a straightforward generalisation here: at the phonemic level obstruent clusters have uniform voicing in English. Either all members of the cluster are [– voice], as in (8.20a), or they are all [+ voice], as in (8.20b). 'Mixed voice' clusters of [– voice] + [+ voice], or [+ voice] + [– voice], as in (8.20c), are ill-formed phonemically, i.e. do not occur; phonetically, however, there may be devoicing of the second segment of the final cluster in words like 'robbed', as discussed in Section 3.1.4.

So what is the relevance of this to deciding which phoneme a stop preceded by /s/ should be grouped with? If we choose the voiced phoneme, i.e. say that the oral stop in 'spin' is some kind of /b/, then the underlying representation of 'spin' will be /sbɪn/. If this is so, then we must allow three (and only three) 'mixed voice' clusters (/sb, sd, sg/ as in 'spin, stick, skate'), and we can no longer maintain the generalisation illustrated in (8.20). That is, the statement about cluster voice agreement becomes apparently no more than a tendency, and we have the problem of accounting for the fact that of the many possible mixed voiced clusters, some of which are illustrated in (8.18c), only three, /sb, sd, sg/, are ever attested in English.

On the other hand, if we choose the voiceless phoneme, and say that 'spin' is underlyingly /spɪn/, then the generalisation remains exceptionless, since the three clusters under consideration will be /sp, st, sk/ and thus no longer counterexamples to the cluster voice agreement statement. In this instance, then, our analysis is determined not by the commutation test, nor by considerations of phonetic similarity – since neither of these will prefer one option over the other – but in wider terms of the overall patterns found in the phonological system: in terms of pattern congruity. Choosing voiceless phonemes for these stops gives a more revealing, economical and elegant statement of the behaviour of obstruents in English.

8.5 Summary

In this chapter we have seen that some surface phonetic speech sounds – phones – can be grouped together in terms of their behaviour in the language as being distinct from other groups of phones. They can be thought of as both phonetically different, but at the same time phonologically the same. The underlying, abstract, cognitive entities we call phonemes; allophones are the surface, physical sounds which represent these underlying organisational units. Linking the two levels we have a set of statements specifying which of the allophones of any particular phoneme will occur in a specific context; that is, a set of rules describing the distribution of allophones.

One of the tasks facing a phonologist working with any particular language is thus to determine what the underlying phonemes of that language are and what the set of rules linking the phonemes to their allophones is. While there are no hard and fast 'discovery procedures' which will ensure the right answer every time, we have seen that certain techniques – such as subjecting the phonetic data to the commutation test, supplemented by notions like phonetic similarity, process naturalness and pattern congruity – allow phonologists to propose phonemic inventories on the basis of the distributional patterns exhibited by the phones of the language under investigation. Our focus now turns to the links between phonemes and allophones: to the rule statements.

Further reading

Most recent textbooks include discussion of phonemic analysis. See, for example, Gussmann (2002), Spencer (1996), Kenstowicz (1994), Carr (1993) and Durand (1990).

Exercises

1   Scottish English (Germanic)
    Consider the distribution of [w] and [ʍ] in the following data. Are the phones allophones of the same or different phonemes? Why? If they are allophones of a single phoneme, give a rule to account for the distribution.

a.	ʍaˑe	why	h. we:	way
b.	ʍɪʧ	which	i. wɛðʌɾ	weather
c.	ʍʌɪt	white	j. wɔnt	want
d.	ʍeɫz	whales	k. wɪʧ	witch
e.	ʍɪp	whip	l. wʌɪp	wipe
f.	əʍʌɪɫ	awhile	m. weɫz	Wales
g.	ʍɛðʌɾ	whether	n. əwɔʃ	awash

2   Spanish (Romance; Spain, Latin America)
    Examine the following Spanish data from Quilis and Fernández (1972), focusing on the sounds [b], [β], [g], [ɣ], and answer the questions below. Note: [β] = voiced bilabial fricative; [ɣ] = voiced velar fricative.

a. bomba	'bomb'	e. benga	'(s/he) comes'
b. beɣa	'plain'	f. boβa	'foolish'
c. tuβo	'tube'	g. gato	'cat'
d. paɣa	'pay'	h. tumbo	'fall'

    i.   Can you identify any relationship between the sounds [b], [β], [g] and [ɣ]? If so, what sort of relationship is it? If not, why can we say there is no relationship?
    ii. Depending on your answer to (i), either write a rule to capture the relationship(s) you have observed, or list the environments that lead you to believe that the sounds are not related.
    iii. What might we expect of the sounds [d] and [ð] in Spanish? Why?
    iv. Compare your answer in (iii) with the following data.

i. rondar	'to patrol'	k. roðar	'to roll'
j. dar	'to give'	l. deðo	'finger'

v. Do the data bear out your expectation? Explain.

vi. Make a general statement about the relationships holding between the sounds [b], [β], [g], [ɣ], [d] and [ð].

3 Korean (isolate; Korea)

Examine the following (non-standard) Korean data and answer the questions below. Note: tones are not indicated.

a. satan	'division'	k. ʃesuʃil	'washroom'
b. ʃeke	'world'	l. inzwetʃa	'publisher'
c. ʧaŋza	'business'	m. paŋzək	'cushion'
d. inza	'greetings'	n. ʃihap	'game'
e. ʃekum	'taxes'	o. sosəl	'novel'
f. sæk	'colour'	p. su	'number'
g. sæ	'new'	q. ʃiktaŋ	'dining room'
h. pʰuŋzok	'custom'	r. sul	'wine'
i. ʃilsu	'mistake'	s. jəŋzuʧuŋ	'receipt'
j. susul	'operation'	t. ʃinpu	'bride'

i. On the basis of the data above, are the sounds [s], [z] and [ʃ] in Korean all allophones of the same phoneme? Are any, or all, of them separate phonemes?

ii. Justify your answer to (i) by discussing the evidence you used to determine the status of [s], [z] and [ʃ].

iii. Depending on your answers to (i) and (ii), provide either a rule or a list of contrasting environments expressing the distribution of [s], [z] and [ʃ].

iv. If [s], [z] and [ʃ] are allophones of a single phoneme, which would you choose to represent that phoneme? Justify your answer.

4 American English (Germanic)

Consider the distribution of [uː] and [ʊ] in the data below, which comes from a single speaker of American English.

a. ruːm	room	k. rʊt	root
b. luːt	loot	l. wʊd	wood
c. huːf	hoof	m. rʊk	rook
d. zuːm	zoom	n. sʊt	soot
e. puːl	pool	o. kʊd	could
f. ruːt	root	p. rʊf	roof
g. kuːd	cooed	q. hʊf	hoof
h. wuːd	wooed	r. rʊm	room
i. suːt	soot	s. pʊl	pull
j. ruːf	roof	t. gʊd	good

i. Look for evidence of contrastive distribution, complementary distribution and/or free variation. Which do you find?

ii. In what way is the evidence concerning the number of phonemes involved apparently contradictory?

131

iii. How should this contradiction be resolved (i.e. how many phonemes are represented by the phones [uː] and [ʊ], and why)?

5 Plains Cree (Algonquian; North America)
In the following data from Wolfart (1973), examine the sounds [p], [b], [t] and [d], and answer the following questions.

a.	pahki	'partly'	l.	tahki	'all the time'
b.	niːsosaːp	'twelve'	m.	mihtʃeːt	'many'
c.	taːnispiː	'when'	n.	nisto	'three'
d.	paskuaːu	'prairie'	o.	tagosin	'he arrives'
e.	asabaːp	'thread'	p.	miːbit	'tooth'
f.	siːsiːp	'duck'	q.	nisida	'my feet'
g.	waːbameːu	'he sees him'	r.	meːdaueːu	'he plays'
h.	naːbeːu	'man'	s.	kodak	'another'
i.	aːbihtaːu	'half'	t.	nisit	'my foot'
j.	nibimohtaːn	'I walk'	u.	nisiːsiːbim	'my duck'
k.	siːsiːbak	'ducks'	v.	iskodeːu	'fire'

i. Are [p], [b], [t] and [d] in complementary or contrastive distribution? How many phonemes do we need to posit to account for the distribution of these four sounds? What are they?

ii. If you answered 'complementary distribution' to (i), above, write the rule to express the distribution of [p], [b], [t] and [d]. If you answered 'contrastive distribution', list the environments in which we find a contrast.

iii. Recalling the behaviour of [p, t, k] as a set in English with respect to aspiration, what might we expect in Cree, based on our observations of the data above, with respect to the relationship between [k] and [g]? Is there any evidence in the data that [k] and [g] conform to our expectations?

iv. Given the words of Cree below, can you fill in the blanks with one of the sounds indicated? If not, why not?

a. waː__amon	(p/b)	'mirror'	d. __iːkwaj	(k/p)	'what'
b. nis__a	(t/k)	'goose'	e. os__i	(k/g)	'young'
c. __aːni	(t/d)	'which'	f. oː__a	(d/b)	'here'

9

Phonological alternations, processes and rules

The previous chapter was concerned with establishing the phonemic system which underlies the phonetic inventory of a language; that is deciding what the underlying set of contrasts is. Mention was also made (in Section 8.3) of the need to link the two levels formally via a set of rules which account for the particular allophone of a phoneme occurring in any specific environment. This chapter takes a closer look at this part of the phonological component of the grammar, starting with some discussion of the range of phenomena we have to account for as phonologists, and moving on to a more formal explication of the conventions of rule writing.

9.1 Alternations vs. processes vs. rules

Much of the focus of recent phonological thinking concerns the characterisation of predictable alternations between sounds found in natural languages. We've already seen many examples of these alternations, such as that between [p] and [pʰ] in English. Under specific conditions, there is an alternation between these phones: we get one, [p], and not the other, [pʰ], after [s], as in [spɪt], not *[spʰɪt]. That is, while at the underlying (phonemic) level there is only one element, /p/, there is an alternation in the representation of this element on the surface (phonetic) level between [p] and [pʰ], which is determined by the environment in which the phoneme occurs.

We can characterise such alternations in terms of being caused by, or being due to, some phonological process. In this particular case, we might call the process involved 'aspiration'; in English, a voiceless stop is aspirated when it occurs in absolute word-initial position before a stressed vowel (i.e. not following [s]).

We can represent processes, and thus characterise the alternations that result from them, by means of rules. Rules, as we have seen in Section 8.3, are formal statements which express the relationship between units on the different levels of the phonological component. In the case of aspiration in English, we might have a rule such as:

$$(9.1) \quad \begin{bmatrix} -\text{cont} \\ -\text{voice} \\ -\text{del rel} \end{bmatrix} \rightarrow [+\text{spread glottis}] \; / \; \# \, \underline{\quad} \begin{bmatrix} +\text{syll} \\ +\text{stress} \end{bmatrix}$$

The feature [spread glottis] is used to characterise glottal states, including that for aspiration. The rule in (9.1) is a formal statement of the set of phonemes affected (voiceless stop phonemes), the change which occurs (such stops are represented by the aspirated allophones) and the condition under which such a change takes place (after a word boundary – # – and before a stressed vowel). Note that the facts of aspiration in English are somewhat more complex than our rule suggests, in that aspiration occurs before any stressed vowel, even when the stop is not word-initial, as in 'a[pʰ]art'. A fuller account involves reference to syllable boundaries; see Section 10.4.

It is the identification of such alternations, and of the phonological processes behind them, and the formalising of the most appropriate rules to capture them, that are the main thrust of much of *generative phonology*. These alternations are a central part of what native speakers 'know' about their language, and the goal of the generative enterprise is the formal representation of such knowledge (see Section 1.2).

9.2 Alternation types

Phonological alternations come in many shapes and sizes and the processes behind them are equally varied, as are the kinds of factor which condition them. Consider the following sets of data from English; in what ways do the alternations represented in (9.2) differ from one another?

(9.2) a. [wɪt] vs. [wĩn]
           [tʰuːɫ] vs. [tʰũːm]

       b. 'i[n]edible, i[n] Edinburgh' vs.
           'i[m]possible, i[m] Preston' vs.
           'i[ŋ]conceivable, i[ŋ] Cardiff'

       c. 'rat[s]' vs. 'warthog[z]' vs. 'hors[ɪz]'
           'yak[s]' vs. 'bee[z]' vs. 'finch[ɪz]'

       d. 'lea[f]' vs. 'lea[v]es'
           'hou[s]e' vs. 'hou[z]es'

       e. 'electri[k]' vs. 'electri[s]ity'
           'medi[k]al' vs. 'medi[s]inal'

In (9.2a), we see an alternation between purely oral vowel allophones – [ɪ] and [uː] – which occur before an oral segment, and nasalised vowel allophones – [ĩ] and [ũː] – which occur before a nasal segment. In (9.2b) there is an alternation between different realisations of the final nasal consonant in both the prefix 'in-' and the preposition 'in'; it agrees in place of articulation with a following labial or velar consonant. In (9.2c) we see different realisations of the plural marker – orthographic '(e)s' – which may be [s], [z] or [ɪz], depending on the nature of the preceding segment. In (9.2d) there is an alternation in voicing for a root final fricative, voiceless in the singular, voiced in the plural. Finally, in (9.2e) we see alternation between a stop vs. fricative for the segment represented orthographically by the 'c' in 'medical' and 'medicinal' and by the second 'c' in 'electric' and 'electricity'.

These sets of alternations are different from each other in a number of ways. The type of alternation involved can vary: one or more of the allophones involved in the alternation may be restricted to just one set of environments – like nasalised vowels in English in (9.2a), which only occur before nasal consonants – or the allophones may occur 'independently' elsewhere – and represent a different phoneme, as in the [m] of 'i[m] Preston', which occurs 'in its own right' in words like 'ru[m]'. Or the factors conditioning the alternation may vary. The alternation may occur whenever the phonetic environment is met (as in vowel nasalisation or nasal place agreement). On the other hand, the alternation may be more restricted, and may only be found in the presence of particular suffixes (like the plural) as in (9.2c), or even particular lexical items, as in the [k] vs. [s] alternation in 'electric/ity' in (9.2e). In both these cases, the phonetic environment by itself is not sufficient to trigger the alternation; if it were, words like 'dance' or 'rickety' would be impossible in English – 'dance' has [s] following a voiced segment (compare 'dens'), 'rickety' has medial [k] not [s] (compare 'complicity'). Further, the alternation may be 'optional' – or at least determined by factors other than the immediate phonetic environment – like the variation in the final consonant of the preposition 'in', which typically happens in faster speech styles rather than in slower ones (where the nasal may not necessarily assimilate). The following sections deal with each of the types of alternation in (9.2) in turn.

9.2.1 Phonetically conditioned alternations

Alternations like those in (9.2a) – and (9.2b), assuming normal speech style, given the observation about slow speech immediately above – can be characterised as being conditioned purely by the phonetic environment in which the phones in question occur, with no other factors being relevant. If a vowel phone in English is followed by a nasal consonant, the vowel is nasalised (see Section 4.3), irrespective of anything else (such as morphological structure). Indeed, it is very difficult for English speakers to avoid nasalising vowels in this position, hence the designation of such alternations as 'obligatory'; there are unlikely to be any exceptions to this process. Note, however, that this particular alternation is not universally obligatory; in French, vowels in this position are not nasalised – [bɔn] not *[bɔ̃n] for *bonne* 'good (feminine)'.

Similarly, for (9.2b), in English the alveolar nasal /n/ assimilates to the place of articulation of a following labial or velar consonant (see Section 3.4.1), whether this is within a word or across a word boundary. Again, this is difficult for speakers to avoid, although it is somewhat easier than with vowel nasalisation, possibly due to the influence of the orthography. As with vowel nasalisation, this assimilation is not universal; it does not, for instance, occur in Russian – [funksjə] ('function') not *[fuŋksjə] – compare English [fʌŋkʃən].

Other alternations of this sort in English include aspirated vs. non-aspirated voiceless stops discussed above, the lateral and nasal release of stops (see Section 3.1.2), 'flapping' in North American, Northern Irish and Australian English (see Section 3.1.6), clear vs. dark /l/ (see Section 3.5.1.1) and intrusive 'r' in non-rhotic Englishes (see Section 3.5.2.1).

9.2.2 Phonetically and morphologically conditioned alternations

The alternations in (9.2c) are also clearly motivated by the phonetic environment; the form of the plural is dependent on the nature of the final segment of the noun stem. If the noun ends in a sibilant, i.e. [s], [z], [ʃ], [ʒ], [tʃ] or [dʒ], the plural takes the form [ɪz]. If the final segment is a voiceless non-sibilant, the plural is a voiceless alveolar fricative [s]. If the final segment is a voiced non-sibilant, the fricative is voiced [z].

However, unlike the alternations in (9.2a) and (9.2b) discussed above, the alternations in (9.2c) do not necessarily occur whenever the phonetic environment alone is met. If they did, forms like [fɛns] 'fence' or [beɪs] 'base' would be impossible, since they involve sequences of a voiced segment followed by a voiceless alveolar fricative. So the phonetic environment cannot be the only relevant conditioning factor; something else must be taken into account as well. The 'something else' in this instance is clearly the internal complexity of the words, in that the plural marker 's' has been added. The word can be seen to consist of two separable units, known as morphemes – e.g. 'fen+s' consists of the stem 'fen' plus the plural marker '-s'. Words like 'fens' are said to be morphologically complex. The final fricative only agrees in voice with the preceding segment if it represents the plural marker, i.e. if there is a morpheme boundary between the two segments. Thus voicing agreement will occur in 'fens' (fen+s, where '+' indicates a morpheme boundary) and in 'bays' (bay+s), giving [fɛnz] and [beɪz]. On the other hand, 'fence' and 'base' are both morphologically simple forms: they have no internal morphological boundaries, and thus no voicing agreement takes place. For a fuller treatment of plural formation, see Section 11.2.

Like the alternations discussed in Section 9.2.1, this type of alternation is obligatory and automatic; it occurs whenever both the phonetic and morphological conditions are met. Speakers never say things like *'wartho[gɪz]' or *'ra[tz]', and the alternations will occur even with completely new words; if we were to launch some product called a 'plotch', the plural would have to be 'plo[tʃɪz]', and not *'plo[tʃz]' or *'plo[tʃs]'. When an alternation behaves in this predictable, automatic manner, applying freely to new forms, it is known as **productive**.

Other alternations of this kind in English include the [t/d/ɪd] forms of the past tense, as in 'stro[kt]', 'rou[zd]' and 'wan[tɪd]'.

9.2.3 Phonetically, morphologically and lexically conditioned alternations

Consider now the alternations in (9.2d) and (9.2e). Here there is clearly some phonetic conditioning: fricatives are voiced between voiced segments (voicing assimilation) in (9.2d), and a velar stop [k] is fronted and fricativised to an alveolar fricative [s] before a high front (that is palatal) vowel segment in (9.2e). The latter is also a kind of assimilation, though somewhat more complex, involving both manner and place of articulation – the term for this particular process is *velar softening*.

There is also clearly some morphological conditioning in that, for instance, [beɪsɪs] 'basis' and [kɪt] 'kit' are both well formed (they don't become *[beɪzɪs] and *[sɪt] respectively, even though their phonetic environments are the same as those involved in the alternations above). But even stating that there must be a morpheme boundary after the final fricative in cases like 'leaf' or after the final stop in cases like 'electric' is insufficient, since we don't get these alternations with, for example, 'chie[fs]' (not *'chie[vz]') or with 'li[k]ing' (not *'li[s]ing').

In these cases we must, thus, also specify the particular (set of) lexical items the alternation is relevant for: only some of the fricative final nouns in English show voicing assimilation and only some [k]-final stems exhibit velar softening. Furthermore, unlike the alternations in the previous two sections, alternations involving lexical conditioning are not typically productive (or are at best intermittently so); a new product called a 'plee[f]' would have the plural 'plee[fs]' rather than 'plee[vz]'.

Other alternations of this type in English include the so-called **vowel shift** or **trisyllabic shortening** pairs like 'rept[aɪ]le'/ 'rept[ɪ]lian', 'obsc[iː]ne'/ 'obsc[ɛ]nity', 'ins[eɪ]ne'/'ins[æ]nity'. Such alternations are often the 'fossilised' remains of alternations/processes which were once productive at an earlier point in the history of the language, but have since died out. The pairs given immediately above are due to a series of changes during the history of English, including the late Middle English 'Great Vowel Shift', hence one of the names given to the alternation.

9.2.4 Non-phonological alternations: suppletion

Consider finally alternations like 'mouse' vs. 'mice', or 'go' vs. 'went'. Are these the same kind of alternations as those we have looked at in the preceding sections? They might at first glance seem to be like the last set described in Section 9.2.3, in that while there is morphological conditioning (plural and past tense, respectively) we must also refer to specific lexical items, since the alternations do not generalise over all similar forms, or extend to new ones (the plural of 'grouse' isn't 'grice', the past tense of 'hoe' isn't 'hent' or some such). Importantly, however, there is one crucial type of conditioning which is absent here: there is no phonetic conditioning of any obvious sort which might help predict the alternations involved. That is, there are no general phonological processes involved in getting from 'mouse' to 'mice' or from 'go' to 'went'. These forms must be learnt by the speaker on a one-off basis, as exceptions to a rule (hence children acquiring English often produce 'regularised' forms like 'mouses' and 'goed'). See Section 11.4.1 for further discussion.

The introduction to a set of alternations (a paradigm) of a form that is

137

not obviously related, as in the instances here, is known as *suppletion*, and is not part of our phonological knowledge (since it has no phonological basis). It thus need not be dealt with by the phonological component.

Still, it might be thought that alternations like 'mouse/mice' are more like those in Section 9.2.3 than the clearly unrelated 'go/went' type, in that there is some obvious relation between the forms: only the vowel is different, rather like 'inane/inanity' (and furthermore, like the trisyllabic shortening pairs, the 'mouse/mice' alternations are the fossilised remains of an earlier process, Old English i-mutation). There is at least one important difference, however: for 'inane/inanity' it is the addition of two extra syllables to the stem which triggers the alternation (hence the term 'trisyllabic shortening', since the alternating vowel is now the first of three syllables). For 'mouse/mice', on the other hand, there is no phonetic or phonological change to trigger the alternation. It is solely dependent on being a plural form of one of a small set of English nouns.

9.3 Formal rules and rule writing

In the previous two sections of this chapter, and indeed throughout this book, we have been concerned with looking at the kinds of things that speech sounds do in language, the changes they undergo and the processes that occur. In a certain respect this is only half the picture since, beyond simply observing what goes on, the phonologist wants both to characterise or represent these processes and to try to understand how they work. The rest of this chapter will focus on representing these processes. However, this will be only one sort of representation, and a fairly basic sort of representation besides. In the following chapters we will see why the representations here are not the entire story and why they need to be improved on.

At this point you might wonder why, if the representations we're about to examine are inadequate, do we bother with these and not go straight on to other ways of representing phonological processes that may capture greater generalisations. There are two reasons for this. First of all, the kinds of rules and rule formulation we'll deal with in this chapter pre-date the fuller representations we'll see in Chapter 10 and some of the more general concerns we look at in Chapters 11, 12 and 13. Understanding the formalisms presented here enables you to start reading some of the older papers on phonology that would be inaccessible if you understood only where phonology currently stands. Second, dealing first with more 'basic' sorts of representation helps us see where modern phonology has come from and why richer representations are needed.

9.3.1 Formal rules

In Chapter 8 we looked at the fundamentals of rule formulation, that a rule in phonology consists of some phonological element (A) – typically a segment or a feature – which undergoes some change (B) in a particular environment:

(9.3) $A \rightarrow B \ / \ X \ \_\_ \ Y$

The rule in (9.3) represents the state of affairs in which A becomes B between X and Y. We could take as a concrete example the flapping rule of American English (see Section 3.1.6), according to which a /t/ is pronounced as a flap [ɾ] when it occurs between two vowels, V, provided that the second vowel is not stressed. So, A = /t/, B = [ɾ], X = V, Y = [+ syllabic, – stress] as shown in (9.4):

(9.4) $/t/ \rightarrow [\text{ɾ}] \ / \ V\_\_ \begin{bmatrix} + \text{ syllabic} \\ - \text{ stress} \end{bmatrix}$

This rule applies to forms like /ˈbɪtəɹ/, /ˈleɪtəɹ/, /ˈætəm/, /ˈɹɪkɪtiː/ which surface as [ˈbɪɾəɹ], [ˈleɪɾəɹ], [ˈæɾəm], [ˈɹɪkɪɾiː] respectively.

We also saw in Chapter 8, as in (9.4), that the bits of phonology represented by A, B, X, Y are either segments, or features associated with segments. That is, they are either complete feature matrices or individual features. As a further example, we might have a rule like that in (9.5):

(9.5) $/t/ \rightarrow [ʔ] \ / \ V \_\_ \#$

This rule would capture the process found in many varieties of English by which a /t/ becomes a glottal stop after a vowel at the end of a word, e.g. in words like 'cat' and 'hit': /kæt/ and /hɪt/ which surface as [kæʔ] and [hɪʔ] (see the discussion in Section 3.1.5). That is, phoneme /t/ is realised as the allophone [ʔ] when preceded by a vowel and followed by the end of a word.

More often than not rules are written in terms of the relevant features, not whole feature matrices represented by segments (see Section 8.4). The rule for glottalisation we have just seen can also be recast in (9.6) using the feature [constricted glottis], where the '+' value indicates glottal closure.

(9.6) Glottalisation: $\begin{bmatrix} - \text{ cont} \\ + \text{ ant} \\ + \text{ cor} \\ - \text{ voice} \end{bmatrix} \rightarrow \begin{bmatrix} - \text{ ant} \\ - \text{ cor} \\ + \text{ const glottis} \end{bmatrix} / [+ \text{ syll}] \_\_ \#$

A further example of the use of features in a rule can be seen with words such as [mɪntʔ], [tækʔ] and [mæpʔ], where a final voiceless stop is glottalised – reinforced rather than replaced by a glottal stop (see Section 3.1.5). Thus we might write the rule as in (9.7).

(9.7) $\begin{bmatrix} - \text{ continuant} \\ - \text{ voice} \end{bmatrix} \rightarrow [+ \text{ const glottis}] \ / \ \_\_ \#$

As we saw in Chapter 7, using features, rather than segments, allows us to capture greater generalisations. Using features in rules expresses these generalisations. In this case using the features [– continuant] and [– voice] allows the rule to express a process affecting the entire class of voiceless stops of English, where a segment-based attempt would require several rules, one for each stop.

(9.8)   a. /p/ → [p$^{?}$] / __ #
        b. /t/ → [t$^{?}$] / __ #
        c. /k/ → [k$^{?}$] / __ #

In other words, the rule in (9.7) accounts for final glottalised /p, t, k/ in any word. If we could only use segments in a rule, not features, we would need three rules. Formally, there is no reason why just these three segments should be affected. Why, for example, do we not find something along the lines of [æ] → [p$^{?}$]?

By including a feature in the rule we capture the generalisation that all voiceless stops do this, so the process is one affecting the *class* of voiceless stops, not an apparently random set of segments.

9.3.1.1 Parentheses notation

In addition to these basic rules, there are also notational devices and conventions used to express more complex relationships and operations. One of these conventions involves parentheses – ( ) – which are used to enclose optional elements in rules. The rule in (9.9) shows that A becomes B either between X and Z or between XY and Z. The optional element is Y, which may or may not be present.

(9.9)   A → B / X(Y) __ Z

Although this is written as a single rule, it in fact encodes two separate but related rules, namely A → B / X __ Z and A → B / XY __ Z.

To illustrate the application of parentheses notation let us look at 'l-velarisation' in English. In Section 3.5.1 we saw that most varieties of English have a clear *l* – [l] – and a dark or velarised *l* – [ɫ]. So words like 'leaf' have a clear *l* and words like 'fell' and 'bulk' have a velarised *l*. The distributional facts are actually more complex than this and we return to a more complete characterisation of l-velarisation in Section 10.1. These two words – 'fell' and 'bulk' – show l-velarisation occurring either at the end of a word, or before a consonant at the end of a word. That is, there is an optional consonant which may intervene between the /l/ and #:

(9.10)   /l/ → [ɫ] / __ (C) #

The parentheses here indicate that there may or may not be a consonant between the lateral and the end of the word.

9.3.1.2 Braces

Another notational device used in linear rule writing is brace notation, also known as curly brackets: { }. Brace notation represents an either/or relationship between two environments. In other words, the same process occurs in two partially different environments and the rule captures the fact that it is the same process, despite the difference in environment.

(9.11) $A \rightarrow B / \begin{Bmatrix} X \\ Z \end{Bmatrix}$ __ Y

The rule in (9.11) shows that A becomes B either between X and Y or between Z and Y. In other words, A → B / X __ Y or A → B / Z __ Y. Note that in (9.11) parentheses have not been used. Therefore either X or Z must be present; both cannot be absent. Recalling the rule in (9.5) glottalising final-t, we also find that /t/ → [ʔ] /__ C, as in 'petrol' [pɛʔɹəl]. Since this 't' isn't at the end of the word we appear to have an either/or environment: either before the end of a word or before another consonant (in fact, there is more to it than this: see Section 10.4.1).

(9.12) $\quad$ /t/ → [ʔ] / __ $\left\{ \begin{matrix} C \\ \# \end{matrix} \right\}$

Here we see that /t/ surfaces as glottal stop [ʔ] either before another consonant or before the end of the word.

Both parentheses and braces can appear in the same rule, allowing overlapping environments to be captured in terms of a single rule. Take, for example, the rules in (9.13).

(9.13) $\quad$ A → B / X __ Y
$\qquad$ A → B / XZ __ Y
$\qquad$ A → B / X __ #
$\qquad$ A → B / XZ __ #

These rules can be collapsed into a single rule, as in (9.14).

(9.14) $\quad$ A → B / X(Z) __ $\left\{ \begin{matrix} Y \\ \# \end{matrix} \right\}$

The use of devices like parentheses and braces increases the power of the model and allows us the capacity to formulate rules of greater complexity. This rule captures the generalisation that there is some process which changes A to B and that this process occurs in a number of different environments. The advantage of this over the list of rules in (9.13) is this: by expressing this change as a single rule we are presumably saying something important about the relationship between A and B that is not captured by a list. In the list there is no reason that each of the four rules should involve A → B: in the single rule each of the four statements must involve A → B.

9.3.1.3 Superscripts and subscripts

Superscript and subscript numbers associated with variables let us express minimum and maximum numbers of segments relevant to a given environment. Let's imagine that our basic rule of A → B / X __ Y turns an /i/ vowel into an [ɪ] after any consonant (C) and before any double consonant; that is, the Y variable has to be at least two consonants. So an imaginary word like /nis/ would be pronounced [nis], while a word like /nist/ would be pronounced [nɪst]. We can represent this as in (9.15).

(9.15) $\quad$ /i/ → [ɪ] / C __ C_2

The subscript indicates the minimum number of elements required for the rule to apply. Thus this rule states that /i/ becomes [ɪ] when followed by a minimum of two consonants.

Imagine another rule which has the effect of turning an /i/ vowel into an [ɪ] before a single consonant, but not before more than one. In other words, the rule applies before a minimum *and* maximum of one consonant, as in (9.16).

(9.16)   /i/ → [ɪ] / C __ C_1^1

The superscript indicates the maximum number of elements allowable for the rule to apply. According to this rule /nis/ would surface as [nɪs], but /nist/ would be [nist] since /nist/ exceeds the maximum number of consonants specified. In other words, the rule does not apply in the case of /nist/ since the structural description of the rule is not met. Thus, superscript and subscript numbers associated with elements in a rule allow us to specify the number of such elements in a particular environment. Note that there is some overlap with parentheses: C_0^1 represents the same thing as (C).

9.3.1.4 Alpha-notation

Consider the following words of English: 'unproductive' [ʌmpɹə'dʌktɪv], 'indeed' [ɪn'diːd], 'include' [ɪŋ'kluːd]. Note that in each case the nasal stop shares the same place of articulation with the consonant which follows it (see Section 3.4). Recalling the discussion of features in Chapter 7, we see that [p], [d] and [k] can be distinguished using the features [± coronal] and [± anterior] (see Section 7.3.3):

(9.17)   [p] = [+ ant, – cor]
          [d] = [+ ant, + cor]
          [k] = [– ant, – cor]

It is the values of [± ant] [± cor] which [m], [n] and [ŋ] share with [p], [d] and [k] respectively.

(9.18)   [m] = [+ ant, – cor]
          [n] = [+ ant, + cor]
          [ŋ] = [– ant, – cor]

In order to capture the generalisation that /n/ surfaces as [m], [n] or [ŋ], depending on the feature specifications for [anterior] and [coronal] of the following segment, we need some way of matching the features involved.

Note that we cannot capture this assimilation as a single feature-matching process by using '+' and '–', since the realisation of /n/ as [m] requires a change from [+ cor] to [– cor] with [+ ant] remaining constant, while the realisation of /n/ as [ŋ] requires not only a change from [+ cor] to [– cor] but also a change from [+ ant] to [– ant]. If we were to use '+' and '–' a separate rule for each assimilation would be required.

This kind of feature-matching generalisation is precisely what *alpha-notation* allows us to capture. Replacing the '+' or '–' value of regular feature specification, alpha (α) represents *either* '+' or '–', matching the value of an occurrence of the feature in question elsewhere in the rule.

Taking the example of nasal assimilation, we can characterise what is going on in the following way. By using two Greek letter variables (represented by α and β) we can match the value for these features between the consonant and the nasal:

(9.19)

$$/n/ \rightarrow \begin{bmatrix} \alpha \text{ ant} \\ \beta \text{ cor} \end{bmatrix} / \underline{} \begin{bmatrix} + \text{ cons} \\ \alpha \text{ ant} \\ \beta \text{ cor} \end{bmatrix}$$

This rule states that the values for [anterior] and [coronal] of the nasal stop must match the values for [anterior] and [coronal] of the following consonant. Note that by using α and β, the values for [anterior] and [coronal] are independent of each other. Had we used only α, then the values for [anterior] and [coronal] would have to match each other as well: [α ant, α cor] means that if the value for [anterior] is [– anterior], then the value for coronal is [– coronal]. If α happens to stand for '–' anywhere in a rule, it stands for '–' everywhere in a rule; likewise, if α happens to stand for '+' anywhere in a rule, it stands for '+' everywhere in a rule. Using both α and β allows each feature to be specified independently without affecting other features. If more than two features need to be specified independently the rest of the Greek alphabet can be used, i.e. γ, δ, ε, etc.

9.4 Overview of phonological operations and rules

In this section we review basic phonological operations and how those operations are represented in the type of rule we have been considering. These operations include deletion and insertion, and feature-changing rules, such as assimilation and dissimilation.

9.4.1 Feature-changing rules

In previous sections we have seen rules which affect individual features or small groups of features, such as nasal assimilation, in which the specifications for the features [anterior] and [coronal] match between a nasal stop and a following obstruent. Such rules are known as *feature-changing rules*. Another kind of feature-changing rule is the mirror image process of *dis*similation, in which two adjacent segments which share some feature (or features) change to become less like each other. The pronunciation of 'chimney' as [ʧɪmliː] can be characterised as nasal dissimilation, in which the underlying sequence of /...mn.../ dissimilates to a sequence of [...ml...]. In terms of a rule this could be expressed as follows.

(9.20)   [+ nasal] → [– nasal] / [+ nasal] ___

Other feature-changing operations include processes like flapping and glottalisation (discussed earlier in this chapter).

143

9.4.2 Deletion

As distinct from feature-changing rules, there are other rules which manipulate entire segments, i.e. whole feature matrices. **Deletion** is expressed in terms of a segment 'becoming Ø' (zero). In (9.21) we see an abstract rule expressing the loss of A at the end of a word following B.

(9.21) $A \rightarrow \emptyset \,/\, B \,\_\_\_\, \#$

This could be a variety of English in which a word-final coronal stop is deleted in a cluster, e.g. 'hand' [hæn], 'list' [lɪs], 'locust' ['loʊkəs].

(9.22) $\begin{bmatrix} - \text{syll} \\ + \text{cons} \\ + \text{ant} \\ + \text{cor} \end{bmatrix} \rightarrow \emptyset \,/\, \begin{bmatrix} - \text{syll} \\ + \text{cons} \end{bmatrix} \_\_\_ \#$

According to (9.22) a consonant is deleted at the end of a word when it follows another consonant. Here the /d/ of /hænd/ and the /t/ of /lɪst/ are deleted word-finally: /hænd/ → [hæn] and /lɪst/ → [lɪs].

9.4.3 Insertion

An *insertion rule*, again manipulating an entire feature matrix, is the mirror image of a deletion rule, so inserting some segment A would be expressed by starting with zero: $\emptyset \rightarrow A$. As a concrete example we might consider varieties of English (e.g. Geordie) in which a schwa is inserted into a final liquid + nasal cluster, e.g. /fɪlm/ becomes [fɪləm]. This can be stated as in (9.23).

(9.23) $\emptyset \rightarrow ə \,/\, \begin{bmatrix} + \text{cons} \\ + \text{son} \\ - \text{nos} \end{bmatrix} \_\_\_ \begin{bmatrix} + \text{cons} \\ + \text{nas} \end{bmatrix} \#$

Here we see that schwa is inserted between a liquid and a nasal at the end of a word.

9.4.4 Metathesis

Metathesis refers to the reversal of a sequence of elements, typically whole segments, in a word. In many Scottish varieties, words such as 'pattern' [patəɹn] or 'modern' [mɔdəɹn] have alternate pronunciations [patɹən] and [mɔdɹən]. In both of these cases, a sequence of vowel + /ɹ/ is reversed. This can be represented abstractly by assigning a number (known as an *index*) to each of the segments involved, and showing the original, underlying order to the left of the arrow, and the new, metathesised order on the right:

(9.24) $C_1 C_2 V_3 C_4 \rightarrow 1\ 3\ 2\ 4$

In the case of 'pattern' then, the rule would be as in (9.25).

(9.25) $/\text{p a t}_1\, ə_2\, ɹ_3\, n_4/ \rightarrow 1\ 3\ 2\ 4$ $[\text{p a t}_1\, ɹ_3\, ə_2\, n_4]$

Here, the /ɪ/, indexed as 3, is shown to reverse with the /ə/, indexed as 2. It should be noted that, unlike feature changing, deletion and insertion processes, metathesis is relatively uncommon, and rarely systematic in its application, being typically found in a small number of specific lexical items rather than across all potential targets.

9.4.5 Reduplication

One final process to look at is **reduplication**, a process involving both phonology and word formation. Reduplication entails copying all or part of word, then attaching the copy to the original word. English has very little evidence of reduplication, apart from some reduplicative compounds, e.g. 'helter-skelter', 'pooh-pooh' and some infantile words such as 'weewee'. While this phenomenon is not common in English or other European languages, some languages – e.g. Samoan (Samoa), Tagalog (Philippines), Dakota (North America) – use reduplication extensively to indicate morphological categories like tense and number. Consider, for example, Samoan, in which the stressed syllable of a singular verb may be repeated (without the stress) within the original word, immediately before the stressed syllable, to yield a new plural verb form: so [ma.ˈtu.a] 'he is old', [ma.**tu**.ˈtu.a] 'they are old', or [a.ta.ˈma.ki] 'he is wise', [a.ta.**ma**.ˈma.ki] 'they are wise' (where the reduplicated material is in bold, the dot indicates a syllable boundary and ˈ marks the beginning of a stressed syllable). This may be expressed in rule form, again using indices on segments, as for the characterisation of metathesis in the preceding section, as:

(9.26) C_1 V_2 $\rightarrow$ 1 2 1 2
$\quad$ [+ stress] $\quad$ [- stress]

In the case of [a.ta.ˈma.ki], the effect would be as in (9.27)

(9.27) /a.ta.m_1 a_2. ki/ $\rightarrow$ 1 2 $\quad$ 1 2 [a.ta.ma.ˈma.ki]
$\quad$ [+ stress] $\quad$ [- stress]

Here, the sequence /ma/ is reduplicated (without stress) immediately before the stressed /ˈma/.

9.5 Summary

In this chapter we have considered the different types of phonological alternations and processes found in languages. We have also examined how these alternations and processes may be expressed in terms of formal notation as rules. These rules provide a way of linking the underlying phonemic level with the surface phonetic level. In the next chapter we examine the nature of the phonological structures on which such rules operate.

Further reading

At the core of early generative phonology, focussing on rules and representations, is Chomsky and Halle (1968) which is, however, rather daunting. More accessible and recent works on generative phonology include Spencer (1996), Kenstowicz (1994), Carr (1993), Durand (1990), and Gussenhoven and Jacobs (2005).

Exercises

1 Alabaman (Muskogean, North America; from Rand 1968)
   Consider the data below from Alabaman. (A stop followed by ⌐ is unreleased.)

a. ĩnkʰaː	'give'	l. tʰaːtʰaː	'father'
b. pʰosnoː	'we'	m. tʰãnkʰaː	'dark'
c. hip⌐loː	'snow'	n. slot⌐kʰaː	'full'
d. ok⌐kʰiːtʰat⌐kʰaː	'see'	o. hoːmaː	'bitter'
e. kʰolbiː	'basket'	p. pʰiːtʃiː	'mother'
f. tʰot⌐tʃĩnnaː	'three'	q. ĩmpʰiːtʃiː	'breast'
g. hat⌐kʰaː	'white'	r. it⌐tʰoː	'tree'
h. tʰĩnnaː	'dull'	s. ik⌐baː	'hot'
i. hõmmaː	'red'	t. pʰaːniː	'creek'
j. kʰop⌐liː	'water glass'	u. ik⌐fiː	'belly'
k. ok⌐tʃak⌐kʰoː	'green/blue'		

   i.   Determine the rules that govern the variation in the voiceless stops.
   ii. Is vowel length distinctive in Alabaman? If so, express the distribution in terms of a rule.
   iii. Is the occurrence of oral vs. nasal vowels predictable? If so, express the distribution in terms of a rule.

2 In French non-sonorant consonant clusters both members of the cluster agree in voicing, with the first segment assimilating to the second if necessary: /bs/ becomes [ps] as in [ɔpsɛʀve] 'observe'; /kd/ becomes [gd] as in [anɛgdɔt] 'anecdote'. Such clusters also include /bt/ → [pt], /gs/ → [ks], /kb/ → [gb], /tz/ → [dz]

   i. Express this relationship first as two rules, one spreading [+ voice] leftwards, the second spreading [– voice] leftwards
   ii. Generalise over these two rules by writing a single rule to express this voicing assimilation, regardless of whether it involves [+ voice] → [– voice] or [– voice] → [+ voice]

3 Zoque (Mixe-Zoque, Mexico)
   In the data below, what is the relationship between the voiced and voiceless stops and affricates [p]/[b], [t]/[d], [c]/[ɟ], [k]/[g], [tˢ]/[dᶻ] and [tʃ]/[dʒ]. (N.B.: [c] and [ɟ] are palatal stops.) If each member of the pair is the allophone of a distinct phoneme, give your evidence for that

conclusion. If both members of each pair can be related to a single phoneme, state the underlying representation for each pair and give a rule to characterise their distribution.

a. kaʔnʤi	'turkey'	j. cenba	'he sees'
b. kaŋ	'jaguar'	k. netˢ	'armadillo'
c. xuʔci	'vulture'	l. nəmɟeʔtu	'he also said'
d. mbama	'my clothing'	m. liŋba	'to slash'
e. ndᶻin	'my pine'	n. ɲiçpu	'he planted it'
f. təʔŋguj	'bell'	o. ʧehʧaxu	'he frightened him'
g. petpa	'he sweeps'	p. ʔanemuʧ	'tortilla'
h. təpceʔtu	'he jumped'	q. tiŋdiŋ	'thick'
i. ŋgama	'my field'	r. ɲʤiŋu	'you bathed'

4   Scottish English (Germanic)
Consider the distribution of long and short vowels in the following data. What factors determine vowel length? How might this be expressed as a rule? What problems are there with this rule as regards natural classes?

a. bliːɹ	beer	bin	bean	ʃɨɬ	feel
b. bik	beak	liːv	leave	iːz	ease
c. ɾʉm	room	mʉːv	move	brʉː	brew
d. sʉːð	soothe	sʉp	soup	mʉːɹ	moor
e. ʍeɬ	whale	weː	weigh	sket	skate
f. wef	waif	beːð	bathe	des	dace
g. ɬʊd	load	noːz	nose	ɾʊb	robe
h. poːɹ	pore	bloː	blow	gost	ghost

Now consider the pairs below. How do they affect your analysis? Can your rule be amended to account for them, or must the analysis be abandoned in favour of phonemic, i.e. non-predictable, vowel length in Scottish English?

i. nid	need	niːd	kneed
j. brʉd	brood	brʉːd	brewed
k. wed	wade	weːd	weighed
l. od	ode	oːd	owed

10

Phonological structure

In Chapters 7 to 9, we have been assuming a relatively straightforward view of phonological structure; the smallest phonological element has been the binary distinctive feature (Chapter 7). An unordered list, or matrix, of these distinctive features, each given a value of '+' or '–', characterises the largest phonological element, the segment (or phoneme), as in (10.1).

(10.1)

$$
\begin{array}{l}
/p/ \\
- \text{ syll} \\
+ \text{ cons} \\
- \text{ son} \\
- \text{ cor} \\
+ \text{ ant} \\
- \text{ cont} \\
- \text{ nas} \\
- \text{ stri} \\
- \text{ lat} \\
- \text{ del rel} \\
- \text{ high} \\
- \text{ low} \\
- \text{ back} \\
- \text{ round} \\
- \text{ voice}
\end{array}
$$

As we have seen in Chapters 8 and 9, phonological rules make reference to these features, either in terms of individual features such as [– voice] (in, say, a rule devoicing final obstruents), small groups of features such as [– high, + low, – back] (in a rule which raises front vowels), or the whole matrix in a rule which refers to a whole segment (e.g. a deletion rule). The only other elements available for use in rule specifications have been morphological and syntactic boundaries, indicating positions like morpheme-final (__+), or word-initial (#__). This type of phonological representation is characterised as being 'linear', in that reference can only be made to the particular linear sequence or string of feature specifications and boundaries that make up the environment for a particular phonological process. That is, rules may only make reference to 'flat' sequences of segments (plus boundaries); no other information, such as syllable structure, can be incorporated into the rule. For example, the rule expressing word-final devoicing, as in German, or Yorkshire English, is in fact a statement expressed in terms of linear order: if we find a stop, i.e. a segment characterised as [– continuant], followed by a word-boundary, #, the stop will be voiceless, as in (10.2).

(10.2)   [– continuant] → [– voice] / _#

However, at various points in the preceding chapters, we have also had cause to refer to other notions concerning phonological structure. In Chapter 7, for instance, we talked of groupings of features referring to particular aspects of the make-up of a segment (such as 'place features' or 'manner features'), and in Chapter 6, we discussed structures larger than the segment, like the syllable and the foot. We have not thus far incorporated such notions into the formal characteristics of the phonological component, however. In the following sections, we look at some arguments for extending the model of phonological representation in just these ways. This takes the model beyond simple linearity and allows reference to a wider range of phonological structures. Section 10.1 looks at some general arguments for 'richer' phonological structure, Section 10.2 looks again at segment internal structure, Section 10.3 looks at the notion of 'independent' features, not necessarily tied to a single segment, and Section 10.4 looks at the importance of constructs like the syllable – phonological structure above the level of the segment.

10.1 The need for richer phonological representation

While there are quite a number of phonological operations that can be expressed adequately in terms of linear order or adjacency, there are also many common processes which either cannot be captured purely by reference to strings of adjacent elements, or for which any such linear rule is not very insightful, i.e. the linear formulation tells us little about the nature of the process it is describing.

Consider for instance the data in (10.3), which we discussed in Section 9.2:

(10.3)   i[n ɛ]dinburgh
          i[n d]erby
          i[m p]reston
          i[ŋ k]ardiff

Here, an underlying /n/ surfaces as [n] when preceding a vowel or a coronal consonant, as [m] when preceding a labial consonant, and as [ŋ] when preceding a velar consonant. Using 'Greek-letter variables' (see Section 9.3.1.4), this can be given a straightforward linear characterisation, as in (10.4).

(10.4)
$$[+ \text{nasal}] \rightarrow \begin{bmatrix} \alpha \text{ coronal} \\ \beta \text{ anterior} \end{bmatrix} / \_\_ \begin{bmatrix} + \text{consonantal} \\ \alpha \text{ coronal} \\ \beta \text{ anterior} \end{bmatrix}$$

While this rule does indeed characterise the process, it doesn't actually tell us very much about what is going on. All it says is that two apparently random features in a consonant must have the same specification in a preceding nasal (i.e. the nasal must agree with the following consonant in its values both for [coronal] and for [anterior]). In purely formal terms, the rule might equally well have been:

(10.5)
$$[+ \text{nasal}] \rightarrow \begin{bmatrix} \alpha \text{ voice} \\ \beta \text{ back} \end{bmatrix} / \underline{\quad} \begin{bmatrix} + \text{consonantal} \\ \alpha \text{ voice} \\ \beta \text{ back} \end{bmatrix}$$

The difference is of course that (10.5) is not a particularly likely rule; we would not expect both voicing and backness to be related in any way. On the other hand, the kind of process shown in (10.4) is very common in many languages. What the formulation in (10.4) lacks is any indication that the features specified with variables are in some way related, and not just a random pair like those in (10.5). That is, we want to be able to express formally that it is place of articulation assimilation that is occurring here. The rule in (10.4) cannot do this insightfully, since there are no relations expressible between features if all features are simply part of an unordered, unstructured matrix. The involvement of two features in some process might well be accidental. Nothing about the organisation of the matrix suggests that [anterior] and [coronal] should be in any way related, any more than any other two features, like [voice] and [back]. If, however, features were formally grouped together in some way, such that [anterior] and [coronal] belonged to the same set, whereas [voice] and [back] belong to separate subgroupings, then the difference between (10.4) and (10.5) would become clearer. The features [anterior] and [coronal] would no longer be a random combination, since both would belong to the same subset of features (which might be labelled something like 'place'). The rule could then be reformulated to refer to the subset as a whole:

(10.6) $[+ \text{nasal}] \rightarrow \alpha \text{ [place]} / \underline{\quad} \begin{bmatrix} + \text{consonantal} \\ \alpha \text{ [place]} \end{bmatrix}$

No such reformulation would be possible for (10.5), since [voice] and [back] would not be in the same subset; while [back] would presumably be in the 'place' subset, [voice] wouldn't. Section 10.2 looks at some proposals for exactly how the features should be divided up into subgroupings.

Another way in which it has been suggested that the characterisation of phonological structure should be enriched has to do with data like the following, from Desano (a South American Indian language).

(10.7)   a. [waɪ]   fish   b. [w̃ãĩ]   name
            [jɨ'ɨ]   I   [mɨ̃'ɨ̃] you
            [baja] to dance   [õã]   to be healthy

In Desano, in any one word all voiced segments are either non-nasal as in (10.7a) or nasal as in (10.7b). Combinations of oral and nasal voiced segments within the same word are not allowed, so *[mi̧] or *[bi̧] are not possible Desano words. Further, this restriction also applies across morpheme boundaries, as (10.8) shows.

(10.8)   a. [baja+ri] do you dance?
         b. [õã+nĩ]   are you healthy?

Here the interrogative particle is [ri] after an oral stem and [nĩ] after a nasal stem. To capture this in terms of a linear rule would be both complex and somewhat arbitrary; we might randomly choose the first segment of the stem for words like those in (10.7b) and (10.8b) as being underlyingly [+ nasal], and then have a rule like (10.9) to 'spread' nasality to the segments following.

(10.9)   [+ voice] → [+ nasal] / [+ nasal] __

Note that this rule would have to apply over and over again – so-called 'iterative rule application' – until it reached the end of the word. Or we might stipulate that sequences like (10.10) are ungrammatical.

(10.10) $*\begin{bmatrix} + \text{voice} \\ + \text{nasal} \end{bmatrix} \begin{bmatrix} + \text{voice} \\ - \text{nasal} \end{bmatrix}$ $*\begin{bmatrix} + \text{voice} \\ - \text{nasal} \end{bmatrix} \begin{bmatrix} \text{I voice} \\ + \text{nasal} \end{bmatrix}$

We would then need a rule like (10.9) to deal with the morphologically complex forms in (10.8). Whatever way we choose, however, it will not encapsulate the basic insight into what occurs in Desano, which is that the feature [nasal] is not associated with individual segments (as it is in English), but rather is associated with the whole word. It is the *word* as a whole that is [I nasal] or [– nasal], as distinct from any individual segment. This indicates that sometimes (as in the case here) features seem to operate independently of specific segments, associating instead with a whole string of segments at the same time. Section 10.3 examines this idea in more detail.

A third area in which we might want to recognise richer phonological structures has to do with elements which are larger than individual segments. Recall from the discussion of laterals in Section 3.5.1 that most varieties of English have two *l*-sounds, the 'clear' *l* in 'leaf' [liːf] and the 'dark' or velarised *l* in 'bull' [bʊɫ]. From these examples it could be assumed that at the beginning of a word /l/ surfaces as [l], while at the end of a word it appears as [ɫ]. However, it is not as simple as that, since we find instances of clear *l* in non-word-initial position, as in 'yellow' and 'silly'. We also find instances of dark *l* in non-word-final position, as in 'fullness' and 'film'. Indeed a single stem may alternate between clear *l* and dark *l*, compare 'real' [ɹiːəɫ] and 'reality' [ɹiːˈalɪtiː], 'feel' [fiːəɫ] and 'feeling' [ˈfiːlɪŋ]. Thus, a more precise statement of the distribution of clear and dark *l* might be that dark *l* is found preceding a consonant and word-finally, and clear *l* is found elsewhere.

We said in Section 9.3.1.1 that l-velarisation is more complex than was illustrated there. We can capture a bit more of its complexity using a rule along the lines of (10.11).

151

(10.11)   /l/ → [ɫ] / __ $\left\{ \begin{matrix} C \\ \# \end{matrix} \right\}$

However, this linear rule is still not very insightful. A better way of approaching the problem might be in terms of syllables (see Section 2.3 and Chapter 6). Note that the occurrence of velarised and non-velarised *l* depends on where that /l/ appears in a syllable. At the beginning of the syllable, that is in the onset, /l/ surfaces as non-velarised [l]. At the end of the syllable, or when the /l/ is itself syllabic, /l/ surfaces as [ɫ] or [ɫ̩], compare [.liːf.], [.bʊɫ.], [.'bʌn.dɫ̩.] (where a dot indicates a syllable boundary).

Similarly in the alternations involving 'real' and 'feel' where the /l/ appears word-and syllable-finally it surfaces as [ɫ] – [.ɹiː.əɫ.] and [.fiː. əɫ.] – while in 'reality' and 'feeling' the /l/ appears at the beginning of a syllable and is non-velarised [l] – [.ɹiː.'a.lɪ.tiː.] and [.'fiː.lɪŋ.].

With this in mind, the velarisation rule we formulated above could be rewritten as in (10.12).

(10.12)   /l/ → [ɫ] / __ (C) .

This rule allows us to express the generalisation that phoneme /l/ surfaces as velarised [ɫ] at the end of a syllable, i.e. in the coda. Section 10.4 looks at proposals for how suprasegmental structure, specifically syllables and feet, might be incorporated into the phonology.

We can thus see that a solely linear approach to phonological structure is insufficient. Much of recent phonological theory therefore adopts what is commonly known as a 'non-linear' view of phonology, involving concepts of the sort briefly surveyed above. These are introduced in more detail in the following sections.

10.2 Segment internal structure: feature geometry, underspecification and unary features

As suggested in the previous section, most current phonological models view the internal structure of segments as rather more complex than simply an unordered, unstructured list of features. Given that phonological processes typically affect some combinations of features rather than others – that is that certain features or groups of features typically co-occur while others do not – it is generally felt that phonological representations should reflect this tendency. If the segment-internal representations are left unstructured, any such recurring co-occurrences appear arbitrary and coincidental.

We saw some evidence for this position in the data in (10.3). In English (and many other languages) a nasal 'adopts' certain feature specifications from the segment following it. The features affected in the rule given in (10.4) are all 'place of articulation' features; that is, the process is one of place assimilation. To anticipate the terminology of the next section, the place features **spread** leftwards from the obstruent onto the nasal; all the other feature specifications for the nasal remain constant. A rule like that in (10.4) fails to capture this insight, since the features referred to are not formally related. A reformulation along the lines of (10.6), which refers specifically to the subgroup of [place] features explicitly excludes the possibility of features from other subgroups being affected by the rule. Note further that the rule in (10.4) would not account for the data in (10.13).

(10.13)   i[ɱ f]iladelphia   i[ɱ v]enice
          i[n̪ θ]irsk   i[n̪ ð]e Hague

In (10.13) /n/ is realised by the labio-dental nasal [ɱ] before [f] and [v], and by the dentalised [n̪] before [θ] and [ð]. These allophones need to be distinguished from [m] and [n] respectively. The features [anterior] and [coronal] cannot do this, since [m] and [ɱ] are both [+ ant, – cor] and [n] and [n̪] are both [+ ant, + cor]. To account for (10.13), further features would need to be added to the rule in (10.4). But since such features would also refer to place, no amendment need be made to the formulation in (10.6). Note that the exact nature of the feature or features necessary to deal with the assimilations in (10.13) is not uncontroversial, but, assuming that they can be considered 'place' features, the point is valid.

In a similar way, some processes only appear to affect the manner of articulation, but not place. Consider the oral stop in the following data from the history of the word for 'food' (cognate with English 'meat') in the Scandinavian languages Old Norse (ON), Old Danish (ODan) and Modern Danish (ModDan):

(10.14)   ON [matr] > ODan [mad] > ModDan [mað]

The same process has affected the stop in the word for 'water' in the Romance languages Latin (Lat), Old Spanish (OSpan) and Modern Spanish (ModSpan):

(10.15)   Lat [akwa] > OSpan [agwa] > ModSpan [aɣwa]

In both these cases, the place of articulation of the segment concerned remains constant. What was originally a voiceless stop – [t] in [matr] and [k] in [akwa] – subsequently became a voiced stop, and has become a voiced fricative in the modern forms. Both (10.14) and (10.15) are instances of what are known as **lenition processes**. Lenition, or weakening, refers to an increase in the vocalic nature of a segment, and typically involves voicing and the gradual widening of the stricture in the oral tract, usually following the paths shown in (10.16).

(10.16)

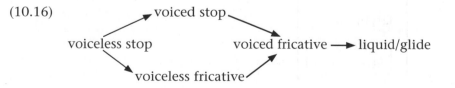

The features we need to refer to here are those associated with manner of articulation – [voice], [continuant], [sonorant], etc. The place specifications remain the same.

A further argument for linking features together formally in some way concerns whether or not certain features are relevant to all segment types. We saw in Chapter 7 that while we want our features to be as widely applicable as possible, some seem to be limited in various ways – their relevance is dependent on the presence of some other feature, or they are restricted to specific segment types. Thus a feature-specification like [+ strident] is only found on obstruents (i.e. sounds which are specified as [– sonorant]); there are no strident liquids, nasals or vowels in human languages. Similarly, the feature [voice] is typically only relevant to consonants (indeed, usually only to obstruents); vowels are not usually (or possibly ever) voiceless at the phonemic level. Simply having an unordered set makes this kind of generalisation awkward to state, since no one relation between features is formally any more likely or unlikely than any other. There is no particular formal reason to link [strident] and [sonorant] rather than say [strident] and [back]. If, however, features are tied together in some way, it becomes possible to capture such 'feature dependencies' directly.

There are various ways of representing such groupings and relations formally. The simplest is to have submatrices within the segment matrix, as in (10.17).

$$(10.17) \quad \begin{bmatrix} \text{place} \\ \begin{bmatrix} \text{anterior} \\ \text{coronal} \\ \text{high} \\ \text{low} \\ \text{back} \\ \text{etc.} \end{bmatrix} \\ \text{manner} \\ \begin{bmatrix} \text{continuant} \\ \text{sonorant} \\ \text{nasal} \\ \text{lateral} \\ \text{etc.} \end{bmatrix} \\ \text{laryngeal} \\ \begin{bmatrix} \text{voice} \\ \text{etc.} \end{bmatrix} \end{bmatrix}$$

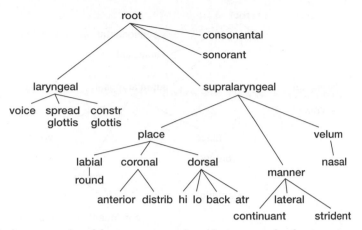

Fig. 10.1 An example of features organised in terms of a feature tree

Rules can then be formulated to refer directly to these submatrices (sometimes known as **gestures**), as in (10.6) above, rather than as an apparently unmotivated list of specific features. Rules would thus not be expected to refer to individual features from more than one submatrix.

A similar, but more widespread, representation, drawing on the notion of features as potentially independent (i.e. not necessarily tied to one particular segment in a string – an idea discussed in Section 10.3), involves organising the features in terms of a tree structure. This type of representation is known as a **feature geometry**, and a typical example is given in Figure 10.1. The **root** is essentially a 'holding position'; the remaining features (or **nodes**) are all associated to this root, giving the specifications for the segment. The tree for the segment /t/ is given in Figure 10.2.

There are a number of things to note about this type of segment characterisation. First, in a tree like Figure 10.2, only those features crucially relevant to the characterisation of the segment in question are shown. Trees like these are referred to as being **underspecified**; we mentioned above that not all features seem relevant to the representation of a particular segment, either because of the type of segment involved – [voice] has no relevance to vowels – or because of the presence of some other feature-specification – [+ sonorant] implies [– strident]. This can be captured by underspecification, in which features that play no distinguishing part in the identification of a segment are not present at the underlying level. These redundant features are filled in later by **default rules**, which assign values to those features not specified in the underlying tree. For example, since /t/ is a coronal sound, there is no need at this level to specify values for any of the features dependent on the other nodes which concern place of articulation, that is [labial] and [dorsal] (see Figure 10.2). These may be filled in later by the default rules. Similarly, since /t/ is specified as [– continuant], the feature [strident] must have the value '–' (since only fricatives can be [+ strident]). This too can be filled in later by the default rules. These default rules are clearly rather different to the kind of rules

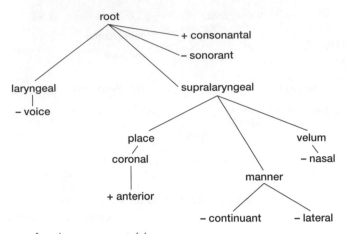

Fig. 10.2 A tree for the segment /t/

we have looked at so far. Rules like those discussed in Chapter 9 have the effect of changing existing feature specifications or inserting and deleting whole segments (see Section 9.4 for discussion of these feature-changing rules). Default rules, on the other hand, *add* new features to a segment and, as such, are often classified as **structure-building rules**, in that they fill in previously absent structure in the characterisation of a segment.

Further, we can distinguish between various levels of feature (or **node types**) in such trees; nodes like [supralaryngeal] or [manner] are *class nodes* (or **organising nodes**), while those like [round] or [strident] are *terminal nodes*. Rules may refer to any type of node, but if a class node is mentioned, then all nodes dependent on that class node are assumed to be involved. Thus, the nasal place assimilation discussed above would involve reference to the [place] node in Figure 10.1. The [place] node specification for the obstruent would replace that originally associated with the preceding nasal, but no other node would be affected. In a similar way, consider a rule which gives a glottal stop [ʔ] for /t/ between vowels, as in [bɪʔə] 'bitter' in many kinds of British English (see Section 3.1.5). Such a rule might involve the deletion of the [supralaryngeal] node, and thus all those features dependent on it. This would leave a stop with no oral place specification; only the root features and those dependent on the [laryngeal] node would remain, resulting in [ʔ].

Note also that class nodes and terminal nodes differ in that while terminal nodes are the familiar binary features, the class nodes are not assigned '+' or '–' values. Class nodes are 'unary' (have one value) and are either present in the tree or not. If a segment, like /t/ in Figure 10.2, is coronal, [labial] and [dorsal] are simply not in the tree (i.e. they are underspecified), rather than being marked as '–'. This may seem like a different way of saying the same thing; whether the tree has a [– labial] node or no [labial] node at all surely comes to the same thing? But in fact there are differences between the two positions. One important difference has to do with a minus value versus nothing at all; if some feature is specified as '–', then it can be referred to in a rule, whereas if the feature simply is not there, it cannot be referred to at all. So, while a rule might refer to [– voice] segments (a devoicing rule would need to do this, for example), no rule could refer to segments in terms of their being underspecified for [labial]; [labial] can only be referred to positively (i.e. when it is specified in the tree). The advantage of this is that the power of the model is constrained; the number of things it can do is reduced. A model which can refer to both [+ labial] and [– labial] segments is less restricted than one which can refer only to the positive specification [labial] (see Chapter 13 for more on the power of models and on constraining excessive power).

Indeed, a number of models of phonological structure have taken this notion of the unary feature (also known as 'monovalent' or 'single-value' features) to its extreme, and characterise *all* aspects of segment structure in terms of unary features, dispensing with the notion of binarity altogether.

While we will not attempt to give a full account of such approaches here, we will look at one particular area, that of characterising vowel systems, in which the use of unary features seems to have some advantages over a binary account.

Cross-linguistically, vowel systems show a preference for the vowels /i/, /u/ and /ɑ/; that is a high front vowel, a high back round vowel and a low back unround vowel. These three vowels seem to show up in all human languages (though the phonetic realisation will vary from language to language), indeed, for some languages these three may be the *only* vowels (as is the case in (Classical) Arabic and many Australian languages). These three are also typically the earliest vowels acquired by children.

Another very common vowel system consists of the basic three vowels plus the mid-vowels /e/ and /o/ (where again the phonetic realisations may vary); Greek, Japanese, Spanish and Swahili are examples of languages with such five vowel systems.

So how might such systems be captured using unary features? If we take the vowels in the basic three-way system as the building blocks, then the simplest system would be represented as comprising the vowel **elements** or **components** |I|, |U| and |A|, where |I| may be glossed as palatality/frontness, |U| as labiality/backness and |A| as lowness. In these terms, the vowel /i/ is represented solely by |I|, /u/ by |U| and /ɑ/ by |A|. (Vertical lines are used to enclose the components.)

The vowels /e/ and /o/ can then be seen as combinations of these basic components; /e/ is a mixture of palatality and lowness, so would be represented as |I, A|, and /o/ is a combination of labiality and lowness, thus |U, A|. A five vowel system of this sort is shown in (10.18)

(10.18) /i/ |I| /u/ |U|

         /e/ |I, A| /o/ |U, A|

              /ɑ/ |A|

157

Support for this idea of combination comes from the fact that in many languages the diphthongs /ai/ and /au/ develop into the monophthongs /e/ and /o/ respectively. In unary feature terms, a sequence |A| |I| /ai/ or |A| |U| /au/ fuses into a single segment |I, A| /e/ or |U, A| /o/ respectively. So, late Middle English 'draw', pronounced /drau/, becomes Modern British English /drɔː/.

More complex systems can be characterised by more complex combinations. A four height system such as /i, e, ɛ, a/, with *two* mid vowels (as found in Danish), would still involve the combination of |I| and |A|, but this time in differing proportions. For /e/ there is a higher proportion of palatality than lowness, for /ɛ/ there is more lowness than palatality. This might be modelled as |I>A| for /e/ and |A>I| for /ɛ/, where '>' indicates greater preponderance of the component to the left. In such cases, the first component in the representation is said to **govern** the second, so for /e/ |I| governs |A| (and equally |A| **depends** on |I|; |I| is the governor or head, |A| is the dependant).

A more complex (and typologically correspondingly less frequent) system involving the front round vowels /y/ and /ø/ (such as French) would involve all three components and the notion of dependency: /y/ might be represented as |I, U| and /ø/ as |I, U>A|.

The idea of dependency or government can be represented graphically by showing the head above the dependant, as in:

(10.19) /e/ |I| /ɛ/ |A| /ø/ |I, U|

             | | |

            |A| |I| |A|

These structures are equivalent to |I>A|, |A>I| and |I, U>A| respectively.

There are a number of advantages that accrue from such an approach, compared to the binary feature characterisation outlined in Chapter 7. Recall that in Section 7.3.6 we discussed the problem of using [+/– high] and [+/– low] when attempting to characterise vowel height. The interaction of these two features predicts an impossible combination ([+high], [+low]) and can thus only deal with three vowel heights, high, mid and low. Both these problems are avoided in the unary system sketched here; the components can combine freely, so no 'impossible' vowels are predicted, and a four height system, as found in e.g. Danish, is captured in a straightforward manner. Further, processes of monophthongisation, like the Middle English example above, can be given an insightful analysis in terms of component fusion. A binary feature account involves a complex and apparently arbitrary set of feature changes. Unary features also automatically embody a degree of underspecification, since they have no 'opposite value' to be filled in later; they are either present in a representation or they are not. We return in Chapter 13 to some further advantages of unary features.

The exact details of feature geometries, underspecification and unary features are a source of debate among phonologists, and many different systems have been proposed. What is important to remember is that expressing relationships between features in terms of the ways in which they interact helps us to characterise more insightfully some of the phonological processes found in languages. So, while the binary features we discussed in Chapter 7 are still relevant, and will still form the basis of analyses in the rest of this book, we would no longer want to say that a segment is simply an unstructured list of all such features. Rather, we would want to say that not all features are necessarily binary, not all are necessarily present underlyingly and that those that are present are 'organised' in some kind of hierarchy or geometry which shows relationships between them.

10.3 Autosegmental phonology

At the beginning of this chapter we saw ways in which a strictly linear approach to phonology – assuming both that segments are distinct from each other and that there is a one-to-one correspondence between segments and features – fails to capture certain important aspects of the phonology of human languages. By recognising concepts such as syllables and featural subgroupings we gain a richer representation and analysis of phonological operations as well as greater insight into phonological relations. In this section we will consider further extensions of these concepts, looking at the correspondence between features and segments.

Consider the English affricates [tʃ] and [dʒ]. Both are considered to have [– continuant] in their feature specifications (see Section 7.3.4). However, consider the phonetic make-up of an affricate. As mentioned in Section 3.2, affricates are similar to a stop followed by a fricative. A stop is [– continuant], but a fricative is [+ continuant]. This is a problem, since in a feature matrix consisting of binary features (see Section 7.2) any given feature must have either the '+' or '–' value, but not both values. In Chapter 7 we characterised affricates as involving the feature [delayed release], without any discussion. This feature allows [tʃ] and [dʒ], [+ del rel], to be distinguished from [t] and [d], [– del rel], but has very little independent motivation. Moreover, it leaves us in the position of having to claim that [tʃ] and [dʒ] are [– continuant] while recognising that phonetically they start off like stops [– cont], but end up like fricatives [+ cont].

There is another class of consonants, found in a number of languages – including Fula (West Africa), Sinhala (Sri Lanka), KiVunjo (Tanzania), Fijian (Fiji) – often referred to as **prenasalised stops**, e.g. [ᵐb], [ⁿd], [ᵑg]. These, like affricates, are phonetically complex segments which behave like single segments. Also, like affricates, they seem to involve the change of a feature, this time [nasal], from one value to another, starting off as [+ nasal] and ending as [– nasal]. If in a given language these segments contrast with [b], [d] and [g] and there are no nasal stops, the feature [+ nasal] could be used to distinguish prenasalised [ᵐb], [ⁿd], [ᵑg] from oral [b], [d], [g]. However, languages with prenasalised stops may also have both the corresponding oral stops – [b], [d], [g] – and the corresponding nasal stops – [m], [n], [ŋ]. As with [del rel], it is not too difficult to invent a feature, call it [prenasalisation], to distinguish [ᵐb], [ⁿd], [ᵑg] from [b], [d], [g] and from

159

[m], [n], [ŋ]. However, this solution sheds no insight into what is going on. It allows us to distinguish the segments involved, but it also masks the problem that exists, namely that [ᵐb], [ⁿd], [ᵑg] are both [+ nasal] and [– nasal].

For the reasons discussed above, both affricates and prenasalised stops pose problems for feature matrices in linear phonology. A linear approach insisting on binary features associated in a one-to-one fashion with segments misses something important about phonological relationships. Affricates and prenasalised stops provide strong evidence that the relationship between (at least certain) features and segments is something other than one-to-one. By making different assumptions we can begin to gain greater insight into the relationships holding between segments and features. Let us assume that we have a row of 'timing slots' representing the linear facts (after all, there must be at least *some* linearity, since speech sounds occur one after the other). For the moment we'll show this as a sequence of Cs and Vs, representing consonants and vowels respectively. So, for the word 'lap' we have a sequence of CVC linked with /l/, /æ/ and /p/.

(10.20)
$$
\begin{array}{ccc}
\text{C} & \text{V} & \text{C} \\
| & | & | \\
\end{array}
$$
'lap' l æ p

Each of the three segmental representations, like C linked with 'l', or V linked with 'æ', can be seen as abbreviations of the feature-geometry trees discussed in Section 10.2. In the following discussion we will omit tree structure and features not relevant to the argument, focusing only on those features which are pertinent. The relevant features will be shown as linked directly to the C and V positions by **association lines**. This approach to phonology is called **autosegmental phonology**. The name derives from the notion of 'autonomous segment' referring to the relative independence of (at least some) features. Any such independent feature linked to a timing slot is said to occupy its own **autosegmental tier**.

Looking at the representation of 'lap' in a little more detail, we can see that features occupying a tier may be associated with more than one timing slot. For example, since both [l] and [æ] are voiced, the feature [+ voice] will presumably be associated with both segments on the [voice] tier:

(10.21)

Just as one feature may be associated with more than one slot, so more than one feature may be associated with a single slot. This gives us a more insightful way of representing complex segments such as the affricates and prenasalised stops we discussed at the beginning of this section. In

(10.22), we see the [continuant] tier representation for the English word 'latch', showing a [– continuant] specification followed by a [+ continuant] specification associated with a single timing slot.

(10.22)

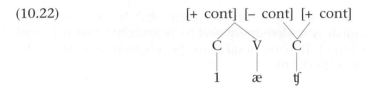

In the same way, assuming that the feature [nasal] is an autosegment, we can represent prenasalised stops as involving a doubly-linked nasal specification exemplified by the Sinhala word for 'blind', [laⁿda] in (10.23a). A variety of complex segments can be handled in this way. For instance, short diphthongs, like those in Icelandic, can be similarly represented, as in (10.23b) [laistɪ] 'lock'.

(10.23)   (a) [– nas] [+ nas] [– nas]   (b)   [+ lo] [+ hi]

```
      C   V   C   V                  C   V   C   C   V
      |   |   |   |                  |   |   |   |   |
      l   a  ⁿd   a                  l   ai  s   t   ɪ
```

This type of multiple association also allows us to represent long segments, i.e. long vowels, diphthongs and geminate consonants. Thus we see in (10.24) autosegmental representations of the words 'bee', 'fly' and Italian *bella* 'pretty'.

(10.24) a. C   V   V   b. C   C   V   V   c. C   V   C   C   V
```
        |    \  /          |   |   |   |          |   |    \  /   |
        b     i            f   l   a   ɪ          b   ɛ     l     a
```

Representations like (10.24a) and (10.24b) show both the similarity and difference between long vowels and diphthongs: they are both associated with two timing slots (hence long), but differ in terms of long vowels sharing a place specification, while diphthongs have two different place specifications.

This approach also lends itself to the representation of assimilation. Coming back to a relatively familiar language, English, we find that many varieties tend to nasalise vowels preceding nasal stops. As mentioned in Section 4.3, a word like 'bin' tends to have a nasalised vowel, under the influence of the following nasal stop: [bĩn]. In autosegmental terms we can show this as a rule of **spreading** as shown in (10.25). Rule formalism in autosegmental phonology is somewhat different to that discussed in Chapter 9. In rules like (10.25) a dotted line indicates the spreading of an autosegment, showing the spread of [+ nas] onto the vowel. The solid line with the bars through it indicates that the feature [– nas] has been **delinked** from (is no longer associated with) the vowel.

161

(10.25)

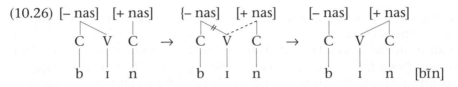

(10.26) shows how this rule applies to the word 'bin'. If we assume that the vowel [ɪ] in English is underlyingly oral, it is associated with [– nas] until the nasality of the following nasal stop spreads to it and causes the association with [– nas] to delink.

(10.26) [– nas] [+ nas]   {– nas] [+ nas]   [– nas] [+ nas]

C V C → C V C → C V C

b ɪ n   b ɪ n   b ɪ n [bĩn]

Another way of dealing with this, employing the notion of underspecification introduced earlier, would be to assume that the vowel is not specified for nasality underlyingly. The [+ nas] feature then simply spreads leftwards onto the vowel with no delinking.

(10.27)   [– nas]   [+ nas]

C V C

b ɪ n [bĩn]

This kind of approach is also applicable to the nasal assimilation data discussed above in Section 10.2. The place node of a nasal preceding an obstruent is delinked and the place node from the obstruent spreads to the nasal, as shown in Figure 10.3. Along with linking and delinking, there are other conventions associated with autosegmental representations. These conventions restrict the power of the model, with the aim of expressing only what we need to about phonological relations.

Among these conventions is the 'no crossing constraint' which prohibits crossing association lines between features on the same tier. This rules out

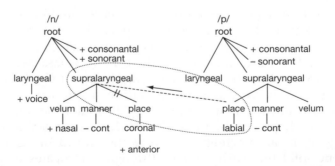

Fig. 10.3 Spreading and delinking

representations like the one in (10.28), in which the plus value for some feature F crosses over the minus value for the same feature.

(10.28)

These sorts of autosegmental representations, recognising that the relationship between features and timing slots in a segmental skeleton is not necessarily one-to-one, help us to gain a clearer insight into phonological relations and help us represent these relations in a way that appears to reflect more appropriately the sound systems of language. As an example of this, let's look at how autosegmental phonology deals with a phenomenon which appears to involve the association of features across a number of segments, namely **vowel harmony**. In some languages, e.g. Finnish, Turkish and Hungarian, there is a very strong tendency for all the vowels in a single word to 'harmonise', that is, to share some feature or features, usually backness or rounding.

In Hungarian vowels must agree for [back]. Thus the word for 'throat' is [torok], while the word for 'Turkish' is [tørøk]. In a linear formulation this would require a complex iterative rule application, copying the value of the feature [back] onto successive vowels. In autosegmental terms one way of representing this is to say that the lexical entries for the words [torok] and [tørøk] have the feature [back] as an autosegment rather than being part of the specification for any particular vowel. In (10.29) capital /O/ represents a mid round vowel underspecified for [back]. Thus it surfaces as [o] when associated with the [+ back] value for the autosegment and as [ø] when associated with [− back].

(10.29) [+ back]   [back]

t O r O k   [torok] 'throat'   t O r O k   [tørøk] 'Turkish'

What is more interesting, however, is what happens when a suffix is added. For example, there is a dative suffix which surfaces as either [-nɑk] or [-nek]. Which form surfaces depends on whether the vowels of the stem to which it is attached are [+ back] or [− back] vowels. So, the word meaning 'to the throat' is [toroknɑk] with all back vowels while 'to the Turk' is [tørøknek] with all front vowels. Represented autosegmentally we can assume that the suffix vowel is underspecified for backness, again using a capital letter – /A/ – but acquires its backness from the specification of the stem.

(10.30)   [+ back]   [− back]

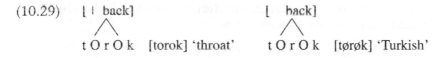

t O r O k + n A k   [toroknɑk]   t O r O k + n A k   [tørøknek]

In this way the formal representations of autosegmental phonology can be extended to a variety of other phenomena, providing not only an analysis of featural changes within a segment, as with affricates and prenasalised stops, but also analyses of harmony phenomena occurring over stretches larger than the segment.

Returning to some data we saw earlier in the chapter, recall that in Desano the word is the domain of nasality and the voiced segments of an entire word are either nasal or oral. In terms of autosegments this can be shown with the feature [+ nasal] associated with the voiced segments of a nasal word, [– nasal] associated with the voiced segments of an oral word.

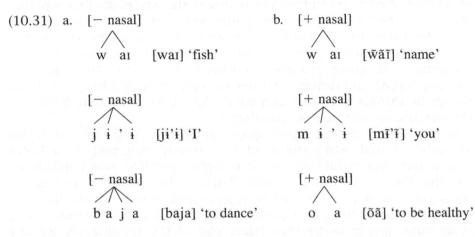

(10.31) a. [− nasal]

w aɪ   [waɪ] 'fish'

b. [+ nasal]

w aɪ   [w̃ãɪ̃] 'name'

[− nasal]

j ɨ ' ɨ   [jɨ'ɨ] 'I'

[+ nasal]

m ɨ ' ɨ   [mɨ̃'ɨ̃] 'you'

[− nasal]

b a j a   [baja] 'to dance'

[+ nasal]

o a   [õã] 'to be healthy'

Unlike the iterative rule application that would be necessary to spread nasality in a linear model, we can represent the [± nasal] value associated with Desano words as the association of a feature with all of the voiced segments in a particular word. This may be particularly appropriate in a case like this, in which the feature in question is associated with the entire word, including any affixes, as seen below.

(10.32)   a.   [− nasal]

b a j a+r i   'do you dance?'

b.   [+ nasal]

õ ã + n ĩ   'are you healthy?'

Here the autosegmental model gives a clear representation of spreading from the stem to the suffix.

Consider, in the light of this, words such as the Desano for 'lizard' [nõhsõ] or 'to know' [mãsĩ], in which nasal and non-nasal segments co-occur. Such words might appear to be counter-evidence to the claim that words in Desano are either completely oral or completely nasal. In fact, the careful reader will have noticed that we said earlier that only the *voiced* segments of the word are susceptible to nasal harmony; voiceless segments like [h] and [s] are thus not affected by the spreading. Segments which are unaffected by some phonological process in this way are said to be **transparent** segments, i.e. in the case here voiceless segments are invisible to the nasal spreading rule, which simply ignores them and spreads the [nasal] specification to the voiced segments beyond.

In other cases, segments may prevent a feature from spreading to all the positions it might be expected to affect. In Section 7.3.5.7, we mentioned the Ghanaian language Akan, in which we said vowels must harmonise within the word for the feature [+/–Advanced Tongue Root]. To recap, [+ATR] vowels in Akan are /i, e, ɜ, o, u/ and [–ATR] vowels are /ɪ, ɛ, a, ɔ, u/. Akan vowel harmony could be represented straightforwardly in autosegmental terms by having an unassociated [ATR] autosegment in the underlying form for the word, which is then linked to all vowels by spreading (consonants are transparent to ATR harmony), as in (10.33), where we again use capitals to indicate vowels which are underlyingly unspecified (in this case, for [ATR]).

(10.33) a. [+ATR]   b. [–ATR]

          E b U O   E b U O
             ↓   ↓

          [+ATR]   [–ATR]
          /⟍\   /⟍\
          e b u o   ɛ b ʊ ɔ

Inevitably, however, the situation is not so simple. Consider the forms [obisaɪ] 'he spreads' and [oɲinsɛɲɪɪ] 'she became pregnant', which mix [+ATR] and [–ATR] vowels within the same word. To account for these words, we must assume that the spreading of [ATR] is in some way blocked from linking the feature to all potential segments. We can do this by having certain vowels linked to a value for [ATR] in the underlying form (as opposed to all vowels being underlyingly unassociated, as in (10.33)). The underlying representations for the 'mixed' ATR words could be shown as in (10.34) (where /a/ and /i/ indicate vowels underlyingly already specified for an ATR value):

(10.34) a. [+ATR] [–ATR]   b. [+ATR] [–ATR]
                      | |
             O b I s a I   O ɲ i n s E ɲ I I

In (10.34a), the [+ATR] feature associated with the word as a whole spreads as expected to /O/ and /I/, but cannot spread to or beyond the pre-linked [–ATR] /a/ (recall the 'no crossing' constraint mentioned above). The [–ATR] specification on /a/ then spreads to the final /I/ in the normal way. This is shown in (10.35):

(10.35) [+ATR] [–ATR]

o b i s a i

A similar account can be given for [oɲinsɛɲɪɪ], whose underlying representation is given in (10.34b). In this case, the pre-linked [+ATR] /i/ prevents the [–ATR] associated with the word from spreading to the first two vowels. Segments which block spreading in this way are known as **opaque** segments.

Especially when combined with the notions of feature geometry, underspecification and unary features outlined in Section 10.2, this kind of autosegmental representation makes possible some interesting claims in terms of phonological structure and description which are unavailable to the purely linear, feature matrix approach introduced earlier in the book.

10.4 Suprasegmental structure

Once autosegments are accepted and the relationship between features and segments is seen as being potentially other than one-to-one, the question that arises is that of phonological structure in general. If it is no longer crucial, or desirable, to refer to adjacent segments in a line, what kind of organisation is there of phonological material into larger units? In the following sections we try to answer that question.

10.4.1 The syllable and its internal structure

We saw in Section 10.1 with the distribution of clear and dark *l* that syllable structure plays a role in phonological processes. In a similar vein, consider the words 'nightly' and 'nitrate'. For many speakers the /t/ in 'nightly' is likely to surface as [ʔ], while in 'nitrate' the first /t/ is aspirated [tʰ].

So, how do we capture this? Without reference to syllable structure we need to show that /t/ is realised as [ʔ] when it appears in two apparently distinct environments, i.e. before another consonant, as in 'nightly' [naɪʔɪ], and when it appears at the end of a word, as in 'cat' [kæʔ]. These two disparate environments can be informally stated in a rule as follows:

(10.36) /t/ → [ʔ] / __ $\left\{ \begin{matrix} C \\ \# \end{matrix} \right\}$

This rule states that /t/ becomes [ʔ] both before another consonant and at the end of a word. Note that this is exactly the environment associated with the distribution of clear and dark *l*. While (10.36) captures the observed behaviour of /t/, it gives us little insight into the nature of the conditioning environment, since it tells us nothing about a possible relationship between a consonant and a word boundary.

Looking at this in terms of syllable structure sheds more light on the nature of the environment. If we look at the words 'nightly' and 'cat' again and consider where the syllable boundaries fall, we find that in both cases

/t/ is immediately before a syllable boundary, i.e. in the coda (see Sections 2.3 and 6.1).

(10.37)   a. [.naɪʔ.lɪ.]   b. [.kæʔ.]

These examples show that rather than referring to consonants and word boundaries the important aspect of the environment is the position of the syllable boundary: /t/ in syllable-final position is glottalised. This can be informally represented as in the rule below.

(10.38)   /t/ → [ʔ] / __ .

If we now consider in the light of this the difference between 'nightly' and 'nitrate', where the /t/ of 'nightly' surfaces as [ʔ] and the first /t/ of 'nitrate' surfaces with aspiration as [tʰ], one might suspect that there is some difference between the sequences /tl/ and /tɹ/ in terms of syllable boundaries and, indeed, there is. Recall from Section 6.1.4 that the position of syllable boundaries is determined in part by onset maximisation, and that this is subject to language-specific phonotactic restrictions on word initial clusters. In English, [tɹ] is a permitted initial sequence, but [tl] is not, due to a phonotactic constraint operating in English; English words cannot begin with the sequence *[tl].

What this means for 'nightly' and 'nitrate' is that a syllable boundary occurs between /t/ and /l/ in 'nightly', but the /t/ and /ɹ/ in 'nitrate' belong to the same syllable: night.ly ~ ni.trate. The /t/ in 'nightly' is syllable-final while the /t/ in 'nitrate' is not. Hence the /t/ in 'nightly' fits the environment for the rule in (10.38) and is thus glottalised. In 'nitrate' the first /t/ is syllable-initial, rather than syllable-final, and so cannot be glottalised.

Further evidence for this account comes from examples like 'patrol' and 'petrol'. There are many varieties of English in which 'petrol' is pronounced with a glottal stop, as ['pʰɛʔɹəɫ], while 'patrol' surfaces with [tʰ] and never with a glottal stop as in [pətʰɹoʊɫ], where the aspiration serves to devoice the following liquid. This is good evidence that it's not merely a question of whether or not the /t/ in question *can* be in an onset with the following consonant, but rather whether it *is* in the onset. As we've seen before, an underlying segment undergoes a particular process depending on where it is in a syllable, since in 'pet.rol' the /t/ is in the coda of the first syllable whereas in 'pa.trol' (for reasons of stress placement) the /t/ is in the onset of the second syllable.

Note that the syllable boundary suggested here for 'petrol', between the /t/ and /ɹ/, runs counter to the principles of boundary placement discussed in Section 6.1.4. Onset maximisation would suggest that in both words both the consonants should be in the onset of the second syllable. However, the differing behaviour of the consonant clusters in 'petrol' and 'patrol' suggests that there might be more to be said here. The fact that the /t/ in 'patrol' can never glottalise indicates clearly that it must be in the onset, but the case of the /t/ in 'petrol' is a little more complex. The fact that it can glottalise suggests it is in a coda, as claimed above. However, in both 'petrol' and 'patrol', the /ɹ/ devoices. This devoicing of a liquid after a voiceless stop (see Section 3.1.3) only occurs in onsets, which suggests that the /t/ in both words is in onset position. So, while the /t/ in 'patrol' is uncontroversially an onset consonant, the /t/ in 'petrol' has characteristics of both onset *and* coda positions. It is thus possible to consider the /t/ in 'petrol' to be **ambisyllabic**, that is simultaneously in the coda of the first syllable (hence it can glottalise) and in the onset of the second syllable (and hence it devoices the following liquid). The syllable boundaries thus overlap in the case of 'petrol', as $[_1$ pe $[_2$t$]_1$rol$]_2$, with the /t/ in both syllables. Note that only the /t/ is ambisyllabic; the /ɹ/ cannot also be simultaneously in the coda of the first syllable since /tɹ/ is not a permitted coda. That the boundaries do *not* overlap in 'patrol', $[_1$pa$]_1[_2$trol$]_2$, has to do with the position of the stress, as we suggested above. Only consonants following stress can be ambisyllabic; onsets of stressed syllables cannot be ambisyllabic.

The notion of ambisyllabicity also helps account for the varying behaviour of /t/ with respect to 'flapping' in North American Englishes (see Section 3.1.6); while the /t/ in 'atom' is realised as a flap, in 'atomic' the /t/ surfaces as aspirated. Given the different stress patterns of the two words, we can see that the /t/ in 'atom' follows the stress, and is thus ambisyllabic, whereas the /t/ in 'atomic' is in the onset of the stressed syllable, and so cannot be ambisyllabic. Given this difference, flapping can be seen as only affecting ambisyllabic stops.

As we discussed briefly in Section 6.1.2, there is more to the role played by syllables than simply the location of syllable boundaries in phonological structure. There is a certain type of speech error, usually called a spoonerism, which consists of the first segment or cluster of a syllable being swapped for the first segment or cluster of another syllable in a phrase. For example, a speaker who wants to say 'round moon' may mistakenly make the transformation as in (10.39).

(10.39)   round moon → mound rune

What has happened here is that the first consonant of each word has been switched, shown schematically in (10.40).

(10.40) C_1V... C_2V...   → C_2V... C_1V ...
          [ɹaʊnd muːn]   [maʊnd ɹuːn]

A spoonerism, however, of 'dear queen' may end up as 'queer dean'.

(10.41) C_1V... C_2C_3V... → C_2C_3V... C_1V...
          [diːɹ kwiːn]   [kwiːɹ diːn]

(For non-rhotic speakers the final segment of 'dear'/'queer' will be [ə].) Significantly, it doesn't end up as *C_1C_2V... C_3V... *[dwiːɹ kiːn], or *C_1C_3V... C_2V... *[dkiːɹ wiːn] or some other combination. This indicates that it's not simply the 'first consonant' or some other specific consonant that is important. Rather, it is some constituent of a syllable that is important,

168

namely the onset, which we can define informally as 'that part of the syllable that occurs before the vowel.'

Spoonerisms thus provide evidence of structure within the syllable. They show that we can manipulate *parts* of syllables in perfectly systematic ways. What we've done in the examples above is to switch onsets while leaving the remainder of the syllable – i.e. the rhyme – intact.

There are several ways of representing the internal structure of the syllable. One of the most common, repeated from Section 6.1.2, is shown in (10.42).

(10.42)

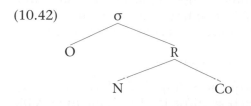

Lower case sigma (σ) stands for 'syllable'. The onset is represented by 'O'. The nucleus, or core, of the syllable is represented by 'N'. 'Co', or coda, is a consonant or consonants following the vowel. 'R' represents the rhyme, the combination of N and Co.

Returning to our spoonerism in (10.41), we can represent this in terms of syllable structure, as shown in (10.43).

(10.43)

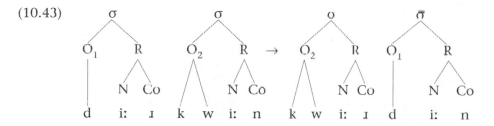

What we see in (10.43) is that the onsets have changed places: the first onset O_1 has traded places with the second onset O_2. In linear terms we would have to characterise this process as moving one, two or three segments before a vowel (since English allows consonants clusters of up to three members to appear word/syllable-initially as in 'ray', 'pray' and 'spray'). In terms of syllable structure we need only say that two onsets have moved.

Recall from Section 6.1.2 that in English, onsets and codas are optional; only the nucleus is obligatory and may be considered to be the **head** of the syllable. By head we mean the obligatory and characterising element of a construction. Without a nucleus there is no syllable. Note also that the nucleus, typically a vowel, is the most prominent segment in the syllable in the sense that it is the most sonorant.

In terms of syllable structure, then, we start to see what processes are involved in t-glottalisation and l-velarisation: when /t/ appears in coda position it may glottalise; when /l/ appears in coda position it velarises.

(10.44)

In the above trees, we ignore issues of ambisyllabicity for ease of exposition.

Syllable structure can also give us interesting insights into **phonotactics**, which is the statement of permissible combinations of segments in a particular language. Consider the underlined parts of following words:

(10.45) sleepwalk lab worker livewire leafworm

In linear terms these words exhibit sequences of [pw], [bw], [vw] and [fw]. At the same time, however, words such as those in (10.46) are impossible words of English:

(10.46) *pwell *bwee *vwoot *fwite

This means that we cannot simply place a restriction on *sequences* of [pw], [bw], [vw] and [fw], since they do occur, as in (10.45). Rather, the restriction is that sequences of a labial segment followed by [w] cannot appear in an onset or in a coda. So it is not the sequence of [pw] etc. that is not permitted, but the occurrence of such a sequence in an onset or a coda. Compare the position of the [pw] in [sli:pwɔk] with that in *[pwɛɫ].

(10.47)

Although the [p] and [w] are linearly adjacent in both (10.47a) and (10.47b), they are in different syllables in (10.47a) – referred to technically as **heterosyllabic** – while in (10.47b) they are in the onset of the same syllable – **tautosyllabic**. It is this second occurrence that is ill–formed in English.

10.4.2 Mora

A rather different type of syllable-internal structure to that described above involves an element called the mora. As we saw in Section 6.2.2, in some languages (e.g. English, Latin and Arabic) stress is sensitive to **syllable weight**. In other words, stress is assigned to particular syllables depending on whether they are **light** – consisting of a short vowel in the nucleus and no coda – or **heavy** – consisting of either a long vowel or diphthong in the nucleus, or having a consonant in coda position. While the light syllable seems to be rather straightforward – (C)V – the heavy syllable can consist of (C)VV, (C)VC – or even (C)VCC. Note the parentheses around the initial C. Onsets appear to be irrelevant to syllable weight. Using the syllable formalism seen above we can represent these syllables as in (10.48).

(10.48)

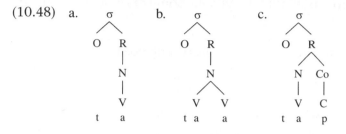

In languages sensitive to syllable weight the syllables in (10.48b) and (10.48c) (as well as VCC) typically behave as a group. In terms of syllable structure there is no clear reason why this should be so: in (10.48b) the nucleus contains two segments; in (10.48c), the nucleus contains one segment and the coda also contains one segment. One might suggest that some notion like 'branching rhyme' is playing a role here but, while 'branchingness' may be relevant, it is the nucleus branching in one case and the rhyme in the other.

So, how can these types of syllable be formalised so that heavy syllables are distinguished from light syllables in a natural way? One way of doing this is to recognise another structural unit, the *mora* (represented by Greek *mu*, μ). The mora is a unit of quantity, with a single vowel – i.e. a light syllable – equalling one μ, while a long vowel and a vowel plus coda consonant – i.e. heavy syllables – each equal two μs:

(10.49)

Note that in (10.49) the onsets attach directly to the syllable node and have no bearing on moraic structure. This is in keeping with the generalisation mentioned above that onsets do not contribute to syllable weight.

Apart from structure between the segment and the syllable there remains the question of suprasyllabic structure, that is structure above the syllable. We turn to this question now.

10.4.3 Foot

Traditional studies of poetic metre have long recognised the foot as an organising structure for combining syllables, or more precisely for combining stressed and unstressed syllables. A stressed syllable combined with any associated unstressed syllables constitutes a foot, with the stressed syllable being the head, since it is the most prominent. Feet may be **leftheaded**, i.e. with the stressed syllable on the left [ˈσσ], or rightheaded [σ ˈσ], they may be **binary** (**bounded**), consisting of two syllables, or **unbounded**, consisting of all the syllables in a particular domain, for instance, a morpheme or word. A **degenerate foot** consists of a single syllable. Some of these structures are illustrated in (10.50).

(10.50)   a. binary rightheaded   b. binary leftheaded

Traditionally, feet like those in (10.50a) are called iambic feet or iambs, while feet like those in (10.50b) are trochaic feet or trochees. (Other sorts of feet also have traditional labels which we won't detail here.) Note that the syllable in (10.50d) is not shown as stressed: since stress is a relative relationship, a single syllable in isolation is neither strong nor weak in relation to another one. This does not preclude a degenerate foot from having stress, as will be evident from the discussion below.

In addition to their metrical function, another reason to identify feet is to allow us to refer to the domain of specific phonological rules. Compare the words in (10.51). (Primary stress is indicated by a superscript ' and secondary stress by a subscript ˌ before the syllable.)

(10.51) [ɪŋk]   'ink'   [ˌɪŋkləˈneɪʃan]   'inclination'
         [ˈɪnˌklaɪn]   'incline' (noun) [ˌɪnˈklaɪn]   'incline' (verb)

Note that in 'ink' and 'inclination' the /n/ obligatorily appears as [ŋ]. In 'incline' (noun or verb) the /n/ may occur as [n] (though it *can* appear as [ŋ] it does not have to). If we look at syllable structure alone, we find that we cannot distinguish between the occurrence of [ŋ] and [n]: leaving aside 'ink', the syllabification of 'inclination' and 'incline' is the same for the relevant parts of the words. The /n/s in question are syllable-final in both cases.

(10.52)   σ   σ   σ   σ   σ   σ
            △   △   △   △   △   △
           ɪ ŋ k lə neɪ ʃ ə n   ɪ n k l aɪ n

At the same time, the difference in occurrence between [ŋ] and [n] cannot be due to stress alone, since the noun and verb forms of 'incline' differ precisely with respect to the stress assigned to the initial syllable.

What *is* different about the words in (10.51) though is the foot structure. Assuming that each stressed syllable (primary or secondary stress) heads its own (possibly degenerate) foot, the words in question differ in whether or not the /n/ at issue is next to the /k/ within the same foot or whether a foot boundary intervenes. When the two segments are in the same foot /n/ surfaces as [ŋ]. When the /n/ and /k/ are in different feet the /n/ may appear as [n].

(10.53)

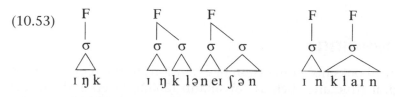

In other words, the velar assimilation of the /n/ to the /k/ occurs obligatorily within a foot but when the /n/ and /k/ are in different feet there is no obligatory assimilation. (Unlike the obligatory assimilation, optional velar assimilation is not foot based, as it can occur across words: 'gree[ŋ] car'.) By recognising the foot as a domain for the application of a phonological rule, we can capture the behaviour of /n/ velarisation. Without recognising the foot we have no insightful way of accounting for this

10.4.4 Structure above the foot

We have seen that nuclei head syllables and stressed syllables head feet. Feet may also be combined into larger constituents where one foot is more prominent than the others. Thus, in (10.54) we have a construction consisting of three feet, the last of which is the most prominent, i.e. the head.

(10.54)

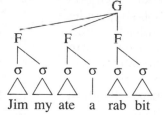

Jim my ate a rab bit

In (10.54) we informally label the structure 'G' for 'group'. The exact nature of structures above the level of the foot is a matter of some controversy which goes beyond the scope of this book. Without going into the specifics of these constituents, phonologists have proposed a hierarchy of ever larger constituents up to and including entire utterances. For the present purposes, what is important is that there is a general recognition of the need for structures above the foot.

10.5 Conclusion

Chapter 10 has dealt with various aspects of phonological structure. Recognising the inadequacy of a phonological model based on segments alone, phonological research has taken two different directions, exploring representations both larger than the segment and smaller than the segment. These representations include autosegments, feature geometry and suprasegmental structures such as the syllable and foot.

In the next chapter we consider how rules and representations are used in derivational analyses and how analyses are evaluated.

Further reading

Most recent textbooks have discussion of extensions to the representation of phonological structure, such as Gussmann (2002), Ewen and van der Hulst (2001), Gussenhoven and Jacobs (2005), Spencer (1996), Kenstowicz (1994), Carr (1993), Durand (1990).

For somewhat more advanced treatments, see Anderson and Ewen (1985), Harris (1994), Durand and Katamba (1995), Clements and Keyser (1990), Halle (1992), and Goldsmith (1990). A number of the papers in Goldsmith (1995) also deal with topics discussed in this chapter.

The Desano data is from Kaye (1989).

Exercises

1   Schwa epenthesis in Dutch (Germanic)
    The following data exemplify a type of optional schwa epenthesis (underlined) in standard Dutch (see Trommelen 1984).

/ɛlk/	a.	'ɛlək 'each'	b. ɛl'kar 'each other'	c. *ɛləkar	
/vɔlk/	d.	'vɔlək 'people'	e. 'vɔlkən 'peoples'	f. *vɔləkən	
/mɛlk/	g.	'mɛlək 'milk	h. 'mɛlkən 'to milk'	i. *mɛləkən	
/warm/	j.	'warəm 'warm'	k. 'warmən 'warm'	l. *warəmən	
/arm/	m.	'arəm 'arm'	n. 'armən 'arms'	o. *arəmən	
/horn/	p.	'horən 'horn'	q. hornən	r. *horənən	
/bɛlx/	s.	'bɛləx 'Belgian'	t. 'bɛlxiə 'Belgium'	u. *bɛləxiə	
/pɛrs/	v.	pɛrs 'press'	w. *pɛrəs	x. *pɛrəsən	
/hɛld/	y.	hɛlt 'hero'	z. *hɛlət	z'. *hɛlədən	

    i.   Describe in words where underlined schwa can be inserted.
    ii. Account for the insertion using a non-linear analysis.

2 Turkish (Altaic; Turkey, N. Cyprus)
   Turkish has the following vowel system:

	front		back	
	unround	*round*	*unround*	*round*
high	i	y	ɨ	u
low	e	ø	ɑ	o

i. Express the vowel contrasts in terms of distinctive features (you should only require three features).
ii. Using the notion of underspecification, suggest URs for the noun stems and affixes in the data.
iii. What processes are operative in the data?
iv. How can these processes be expressed as rules in autosegmental terms?

nominative singular	genitive singular	nominative plural	gloss
a. gyl	b. gylyn	c. gyller	'rose'
d. ʧøl	e. ʧølyn	f. ʧøller	'desert'
g. kiʧ	h. kiʧin	i. kiʧlar	'rump'
j. ɑkʃɑm	k. ɑkʃɑmɨn	l. ɑkʃɑmlɑr	'evening'
m. ev	n. evin	o. evler	'house'
p. demir	q. demirin	r. demirler	'anchor'
s. kol	t. kolun	u. kollɑr	'arm'
v. somun	w. somunun	x. somunlɑr	'loaf'

3 Welsh (Celtic, Wales; from Tallerman 1987)
   Consider the (simplified) data below. There are two alternations occurring: (i) in the initial consonant of the noun stem and (ii) in the final consonant of /ən/ 'my'. How can the alternations be accounted for in autosegmental terms? The citation form (word in isolation) is given first.

a. kɛgɪn	'kitchen'	b. əŋ ŋ̊ɛgɪn	'my kitchen'
c. bʊθɪn	'cottage'	d. əm mʊθɪn	'my cottage'
e. tiː	'house'	f. ən n̥iː	'my house'
g. pɛntrɛ	'village'	h. əm m̥ɛntrɛ	'my village'
i. dəfrɪn	'valley'	j. ən nəfrɪn	'my valley'
k. kəmriː	'Wales'	l. əŋ ŋ̊əmriː	'my Wales'

11

Derivational analysis

The model of the phonological component of a generative grammar that we've been developing to this point can be seen to consist of two parts. First, a set of **underlying representations** (URs) for all the morphemes of the language and, second, a set of **phonological rules** which determine the **surface forms** (i.e. the phonetic forms) for these underlying representations (see Section 8.3). So, for a word like 'pin' the UR, i.e. the phonological information in the lexicon, might be /pɪn/. To this form, rules like 'Voiceless Stop Aspiration' (see Section 3.1.3) and 'Vowel Nasalisation' (see Section 4.3) will apply, giving the **phonetic form** (PF) [pʰɪ̃n]. As in this simple example, underlying forms may be affected by more than one rule; the series of steps from UR to PF is known as a *derivation*, which is the concern of this chapter.

11.1 The aims of analysis

As we discussed in Chapter 1, the aim of a generative grammar is to capture formally the intuitive knowledge speakers have of their native language, i.e. their competence. So what kinds of intuitive phonological knowledge do speakers have? Clearly they have knowledge of which sounds are and are not part of their language, that is the phonetic and phonemic inventories. Remember that by 'knowledge' we mean subconscious and not conscious knowledge: speakers don't – and can't – typically express generalisations about the phonology of their language. So, for instance, English speakers know that the voiced velar fricative [ɣ] is not part of their inventory of sounds, just as French speakers know that [θ] is not part of theirs.

Speakers also know what combinations of sounds can occur in their language, and what positional restrictions there may be on sounds. English speakers know that the only consonant that can precede a nasal at the beginning of a word is the fricative [s]: [snuːp] is fine, but not *[fnuːp], *[knuːp], *[bnuːp] or *[mnuːp]. That is, speakers have a knowledge of the **phonotactics** of their language.

A further kind of speaker knowledge concerns relationships between surface forms: speakers 'know' that some surface forms are related, and that others are not. Speakers consistently and automatically produce the kinds of (morpho)phonological alternations discussed in Section 9.2. They 'know' that although the actual surface nasal segment at the end of the preposition 'in' varies – as in [ɪm boʊɫtən] or [ɪŋ kɪɫmɑːnək] –

underlyingly the preposition has a single UR, which we can represent as /ɪn/. Without being aware of it, speakers produce forms showing the surface variation which is due to the nasal assimilating to the place of articulation of the following consonant. The phonological rules in the phonological component are a way of expressing such knowledge; that is, they provide a formal characterisation of the link between the invariant underlying representations and the set of surface forms associated with them.

A number of assumptions underpin the type of characterisations phonologists propose for rules and derivations. One is that the rules should account for all and only all the data for which they are formulated. That is, they should not also predict the occurrence of forms which are not in fact found in the language. This may sound obvious, but it is by no means trivial. It is of no use to have a nice straightforward rule that does indeed cover the data but which also makes further, wrong, predictions. As a simple example, consider a statement to the effect that each segment in a consonant cluster in English must agree in its value for the feature [voice]; [+ voice][+ voice] and [– voice][– voice] are fine, but *[+ voice][– voice] or *[– voice][+ voice] are ruled out. Such a statement will quite correctly admit the clusters in [æps, æft, ækts, ɛgz, ɛndz], and not allow those in *[æbs, æfd, ægtz, ɛkz, ɛntz]. However, it would also predict that the clusters in [ænts, ɪntʃ, ɪmp, snoʊ] are impossible in English, which is clearly not the case. In this instance the solution is relatively easy to find: the restriction must apply to obstruent clusters only, not all consonant clusters. Constraining a whole series of rules, that is a derivation, to prevent them from allowing ungrammatical forms to surface, however, is a much harder task.

A second underlying assumption behind rule formulation is that the rules, and the derivations they form part of, should be maximally simple, expressing maximum generalisations with minimal formal apparatus. That is, in general, simple, broad rules are preferable to complex, specific ones. One reason for this is a desire for formal economy; the fewer elements in the grammar, the more highly-valued it is (see the discussion in Section 8.4). This is sometimes known as the principle of Occam's Razor: 'don't multiply entities beyond necessity' (i.e. don't build a complex mousetrap involving wheels, pulleys, weights and cogs when a simple box with a one-way door will suffice). A further reason for valuing economy and maximal generalisation has to do with speculations about how we learn language and how the mind is organised; the hypothesis is that we operate both as learners and fully competent speakers by using a relatively small number of broad generalisations, rather than by employing large numbers of less general statements. Some evidence for such a stance can be found in children's speech, for instance. Noun plural forms like 'mans' and 'foots' are often produced by children, presumably because they have formulated a general 'plural = noun + s' rule and then applied it to 'man' and 'foot'. It is only later that the irregular forms 'men' and 'feet' are learnt. Indeed, on many occasions the generalised form persists at the expense of the adult irregular form. If this were not so, the plural of 'book' in Modern English might be expected to be something like 'beek' (compare with 'feet') since in

177

Old English the forms were *bōc* (singular) and *bēc* (plural), exactly parallel to *fōt* and *fēt* in Old English. (The macron above the vowels indicates a long vowel.)

This principle of descriptive economy obviously has to be tempered by concerns like those expressed earlier about accounting for all and only all the data; sometimes a specific, less general rule will be necessary to avoid incorrect surface forms predicted by a more general rule.

So, to recap, the aim of a derivational analysis is to express, in a maximally simple and general way, the relationship between the underlying phonological representations of a language and their surface phonetic realisations. In the next section, we will look at how such an approach might deal with the set of alternations like those involved in regular noun plural formation in English.

11.2 A derivational analysis of English noun plural formation

Consider the plural nouns in the following lists:

(11.1)   a. rats, giraffes, asps, yaks, moths
           b. aphids, crabs, dogs, lions, cows
           c. asses, leeches, midges, thrushes

(Note that in this section we are not considering irregular plural formation, e.g. 'man' ~ 'men', 'child' ~ 'children', 'sheep' ~ 'sheep'.) Given the forms in (11.1), how do we form regular plurals in English? What might seem to be the obvious answer – add '(e)s' – only tells us about the orthography, and so can be discounted. It tells us nothing about the phonology of plural formation, which is what concerns us here. In fact, there are three different surface forms of the regular plural suffix in English, [s] as in (11.1a), [z] as in (11.1b) and [ɪz] – or [əz], depending on the variety of English under discussion – in (11.1c). Furthermore, the occurrence of each of these alternants is completely predictable: if we come across a new noun it can only take one of the three plural forms, and all speakers of English will agree as to which of the three. Thus an invented noun like 'poik' will take [s]; 'crug' will take [z]; and 'rish' will take [ɪz].

So what determines this distribution? When we look at the set of words in (11.1a), those that take [s], we notice that the singular noun ends in a voiceless segment: [t], [f], [p], [k], [θ]. The singular forms of the words in (11.1b), which take [z], end in voiced segments: [d], [b], [g], [n], [aʊ]. And those in (11.1c), which take [ɪz], have singulars which end in one of the sibilants: [s], [z], [tʃ], [dʒ], [ʃ] and [ʒ]. Given this, we can say that the regular plural suffix in English is a coronal sibilant fricative which agrees in voicing with the preceding segment with the proviso that when the root-final segment is also a sibilant, a vowel separates the two sibilants. Our job now is to formalise this insight in terms of appropriate underlying forms and a set of rules to link the URs to the surface forms.

Let us use the forms 'rats', 'crabs' and 'leeches' as exemplars of the three groups in (11.1). First, we need to decide on the UR for the plural morpheme (we will assume that the noun roots have URs equivalent to their surface singular forms since the roots show no surface variation). We might start by considering the surface forms of the plural morpheme. Any of the three surface forms will do in principle, but given the considerations in Section 8.4 concerning choosing underlying forms, we can probably dispense with [ɪz], since it is the least frequent and occurs in the narrowest range of environments. That leaves us with either [s] or [z]; in terms of frequency there is probably not much to choose between them, but [z] does have a wider distribution, occurring after voiced obstruents, sonorants and vowels, while [s] is restricted to positions following voiceless obstruents. This would give some slight preference for /z/ as the underlying representation for the English plural morpheme.

Note, however, that there is another possibility, which employs the concept of **underspecification** introduced in Section 10.2. Since voicing is always determined by the segment which immediately precedes the coronal fricative, we can leave the feature [voice] out of the underlying representation for the plural morpheme, specifying only that it is [+ coronal] and [+ continuant]. Following the conventions of Section 10.2 of using a capital letter to symbolise the underspecified segment, we might represent this as /Z/.

As far as our analysis of English plurals here is concerned, any of (fully-specified) /s/ or /z/ or underspecified /Z/ are possible URs. Using /Z/ prevents us from having to make an essentially arbitrary choice between /s/ and /z/, however. It also allows us to characterise voicing assimilation in a more straightforward way, as we will see below, so in what follows we assume the UR of the plural morpheme to be a coronal fricative not specified for the feature [voice] (and see Section 11.4.2 for some further justification).

This gives us the following URs for the plurals (where '+' indicates a word-internal morpheme boundary):

(11.2)   /ɹæt+Z/   /kɹæb+Z/   /liːtʃ+Z/

We must now consider the rules we need to mediate between these URs and their respective surface forms [ɹæts], [kɹæbz] and [liːtʃɪz]. In these forms the suffix assimilates to the voicing of the preceding segment. So, for [ɹæts] we need an assimilation rule to add the specification [– voice] to /Z/ to give [s], for [kɹæbz] we need the same rule to add the specification [+ voice] to /Z/ to give [z], and for [liːtʃɪz] we need both the assimilation rule to specify voicing and a rule to insert an [ɪ] between the root and suffix.

Let us take the vowel insertion rule first. As we saw above, an epenthetic [ɪ] is found when the root ends in a sibilant ([s], [z], [tʃ], [dʒ], [ʃ], [ʒ]). We thus need some way of specifying this group of sounds as a natural class. We can start by using the feature [strident] to do this (see Section 7.3.4) since the whole set shares the specification [+ strident], but we then need to exclude the [+ strident] [f] and [v] (since we don't get, e.g. *[dʒɪɹæfɪz] for 'giraffes'). This we can do by specifying that the segments referred to in the rule must also be [+ coronal] ([f] and [v] are [– coronal]). These two features are all we need to identify the set – note that we don't need feature specifications like [+ consonantal] or [– sonorant], since these are implied by [+ strident]. Our 'ɪ-epenthesis' rule might thus take the form in (11.3):

(11.3)
$$\varnothing \rightarrow \begin{bmatrix} + \text{syll} \\ + \text{hi} \\ - \text{back} \\ - \text{tns} \end{bmatrix} \bigg/ \begin{bmatrix} + \text{strid} \\ + \text{cor} \end{bmatrix} \quad + \underline{\hphantom{xx}} \begin{bmatrix} + \text{strid} \\ + \text{cor} \end{bmatrix}$$

Note the presence of the word-internal morpheme boundary '+' in the environment of the rule. If there were no such boundary specified, the rule might apply to the [tʃ z] sequence in 'each zoo', wrongly predicting *[iːtʃ ɪzuː]. It is often important to specify the morphological and syntactic conditions as well as the phonological conditions under which a rule is triggered (see the discussion of alternations in Section 9.2). Note further that it suffices to minimally specify the plural morpheme /Z/ just as [+ strid, + cor] because there are no other strident coronal suffixes in English, so the rule could not affect any other strident coronals (but see below for some further comment on this).

We turn now to the voicing specification rule; this might be expressed in either of the forms in (11.4):

(11.4) a. $\begin{bmatrix} + \text{strid} \\ + \text{cor} \end{bmatrix} \rightarrow [\alpha \text{ voice}] / [\alpha \text{ voice}] \underline{\hphantom{xx}}$

      b.
$$[\alpha \text{ voice}]$$

$$x \qquad x$$

$$\begin{bmatrix} + \text{strid} \\ + \text{cor} \end{bmatrix}$$

The version given in (11.4a) expresses the process as a linear rule involving Greek-letter variables; whatever value the immediately preceding segment has for the feature [voice] is copied onto the plural morpheme. In (11.4b) we see the process recast in terms of the autosegmental model outlined in Section 10.3 with the timing slots represented by 'x' rather than Cs and Vs; the [voice] feature from the immediately preceding segment spreads rightwards onto the suffix.

At this point – if you reflect on what counterexamples there might be – you might wonder why (11.4) doesn't apply to a word like 'fence' (UR /fɛns/), wrongly predicting *[fɛnz], or in a sequence like 'that zoo', predicting *[ðæt suː]. Unlike the rule in (11.3), neither of the rule formulations in (11.4) makes reference to morphological or syntactic information, so why are the alveolar fricatives in 'fence' and 'that zoo' not affected by the rule? The reason (11.4) does not apply in cases like 'fence' and 'that zoo' is that the final fricative in the UR /fɛns/ and the initial fricative in the UR /zuː/ are both fully specified for the feature [voice] underlyingly; the voicing assimilation rule in (11.4) is a structure-building rule (see Section 10.2) and so only applies to segments which are underspecified for the feature [voice].

We now have all we need for a full account of regular plural formation in English. Sample derivations are shown in (11.5).

(11.5)	UR	/ɹæt+Z/	/kɹæb+Z/	/liːʧ+Z/
	ɪ-epenthesis			
	rule	—	—	liːʧ+ɪZ
	Voicing			
	assimilation rule	ɹæt+s	kɹæb+z	liːʧ+ɪz
	PF	[ɹæts]	[kɹæbz]	[liːʧɪz]

In (11.5) each rule scans the input UR to see if the form contains the environment which will trigger the application of the rule. If the environment is met, then the rule fires; if the environment is not met, then the form is unaffected. The UR is then passed on to the next rule in the sequence and the scanning is repeated. This next rule applies if its environment is satisfied, otherwise the form is unaffected. This process continues until there are no further rules; at this point we have reached the surface form.

For the moment, let us simply assume that the rules apply in the order given in (11.5) – we will return to the justification for this in Section 11.3. So, in the derivations in (11.5) the UR /ɹæt+Z/ is first scanned by the ɪ-epenthesis rule (11.3). The environment for triggering the rule is not met, since /t/ is not [+ strident], so the form passes unaffected to the voicing assimilation rule (11.4). This time the environment is satisfied: the /Z/ follows a segment specified for the feature [voice]. The rule thus applies to the form, copying (or spreading) the [– voice] specification from the root-final segment to the plural morpheme. No further rules apply, and we have the surface phonetic form [ɹæts]. The UR /kɹæb+Z/ is similarly passed through both rules in turn; it too fails to meet the environment for ɪ-epenthesis but satisfies the conditions for voicing assimilation, which supplies the specification [+ voice] to /Z/, and so the word surfaces as [kɹæbz].

In the case of the UR /liːʧ+Z/, since /ʧ/ is [+ strident] and [+ coronal] the conditions for the ɪ-epenthesis rule are met. The rule applies, inserting a vowel between the final segment of the root and the plural morpheme. This gives the intermediate form 'liːʧ+ɪZ', and it is this intermediate form, not the original UR, that is scanned by the voicing assimilation rule. This means that the [– voice] specification of the root-final /ʧ/ does not copy or spread, since another segment, /ɪ/, now intervenes. It is this segment that gives /Z/ its specification [+ voice] and the form [liːʧɪz] surfaces.

So, with a single UR for the plural morpheme and two simple rules, we can account for the facts of regular noun plural formation in English in a straightforward and elegant manner. Indeed, we can account for rather more than just noun plurals, as we see when we consider the following data:

(11.6) a. (she) walks, hits, coughs
                 hugs, waves, runs, sighs
                 misses, catches, rushes
        b.   coat's, Jack's, wife's
                 dog's, Maeve's, sun's, bee's
                 Chris's, watch's, hedge's

The rules and derivations we have suggested for the plurals can be extended without alteration to cover the 3rd person singular present tense verb suffix (11.6a) and the genitive case marker on nouns (11.6b), assuming both these suffixes to have the same UR as the plural marker, /Z/. Underlying forms like the verb root plus person/tense marker /hɪt+Z/ and /weɪv+Z/, or the noun root plus genitive /kɹɪs+Z/, can be given derivations exactly parallel to /ɹæt+Z/, /kɹæb+Z/ and /liːtʃ+Z/ in (11.5).

11.3 Extrinsic vs. intrinsic rule ordering

We now return to the question of the relative ordering of our two rules, which we earlier simply assumed was as in (11.5), i.e. ɪ-epenthesis before voicing assimilation. In fact, for the analysis presented in the previous section to work, it is crucial that the two rules apply in the order given in (11.5). To see this, consider the derivations in (11.7), where the order of the rules has been reversed.

(11.7)

UR	/ɹæt+Z/	/kɹæb+Z/	/liːtʃ+Z/
Voicing assimilation rule	ɹæt+s	kɹæb+z	liːtʃ+s
ɪ-epenthesis rule	—	—	liːtʃ+ɪs
PF	[ɹæts]	[kɹæbz]	*[liːtʃɪs]

The derivations of /ɹæt+Z/ and /kɹæb+Z/ are unaffected, since only the voicing assimilation rule can ever apply to these URs. The two rules do not interact for these URs, so cannot help in deciding which order is better. The important evidence for ordering comes from /liːtʃ+Z/. This UR meets the environments for both rules because /tʃ/ is both [+ strident] and is underlyingly specified for voicing as [– voice], so either rule could apply first. If, as shown in (11.7), the voicing assimilation rule (11.4) is allowed to apply first, before ɪ-epenthesis, then the plural morpheme /Z/ receives the specification [– voice] from the root-final /tʃ/ and we get an intermediate form 'liːtʃ+s'. This intermediate form is then fed into the ɪ-epenthesis rule (11.3). The form 'liːtʃ+s' meets the environment for the rule: /tʃ/ is [+ strident] and the now [– voice] plural morpheme is still [+ strident] and [+ coronal]. The rule therefore applies, and inserts the vowel between root and suffix. This analysis thus wrongly predicts that the surface form of /liːtʃ+Z/ will be *[liːtʃɪs], with a final voiceless fricative.

We must thus stipulate that the order of our rules is as in (11.5), ɪ-epenthesis before voicing assimilation. Note that there is nothing in the formulation of the rules themselves which determines this order, since in principle either order is possible. Both orders 'work', in the sense that they make predictions about the surface forms for particular URs, but only one order makes predictions that are in line with facts of English plural formation. This type of ordering, imposed on the rules by the analyst, is known as 'extrinsic' ordering, and is opposed to 'intrinsic' ordering. Intrinsic ordering involves ordering of rules by virtue of the nature of the rules themselves, rather than order imposed from outside.

As an example of intrinsic ordering, consider one possible analysis of English [ŋ]. We noted in Section 3.4.1 that [ŋ] has a distribution unlike that of the other nasals [m] and [n] in English; [ŋ] cannot occur word-initially, and in morphologically simple words the only consonants that can follow [ŋ] are [k] or [g] (and indeed in some varieties [ŋ] must be followed by [k] or [g]). One way of dealing with these facts is to suggest that underlyingly there is no phoneme /ŋ/ in English, but rather that all instances of surface [ŋ] are derived from a sequence of /nk/ or /ng/. The lack of other consonants following [ŋ] is thus accounted for, and the non-occurrence of initial [ŋ] can then be seen to be due to a more general ban on underlying initial nasal + oral stop sequences. English has no initial */mb-/ or */nd-/; initial */ng-/ (the underlying source of [ŋ]) would be impossible by the same constraint, hence no initial [ŋ] on the surface.

If we accept this as a hypothesis, we are going to need some rule or rules to link surface forms like [sɪŋ] to URs like /sɪng/. Two things must happen here: the nasal must become velar, and the voiced oral stop must be deleted. We can express the nasal assimilation as (11.8).

$$(11.8) \quad [+\text{nas}] \rightarrow \begin{bmatrix} -\text{cor} \\ -\text{ant} \end{bmatrix} / \underline{\quad} \begin{bmatrix} -\text{cor} \\ -\text{ant} \\ -\text{continuant} \end{bmatrix}$$

That is, /n/ asssimilates to the place of articulation of the following velar stop. (Using the concepts introduced in the preceding chapter, we could equally well express this process in terms of an autosegmental spreading of the place node from the stop to the preceding nasal.) The rule to delete the [g] might look like (11.9).

$$(11.9) \quad \begin{bmatrix} +\text{voice} \\ -\text{cont} \\ -\text{cor} \\ -\text{ant} \end{bmatrix} \rightarrow \emptyset / \begin{bmatrix} +\text{nasal} \\ -\text{cor} \\ -\text{ant} \end{bmatrix} \underline{\quad}$$

That is, /g/ is deleted after the velar nasal [ŋ]. Note the specification [+ voice] in (11.9) – we don't want to delete a following /k/ in words like 'think'. Now, how are these two rules to be ordered with respect to one another? Recall the situation with our two rules for plural formation; either rule could in principle apply first and the order was determined by appealing to the surface forms found in English. Here, however, that is not the case; 'g-deletion' (11.9) cannot apply to the UR /sɪng/, since there is no velar nasal to trigger the deletion. Indeed, g-deletion can never apply to an underlying form, because under the assumptions we're making here no URs can ever have /ŋ/ in them. The velar nasal only ever arises through the application of the assimilation rule in (11.8) – it is always derived from a sequence of /ng/ (or /nk/). The assimilation rule must thus precede the g-deletion rule, since assimilation introduces part of the environment which triggers g-deletion, i.e. the [ŋ]. Further and crucially, the assimilation rule introduces that part of the environment which can only arise from the application of that rule, since there is no underlying */ŋ/. Note, however, that the data relevant to [ŋ] and g-deletion in English are rather more complex than outlined here; g-deletion does not, for instance, remove the [g] in [fɪŋgə]. A full analysis would obviously have to account for such facts.

This is an example of intrinsic ordering: a type of ordering which is determined by the rules themselves, with one rule creating (part of) the conditions for the application of another, and thus necessarily preceding it.

11.4 Evaluating competing analyses: evidence, economy and plausibility

There is always more than one way of looking at something, i.e. more than one way of interpreting a given set of facts. What this means for phonology is that for any set of data there will be more than one analysis available. One of the tasks facing the phonologist is therefore to evaluate competing analyses and to choose between them. In order to compare competing analyses and draw reasonable conclusions there are several issues to take into consideration, including evidence, economy and plausibility. In other words, is there evidence to support one analysis over another? Is one analysis less complex than another, while still accounting for the same range of data? Is one analysis more plausible than another, in that it expresses expected kinds of phonological behaviour? In answering these questions we can begin to evaluate competing analyses. We should also bear in mind, however, that our conclusions will be influenced by our starting point, i.e. our underlying assumptions about the nature of phonology. If, for instance, we didn't value simplicity as a criterion, then the evaluation of two analyses might yield a different result.

11.4.1 Competing rules

One aspect of evaluating a particular analysis entails evaluating rules, that is choosing between two rules which apparently express the same thing. Sometimes it is rather straightforward to choose between two rules.

For example, if two rules account for the same set of data but one of the rules predicts data that aren't found, the choice is easily made. Recall our discussion earlier, in Section 11.1, of voicing in consonant clusters. Don't be misled, though – it's not always easy to see that a particular rule makes incorrect predictions.

As an example, consider the following set of data from Dutch, focussing on the alternation between the voiced and voiceless stops [t] and [d], [p] and [b]. (Note that there is no voiced velar stop in Dutch, only a voiceless velar stop [k]. A bit more will be said about this later.)

(11.10) [hɔnt] 'dog'   [hɔndə] 'dogs'
        [lat]   'load, 3sg.'   [ladə]   'load, 3pl.'
        [xut]   'good'   [xudərə] 'goods'
        [hɛp]   'have, 1sg.'   [hɛbə]   'have, 1pl.'
        [krɑp] 'scratch, 1sg.' [krɑbə] 'scratch, 3pl.'
        [xətɔp] 'worrying'   [tɔbə]   'to worry'

On the face of it, the alternation between these stops could be captured by either of two rules:

(11.11) a. $\begin{bmatrix} + \text{ cons} \\ - \text{ cont} \\ - \text{ voice} \end{bmatrix} \rightarrow [+ \text{ voice}] \ / \ \underline{\quad} \ [+ \text{ syll}]$

b. $\begin{bmatrix} + \text{ cons} \\ - \text{ cont} \\ + \text{ voice} \end{bmatrix} \rightarrow [- \text{ voice}] \ / \ \underline{\quad} \ \#$

According to the first rule, an underlying voiceless stop surfaces as its voiced counterpart before a vowel. According to the second rule an underlying voiced stop becomes voiceless at the end of a word, indicated by the word boundary '#'. As far as the forms in (11.10) are concerned, either rule would account for the data. However, looking just a bit further into Dutch we find words like [latə] 'leave, 3 plural', [lɛtər] 'letter', [hoːpə] 'hope', [stɔpə] 'stop'. Words like these, containing a voiceless stop followed by [ə], count as evidence against rule (11.11a). If (11.11a) were correct, these words would have to appear as *[ladə], *[lɛdər], *[hoːbə] and *[stɔbə]. (Actually, the forms [ladə] and [stɔbə] do exist in Dutch, but they mean 'load, 3 plural' and 'stump' respectively. That is, they are different lexical items and are derived from different underlying representations than the words for 'leave' and 'stop', and are thus irrelevant to the argument here.) On the other hand, examining a full set of Dutch data we never find a word like *[hoːb], i.e. one that ends with a voiced stop (although there are Dutch words which have a final 'd' and 'b' in the spelling). This is evidence supporting rule (11.11b). In this case it is fairly easy to see which rule should be preferred and why: (11.11a) simply makes the wrong prediction, namely that a voiceless stop will not appear before a vowel; contrary to that prediction we find Dutch words containing precisely that sequence. Rule (11.11b) on the other hand seems both to account for the data in question and make no wrong predictions. Note, too, that in this case both rules are equally plausible in terms of expected phonological behaviour: we find languages in the world in which voiceless stops never occur between two vowels – e.g. Cree (North America) – and other languages in which voiced stops systematically undergo final devoicing – e.g. German, Russian. This means that we need to rule out (11.11a) on the basis of making incorrect predictions for Dutch, not because the rule is inherently implausible.

As mentioned above, another criterion available in deciding between two rules is economy: if two rules account for the same set of facts but one rule does it more simply, that rule is to be preferred. For example, in the analysis above of the regular English plural morpheme as underspecified /Z/, rules were given in (11.4) which did not include reference to the morpheme boundary. As discussed there, reference to the boundary is made unnecessary by the difference in application of the voicing rule between underspecified /Z/ and fully specified /s/ and /z/. It is therefore simpler, and preferable, to propose a rule like that of (11.4), than to posit a more complex rule which unnecessarily includes irrelevant information, in this case, the morpheme boundary.

In a related vein, if one rule or analysis captures a greater generalisation that rule or analysis is to be preferred, again since it is simpler in the sense of using less machinery to gain greater coverage. Once more referring to the analysis of the plural morpheme, underspecified /Z/ along with two rules allows us to account not only for the plural morpheme but also for the English 3rd person singular marker and the possessive marker, as illustrated in (11.6). This is clearly more economical and more insightful than proposing separate rules or separate analyses for each of the three forms associated with each of the three markers: plural, 3rd person singular and possessive. The economy is evident but it is also more insightful, since it seems to be telling us something general about English: that a [+ coronal, + strident] morpheme behaves phonologically in a particular way, regardless of what it is marking grammatically.

The question of economy also applies to underlying inventories and specifications. Recall the discussion of intrinsic ordering above, which was exemplified by the interaction of nasal assimilation and g-deletion. It was suggested there that English has no underlying /ŋ/, and that [ŋ] is derived from a sequence of /nk/ or /ng/. Apart from the relevance of this analysis to the question of intrinsic ordering, another aspect of the status of [ŋ] has to do with economy. In the discussion of Occam's Razor above, the idea was that formal mechanisms and rules should be kept as simple as possible. Applying this principle to underlying inventories, if we can dispense with /ŋ/, that's one less phoneme we need to assume as part of the underlying system of English, thus achieving a more economical system. By the same token, the idea of underspecification is driven by economy: the less you have to specify underlyingly, whether phonemes or features, the more economical the system. The underspecification of the plural morpheme as /Z/ together with the ɪ-epenthesis rule is more economical than positing three fully specified allomorphs (surface forms of the plural marker) /-s/, /-z/ and /-ɪz/ together with the rules specifying where each occurs.

The third criterion mentioned above was plausibility. In evaluating analyses it may be possible to choose one analysis over another because one is more plausible than the other. Recall the alternation between [s] and [ʃ] in the Korean data in Exercise 2 of Chapter 8, some items of which are repeated here. (See also discussion of process naturalness in Section 8.4.3.)

(11.12) satan 'division'   ʃesuil 'washroom'   ʃeke 'world'
       ʃihap 'game'   ʃekum 'taxes'   sosəl 'novel'
       sæk 'colour'

Assuming an allophonic relationship between [s] and [ʃ], two analyses are logically possible: either /s/ becomes [ʃ] or /ʃ/ becomes [s]. If we consider /ʃ/ to [s], we find that there is no particular reason why this should occur; there is no apparent phonetic motivation for the alternation and this is not a change that we typically find cross-linguistically. With /s/ to [ʃ], on the other hand, there is a phonetic reason why this might happen: each occurrence of [ʃ] in the data is followed by a non-low front vowel, [i] or [e]. Thus, the occurrence of [ʃ] can be seen as a type of place assimilation to the non-low front vowel, much as in English the /s/ of /ðɪs/ becomes [ʃ] in [ðɪʃjiə] 'this year' (see Section 8.4.3). Cross-linguistically, too, we often find /s/ surfacing as [ʃ] before a non-low front vowel. These considerations – phonetic and cross-linguistic – suggest that it is more plausible to analyse the Korean alternation as a change from /s/ to [ʃ] than a change from /ʃ/ to [s].

As an exercise in implausibility, imagine for a moment a derivational analysis relating the words 'go' and 'went'. On semantic grounds alone one might find an analysis of 'went' from 'go' plausible, since in Modern English 'went' is the past tense form of 'go'. In phonological terms the two could be related, though not simply. Assuming /goʊ/ as the underlying form, there would need to be a rule changing /g/ to [w], possibly by adding labiality to it, since /g/ is a velar and [w] a labial-velar. Then there would have to be another rule changing the diphthong /oʊ/ to the short monophthong [ε]; one might argue that along with the addition of labiality to /g/, adding 'frontness' to it, the backness of /oʊ/ is also fronted to yield [ε]. Finally, the addition of both [n] and [t] would need to be accounted for. Conversely, one could assume /wεnt/ and derive [goʊ]. In either case, a fair amount of machinery is being invoked to account for a single pair of (semantically) related words, which seems rather implausible. In other words, we would need at least four rules to derive 'go' from 'went' or vice versa, yet those rules apply only to this pair of words; they have no generality in English as a whole and offer no insight into the sound system of English.

Moreover, if we briefly consider historical (or diachronic) evidence there's no reason to suppose that 'went' is derived from 'go': historically the words are forms of two unrelated verbs, Old English *gān* 'go' and *wendan* 'wend'.

Somehow the past tense form of *wendan*, i.e. *went* (in Modern English 'wended'), became associated with the verb 'go'. Furthermore, there is also synchronic evidence that 'go' and 'went' are not related phonologically: a child learning English will at some stage form the past tense 'goed'. This suggests that the relationship between 'go' and 'went' must be learned (as distinct from acquired). Thus, even though we could set up the necessary phonological machinery to relate 'go' and 'went', there is very little reason why we should want to, and such an analysis is implausible.

11.4.2 Competing derivations

Apart from the evaluation of individual rules or groups of rules, complete derivations must also be evaluated. In other words, the interrelated sets of rules and representations that make up an analysis are also open to evaluation.

As an illustration, consider again the choices for the UR of the plural morpheme discussed above in Section 11.2. Suppose that we decided to choose a fully specified voiceless /s/ as the UR (this is, as we suggested in Section 11.2, not unreasonable). This would give us the URs /ɹæt+s/, /kɹæb+s/ and /liːʧ+s/ for our three example words. What rules will we need to link these URs to the surface forms? Clearly, the same ɪ-epenthesis rule we gave in (11.3) will still be necessary to insert the vowel in [liːʧɪz]. We will also need to adjust the voicing for the suffix in both [kɹæbz] and [liːʧɪz]. This voicing assimilation rule will not be the same as that in (11.4), since that is a structure building rule which only applies to underspecified segments. As we discussed in Section 11.2, without this restriction on its application the rule in (11.4) would voice the final fricative in 'fence'. So we need a rule to voice /s/ only when it is a suffix, not when it is part of the root. To do this, our assimilation rule must make reference to the morphological boundary in the URs. Possible formulations in line with our earlier rules are given in (11.13): (11.13a) gives the linear formulation, (11.13b) gives an autosegmental version.

(11.13) a.
$$\begin{bmatrix} + \text{ strid} \\ + \text{ cor} \\ - \text{ voice} \end{bmatrix} \rightarrow [+ \text{voice}] \,/\, [+ \text{voice}] +\_\_\_$$

b. [+ voice] [– voice]

$$\begin{bmatrix} + \text{ strid} \\ + \text{ cor} \end{bmatrix}$$

In both versions, note the presence of the word-internal morpheme boundary '+', to prevent the rule from affecting a UR like /fɛns/ 'fence'. Given this rule, we can now account for the URs /ɹæt+s/ and /kɹæb+s/.

Our earlier ɪ-epenthesis rule (11.3) does not apply to either of these forms – shown in (11.14).

(11.14) | UR | /ɹæt+s/ | /kɹæb+s/ |
Voicing assimilation rule	—	kɹæb+z
ɪ-epenthesis rule	—	—
PF	[ɹæts]	[kɹæbz]

However, when we come to /liːʧ+s/ we hit a problem: voicing assimilation can't apply, since /ʧ/ is [– voice]. The UR thus passes unaffected on to ɪ-epenthesis, which does apply, giving the incorrect form *[liːʧɪs].

Reformulating (11.13) using Greek-letter variables – ([α voice] rather than [+ voice]) – as in Section (11.4), won't help; the rule would now simply apply vacuously in the case of /liːʧ+s/, still resulting in *[liːʧɪs]. Similarly, reordering the rules fails to solve the problem; if ɪ-epenthesis applies first it results in the intermediate form 'liːʧɪs'. This form cannot now undergo the voicing assimilation rule in (11.13), since the environment is not met; rule (11.13) requires a sequence of [+ voice] segment followed by a morpheme boundary '+' to immediately precede the suffix /s/. The form 'liːʧɪs', however, has the reverse order; morpheme boundary followed by [+ voice] segment: '+ɪ'. The rule is not triggered, and *[liːʧɪs] would again be the predicted surface form. A third possibility might be to reformulate the ɪ-epenthesis rule to insert the vowel before the morpheme boundary, giving an intermediate form 'liːʧɪ+s'. While this would allow the voicing assimilation rule to apply, since its environment is now met, it makes the rather odd claim that the epenthetic vowel is in some sense part of the stem, rather than part of the suffix. This would entail the singular and plural forms of such words showing stem variation ('liːʧ' vs 'liːʧɪ'); there is no independent evidence for this position (there are no other circumstances under which this purported alternation turns up, for instance), and it certainly fails to mirror native-speaker intuitions about the make-up of words like 'leeches'.

The only remaining way to arrive at the desired form [liːʧɪz] is to postulate a second voicing rule, specifically to deal with those forms which have undergone ɪ-epenthesis. This could be formulated as in (11.15), which again gives both a linear and an autosegmental version.

Here, the order of the morpheme boundary and the voiced segment is the reverse of that in (11.13). The rule will thus not apply to URs like /kɹæb+s/, but will apply to intermediate forms like 'liːʧ+ɪs', giving the correct PF [liːʧɪz]. Full derivations for all three forms are shown below.

(11.15) a.
$$\begin{bmatrix} +\text{ strid} \\ +\text{ cor} \\ -\text{ voice} \end{bmatrix} \rightarrow [+\text{ voice}] \: / \: + \: [+\text{ voice}] \: \_\_\_$$

b. [+ voice] [– voice]

$$+ \quad \text{x} \qquad\quad \text{x}$$

$$\begin{bmatrix} +\text{ strid} \\ +\text{ cor} \end{bmatrix}$$

(11.16)

	UR	/ɹæt+s/	/kɹæb+s/	/liːʧ+s/
ɪ-epenthesis rule		—	—	liːʧ+ɪs
Voicing 1 rule		—	kɹæb+z	—
Voicing 2 rule		—	—	liːʧ+ɪz
PF		[ɹæts]	[kɹæbz]	[liːʧɪz]

Note: Voicing 1 is rule (11.13) and Voicing 2 is rule (11.15).

While this analysis works, there are two points to be made about it in comparison to our earlier analysis in Section 11.2; see again the derivations in (11.5). First, (11.16) involves three rules, where (11.5) involves only two, so on the grounds of economy we might favour our original analysis. Second, the two rules Voicing 1 and Voicing 2 are uncomfortably alike; both voice a suffix segment, and both operate under very similar (though crucially for the analysis slightly different) conditions. We ought to be suspicious of any analysis with rules as alike as this, since it appears that some generalisation (concerning voicing) is being obscured here by having two formally unrelated rules performing essentially the same function.

Such considerations suggest that an analysis involving /s/ as the UR for the plural suffix in English is inferior to one positing an underspecified /Z/, and should thus be rejected.

The principles we have used here to evaluate rules and derivations can also be applied to evaluating whole grammars and theoretical frameworks, and in fact such evaluation is an ongoing part of linguistics. As hypotheses and assumptions are tested, maintained, modified or abandoned, theories of linguistics also change. We will take this up again in Section 13.2.

11.4.3 Admissible evidence

In the sections above we have talked about various criteria for evaluating rules and derivations, such as simplicity, plausibility and generality. In addition to criteria like these there is also the question of evidence, and specifically the question of what kind of evidence we should bring to bear in evaluating phonological analyses and arguments. For a phonological or indeed any linguistic argument, various sorts of evidence may be brought to bear, e.g. empirical, theoretical, corpus internal, corpus external, phonological and non-phonological. There is also the question of counterevidence or counterexamples, both real and apparent. We now consider each of these in turn.

We can all probably agree that some sorts of 'evidence' are inadmissible in support of linguistic analyses. For example, in analysing a set of linguistic data we are concerned with observing what the data have to tell us and not with the opinions or prejudices of some 'higher authority'. In many varieties of American English, as well as in practically all English English varieties, the phonemic contrast between /ʍ/ and /w/ has been lost in favour of /w/, so that 'whale' and 'wail' are homophonous. Nonetheless, one can find primary school teachers in the United States in areas of the country where the contrast has been lost, who try to teach children that 'whale' and 'wail' do not sound the same. If we were trying to establish the phonemic inventory of the variety of English in an area where the /ʍ/ ~ /w/ contrast has merged, our data would tell us that there was a single phoneme /w/. Our teacher, on the other hand, would insist that there are two sounds [ʍ] and [w]. Such a position appears to be based on notions of how people feel a language *should* be rather than how it actually is. Despite the opinion of that higher authority, from an examination of the data we would nonetheless have to conclude that there was only one sound – [w] – derived from /w/. In some cases the 'higher authority' may be a religious leader, insisting that the words of some language must be pronounced in specific ways, both in particular sacred texts and in normal speech, or a pundit decrying the usual pronunciation of 'flaccid' [flæsɪd] which should, according to the dictionary, be [flæksɪd]. Again, the linguist must deal with the data as they are, not as some non-linguist authority wishes them to be.

The observable facts constitute the data, that is the empirical evidence. It is an empirical, testable, observable fact that many varieties of English aspirate voiceless stops word-initially. To test this, one can record an utterance from a native speaker of English then analyse the recording with the help of speech analysis equipment (see, for instance, Fig. 5.9). Such empirical evidence can be used to support a particular analysis, but the phonetic facts themselves do not constitute an analysis. As the system underlying the organisation of the phonological component, phonology is greater than the sum of the phonetic facts.

A further kind of evidence is theoretical. Theoretical evidence refers to support for a particular analysis from some other part of the theoretical framework one is working in. Recall the discussion of syllable structure in Chapter 10. We saw, on the basis of spoonerisms and syllable weight, that there may be some reasons to distinguish two nodes within the syllable, namely the Onset and the Rhyme as in (11.17a), rather than having undifferentiated structure under the syllable node as in (11.17b).

Given this theoretical construct, in other words, a syllable structured in just this fashion, the prediction is made that we should find other phonological sensitivities to the distinction between onset and rhyme. In fact, we appear to. As discussed in Chapters 6 and 10, in some languages

(11.17) a.

(e.g. Latin, Pali and Arabic) stress assignment is sensitive to the distinction between heavy syllables – that is, syllables with either a long vowel or a diphthong in the nucleus or with a consonant in coda position – and light syllables – that is syllables containing a short vowel and no coda. For the present discussion what is important is that the onset appears to play no role in syllable weight. There appear to be no languages in which syllables with an onset consonant attract stress while syllables without an onset consonant do not. So the prediction made by the suggested syllable structure, that the nucleus and coda are more closely associated than the nucleus and onset, is borne out.

The terms *corpus-internal* and *corpus-external evidence* refer to whether the evidence in question is from within the language under consideration (corpus-internal) or from another language (corpus-external). In Chapter 10 we considered evidence for syllable structure in English by looking at English aspirated voiceless stops, glottalisation of /t/, and velarised versus non-velarised /l/. This evidence is corpus-internal – internal to English. Corpus-external evidence in this case would be evidence for syllable structure from other languages. For example, the process in French which derives [ɛ] from /e/ in a closed syllable: *sécher* [se.ʃe] 'to dry' versus *sèche* [sɛʃ] 'dry, feminine', and the rule in Dutch which inserts a schwa between a liquid and a non-dental consonant when they are both in a word-final coda (see Exercise 1 of Chapter 10), e.g. /mɛlk/ ~ [mɛlək], provide corpus-external support for the importance of syllable structure, which parallels what we found for English.

Various other sorts of evidence may be brought to bear on a phonological analysis, including both phonological and non-phonological. The non-phonological evidence must be linguistic, but not directly from the phonological component. We have already seen phonetic evidence supporting phonological analysis – aspiration, lateral velarisation and so on. Historical evidence, in the form of considering the development of English, was mentioned with respect to the (lack of) relationship between 'go' and 'went'. We can also find combinations of various kinds of evidence. For example, there is theoretical support from syntax for the kind of syllable representation we have assumed: syntax, too, deals in hierarchical structures rather than flat ones, e.g. the kind of structure in (11.17a) as opposed to the one in (11.18).

(11.18)

So in syntax we find representations like those in (11.19).

(11.19)

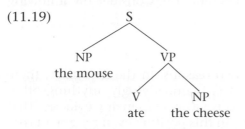

While a syntactic representation is not necessarily relevant to a phonological one, any parallels we can draw between the two components are potentially significant, since our ultimate goal as linguists is to understand language, and the principles holding of one component may well hold of another.

There are thus various sorts of evidence one can use to support a linguistic analysis. Before drawing this section to a close, however, let us consider one further issue: counterevidence, that is data which actually or apparently contradicts our analysis. Recall the discussion of Dutch devoicing of final stops earlier in this chapter. There we rejected an analysis which involved voicing stops before vowels on the basis of data showing voiceless stops before vowels. Such data constitutes actual counterevidence, and prompted us to choose a different analysis based on word-final devoicing. This analysis allowed us to make the statement that in Dutch we never find a word that ends with a voiced stop. Now consider the Dutch data in (11.20).

(11.20)   *had ik* [hɑd ɪk] 'had I'   *heb je* [hɛb jə] 'have you'

The data in (11.20) looks suspiciously like counterevidence, in other words precisely what our rule in (11.11b) claims we *won't* find. Recalling that the other rule we considered, which voiced stops before schwa, fared even worse in terms of accounting for the data, one might wonder whether the examples in (11.20) represent *apparent* counterevidence; that is, evidence that appears to refute the proposed analysis but which on closer inspection can be shown not to contradict it. One of the things we can observe about the data in (11.20), as distinct from the data in (11.10), is that in (11.20) we are looking at phrases, while in (11.10) the data consisted of isolated words. Note, too, that in both cases in (11.20) the segment following the /d/ or /b/ in question is voiced, namely [ɪ] or [j]. One might therefore suspect that there is something else going on here, namely voicing assimilation across word boundaries. In other words, due to the influence of the following voiced segment the /d/ and /b/ in (11.20) are not devoicing. At this point we need to say that either the Dutch devoicing rule is wrong and needs to be modified or replaced, or the rule is fine but is being overridden by a process of voicing assimilation. What kind of evidence do we need to decide between these two possibilities? We could look for further evidence that the devoicing rule is incorrect or we could look for further support that the voicing assimilation analysis is correct. In fact, Dutch provides us with a very convincing piece of evidence that the devoicing rule is correct and that it is overridden by voicing assimilation. Consider the following phrase:

(11.21) *ik ben* [ɪg bɛn] 'I am'

This example is very interesting for two reasons. In the first place, there is no reason to suppose that the *k* in *ik* is underlyingly anything other than /k/, yet it surfaces here as [g]. This is rather convincing evidence that voicing assimilation is occurring, since in this position even a segment that is otherwise always voiceless is voiced. There is one more fact about this [k] ~ [g] alternation that clinches the argument: as mentioned above (in Section 11.4.1), the Dutch phonetic inventory does not include [g] except as a surface allophone of /k/. The Dutch cognates of words of English and German that contain /g/ all surface with [x] (or [ɣ]): English 'good' [gʊd], 'give' [gɪv], German *gut* [guːt], *geben* [gebən], Dutch *goed* [xut], *geven* [xevən]. The only time we find [g] in Dutch is when a /k/ has become voiced, which means that the [g] in *ik ben* must result from voicing assimilation. We can therefore be fairly confident that the [d] and [b] in (11.20) have also been influenced by voicing assimilation. Either devoicing applied and they were subsequently revoiced, or their voicing was maintained, perhaps with devoicing somehow overridden by voicing assimilation. That, however, is a separate issue. What is important here is that the evidence presented by the data in (11.20) is *apparent* counterevidence, and does not affect the devoicing rule. It does, however, indicate that our statement should be revised to read: 'examining a full set of Dutch data we never find a word *in isolation* that ends with a voiced stop'.

11.5 Conclusion

In this chapter we have gone beyond rules alone to consider derivational analysis. After looking at the aims of analysis, we examined a number of issues related to derivational analysis, including extrinsic and intrinsic rule ordering, derivation, and the predictions made by a particular analysis.

Apart from analysis itself we looked at various issues dealing with evaluating competing analyses, from evaluating competing rules to evaluating competing derivations, invoking notions of economy, plausibility and generality. Finally, we examined aspects of evidence, including empirical, theoretical, corpus-internal, corpus-external, phonological and non-phonological evidence, as well as counterevidence, both real and apparent.

Further reading

For a recent textbook treatment of derivational analysis see Gussenhoven and Jacobs (2005). See also the other textbooks referred to earlier: Spencer (1996), Kenstowicz (1994), Carr (1993), Durand (1990).

Exercises

1 Non-rhotic English

Recall the discussion in Section 3.5.2 of the distribution of /r/ in English. We noted there that all varieties of English have pre-vocalic 'r', as in 'raccoon' or 'ca<u>rr</u>ot', but not all have a rhotic in words like 'bea<u>r</u>' or 'ca<u>r</u>t'. Consider the non-rhotic English data below:

A. a. fɑː 'far'   b. fɜː 'fir'   c. ɜː 'err'   d. fiə 'fear'
   e. fɛː 'fair'   f. fɔː 'four'

   g. fɑːm 'farm'   h. kɔːd 'cord'   i. fɜːst 'first'   j. ɜːd 'erred'
   k. fiəs 'fierce' l. skɛːs 'scarce' m. fɔːz 'fours'

   n. fɑːɹəweɪ 'far away'   o. fɜːɹənpaɪn 'fir and pine'
   p. ɜːɹɪzhjuːmən 'err is human' q. fiəɹəvflaɪɪŋ 'fear of flying'
   r. fɛːɹalɪsən 'fair Alison'   s. fɔːɹeɪkəz 'four acres'

   t. fɑːsaɪtɪd 'far sighted'   u. fɜːtɹiː 'fir tree'
   v. fiədɛθ 'fear death'   w. fɛːleɪdi 'fair lady'
   x. fɔːfɛðəz 'four feathers'

i. Given data of this sort, what are the two possible analyses of the [ɹ] ~ ø alternation?
ii. Argue for one of the analyses you mention in (i). Include as much linguistic evidence as you can in support of the analysis you choose.
iii. Is your analysis more easily statable in linear terms or in terms of larger phonological structure? Explain and demonstrate.

Now consider the following:

B. a. ði aɪˈdiəɹ əv ɪt   'the idea of it'
   b. tʃaɪnɔɹ ɔn glɑːs   'china and glass'
   c. ðə səˈnɑːtəɹ ɪn 'ɛf   'the sonata in F'
   d. ðə 'ʃɑːɹ əv 'pɜːʃə   'the Shah of Persia'
   e. ðə lɔːɹ əv 'ɪŋglənd   'the law of England'

iv. Explain how these further observations affect – or do not affect – your analysis. By way of conclusion, present a summary of your analysis, recapitulating why another account of the same data would not be as successful.

2 English past tense formation

In Section 11.2 we looked at an analysis of regular plural formation in English. Look at the data in (a.–j.) below, and suggest ways the analysis in Section 11.2 could be extended to cover English regular past tense formation. Make sure that your analysis can account for the ungrammaticality of the past tense and plural forms in (k.–p.).

a. wɔːkt	'walked'	b. hoʊpt	'hoped'
c. kɹiːst	'creased'	d. ɹʌʃt	'rushed'
e. ɹɒbd	'robbed'	f. bʌgd	'bugged'
g. tiːzd	'teased'	h. seɪvd	'saved'
i. wɒntɪd	'wanted'	j. stʌdɪd	'studded'
k. *feɪsɪd	'faced'	l. *skɹætʃɪd	'scratched'
m. *kɹuːzɪd	'cruised'	n. *dʒʌdʒɪd	'judged'
o. *kætɪz	'cats'	p. *lædɪz	'lads'

3 Canadian French (see Picard 1987; Dumas 1987)

i. Examine the high vowels in the following data. Is the alternation between tense – [i, y, u] – and lax – [ɪ, ʏ, ʊ] – vowels predictable? If so, what is the prediction? If not, demonstrate why it is not predictable. Note: stress is always on the final syllable.

a. plozɪb	'plausible'	i. tʊt	'all' (feminine)
b. by	'goal'	j. vi	'life'
c. kri	'cry'	k. rʊt	'route'
d. tu	'all' (masculine)	l. vɪt	'quickly'
e. sʊp	'soup'	m. lu	'wolf'
f. marɪn	'marine'	n. lʏn	'moon'
g. trʏf	'truffle'	o. ry	'street'
h. rʏd	'rude'	p. ply	'rained'

ii. Now examine the following data. Does the previous observation hold? (Assume that all high vowels pattern the same way.) If not, what modification must be made?

a. vitɛs	'speed'	e. sifle	'whistle'
b. sinema	'cinema'	f. afrɪk	'Africa'
c. afrikɛ̃	'African'	g. sivɪl	'civil'
d. sivilite	'civility'	h. supe	'dine'

iii. Now examine t/tˢ and d/dᶻ (tˢ and dᶻ are dental affricates). Are they phonemes or allophones? If they are allophones, what conditions their distribution? If they are phonemes, demonstrate the contrast.

a. aktˢɪf	'active'	i. tˢy	'you'
b. dᶻi	'say'	j. twe	'you' (obj.)
c. tu	'all' (masculine)	k. deʒa	'already'
d. dɔne	'give'	l. dᶻʏk	'duke'
e. admɛt	'admit'	m. dᶻɪsk	'record' (noun)
f. tɔtal	'total'	n. dʊt	'doubt'
g. tʊt	'all' (feminine)	o. sɔrtˢi	'exit'
h. tˢɪp	'type'		

Finally, there is a process of syncope (= vowel loss) in CF which allows certain vowels to be deleted. Thus given the underlying forms in (p.–s.), the surface forms are as shown:

p. 'difficult' /difisil/ → [dᶻɪfsɪl]
q. 'typical' /tipik/ → [tˢpɪk]
r. 'electricity' /elɛktrisite/ → [elɛktrɪste]
s. 'discotheque' /diskɔtɛk/ → [dᶻskɔtɛk]

iv. Given these forms and your previous observations, what rules are involved and what kind of rule interaction must be taking place? NB: The vowel deletion process itself is very complex. You are not being asked to account for it here.

v. Are the rules ordered? Explain and demonstrate.

12

Constraint-based analysis

The view of phonology presented in this textbook to this point has been **derivational** in nature. That is, the phonetic surface forms of segments and words are derived from abstract underlying representations of those segments and words by applying phonological rules. The goal of phonology is to relate such abstract forms to their concrete realisations. Such derivation, however, is not the only way of expressing those relationships and linking underlying representations with surface forms.

In recent years **non-derivational** approaches to phonology have been developed to relate abstract, underlying phonological structure to the form that actually surfaces without using rules and derivations of the kind we have been looking at so far. One of the attractions of this kind of approach is that it could counter some of the problems associated with derivational phonology if for no other reason than there will be no rules or derivations. Although not the only non-derivational model of phonology, the most successful theory, measured in terms of the greatest number of phonologists working within that framework, is Optimality Theory (OT). In Section 12.1 we give a necessarily brief overview of this model, followed by sections showing how OT works.

12.1 Introduction to optimality theory

Optimality Theory does away with rules and proposes that the relationship between an underlying form and its surface realisation is not derivational in nature. Instead of rules, OT proposes that underlying forms are linked directly to surface forms through evaluation by a set of **constraints**. An example of such a constraint (the effects of which we'll see later in this section) is IDENT-IO(voice). This constraint states that the voicing specification (i.e. [+ voice] or [– voice]) for a segment will be identical in the input – the underlying form – and the output – the surface form.

In OT an underlying form is manipulated in random ways by a function known as 'Generator' (**Gen**). For instance, *Gen* can add, delete or transpose segments, change features, etc. This results in a set of **candidates** – an infinite set of randomly generated outputs from a single underlying form. One of these candidate outputs will be selected as **optimal**. This is done through evaluation of the candidate set by the set of constraints contained in the function 'Evaluator' (**Eval**). So, for an underlying form like /kæt/, *Gen* might produce candidates like [kæt], [kʰæt], [kæ], [ækt], etc., and *Eval* would choose [kʰæt] as the optimal form.

The constraints evaluate the wellformedness of each candidate (for instance, how well the candidate conforms to expected syllable structure, phonotactics, resemblance to the input, and other criteria) and determine which candidate in the set is the 'most harmonic', in other words which candidate fares best relative to the set of constraints. It is the most harmonic, or optimal, candidate that should surface as the concrete instantiation of the underlying representation in question. The diagram in (12.1) shows a graphic representation of OT:

(12.1) Diagram of Optimality Theory

The input form is acted upon by *Gen*, which produces the candidate set. The candidate set produced by *Gen* is then evaluated by *Eval*, which yields an output form, in other words the surface form.

There are three things to note at this point about the constraints used in OT. First of all, the constraints in Optimality Theory are violable. Simply not conforming to a particular constraint does not by itself necessarily disqualify a specific output candidate from being the actual surface form. A second characteristic of OT constraints is that they are not all of equal importance: they are ranked in a hierarchy for a given language, meaning that some constraints are more important than others in that language and that the violation of a particular constraint may be more important than the violation of some other specific constraint(s). Thirdly, the constraints of OT are assumed to be universal. All human languages share the same set of phonological constraints; languages differ in how the constraints are ranked. Indeed, it is the ranking of the set of universal constraints that yields phonological differences between languages.

The constraints themselves are of three basic types or families: *markedness constraints*, *faithfulness constraints* and *alignment constraints*. Markedness constraints deal with specific structural configurations; for instance NoCoda expresses the universal tendency for languages to prefer syllables without codas. Onset is the constraint expressing the cross-linguistic tendency for languages to prefer syllables with onsets (see the discussion of these tendencies in Chapter 6.1.5). The faithfulness constraints seek to ensure that outputs are 'faithful' to inputs, in the sense that output segments match input segments; an output is less faithful to an input if, compared with that input, it has had segments deleted or added or changed in some way. (Faithfulness constraints are sometimes referred to as 'correspondence constraints'.) The third type, alignment constraints, are used to ensure structural alignment between different linguistic structures, for instance making sure that the right edge of a word coincides with the right edge of a syllable.

Consider how this would work when comparing final devoicing in German with the absence of final devoicing in English. In German, the voiced stops /b, d, g/ surface as voiceless [p, t, k] when they appear at the end of a word. So, the German word *Bad* 'bath' is pronounced [bɑt], yet the related verb *baden* 'to bathe' is [bɑdən] with a [d]. Likewise, the word *Burg* 'fortress' is pronounced [buʀk], with final [k], yet the plural *Burgen* is [buʀgən], with a [g]. The predicate adjective *gelb* 'yellow' is [gɛlp], with a final [p], yet the feminine attributive form of the adjective is *gelbe* [gɛlbə], with a [b].

By contrast, in English /b, d, g/ show up as [b, d, g], even word-finally, e.g. in *crab* [kɹæb], *bed* [bɛd] and *bug* [bʌg]. In Optimality terms this can be seen as a case of input–output faithfulness being more important (more highly ranked) in English than the phonetic tendency towards final devoicing, whereas in German final devoicing is more important than faithfulness to the underlying form. Here we'll use the constraint label IDENT-IO(voice) to stand for the faithfulness constraint ensuring that outputs match inputs in terms of voicing; we'll use NoVoicedCoda to refer to the markedness constraint governing the cross-linguistic tendency towards final devoicing. To express the German case, the **tableau** – the primary way of representing phonological operations in OT – would look like this.

(12.2) Tableau of German *Bad* [bɑt] 'bath'

Input: /bɑd/	NoVoicedCoda	IDENT-IO(voice)
bɑd	*!	
☞ bɑt		*

In order to understand this representation, let us first consider the formalisms associated with OT. Each underlying form is said to be parsed into a number of candidate analyses (the 'candidates' mentioned above) by *Gen*. Each candidate is then evaluated in terms of wellformedness constraints – the markedness, faithfulness and alignment constraints. This is the task of *Eval*, to sort through all the candidates posited by *Gen* to find the most harmonic, i.e. the correct surfacing form. To represent the operation of *Eval* graphically, the most plausible candidates are shown in a **tableau** (as in 12.2) which compares the evaluation of each candidate against the relevant constraints. The constraints are arranged across the top of the tableau in a hierarchy of decreasing importance from left to right. Selection of the most harmonic candidate, indicated with a pointing finger (☞), rests on constraint violation relative to the importance of the constraints that are violated.

Looking specifically at the tableau in (12.2), in the upper left-hand corner is the input. Here this is telling us that the assumed input form is

/bad/. At the top of the tableau, to the right of the input, the constraints are listed by importance, left to right. They are separated in (12.2) by a solid vertical line – that indicates that the leftmost constraint, NOVOICEDCODA, is more important than IDENT-IO(voice). The column beneath the input lists the candidates under consideration, here [bad] and [bat]; the pointing finger shows us that [bat] is the correct surface form and is selected by the constraints.

Specifically, in the tableau in (12.2) two of (the infinite set of) candidates generated by *Gen* from the input /bad/ are evaluated by the constraints NOVOICEDCODA and IDENT-IO(voice). Despite the fact that the candidate [bad] is more faithful to the input, [bat] is selected as the optimal candidate. This is because NOVOICEDCODA is more highly ranked than IDENT-IO(voice). An asterisk in a cell indicates a violation of the constraint by the candidate shown; an exclamation mark following an asterisk indicates a 'fatal violation', in other words a violation that serves to distinguish between two candidates by eliminating one of them. Shading in a cell indicates that that cell is irrelevant to any further evaluation of the candidates. It's important here to note that the winning candidate, [bat], does in fact violate a constraint, IDENT-IO(voice). However, the competing candidate [bad] violates a more highly ranked constraint, so [bat] is still the winner.

If we now compare a tableau for English *bed*, we see that the same constraints must be ranked in the opposite order: IDENT-IO(voice) above NOVOICEDCODA. (Remember that constraints are held to be universal. So even in the absence of evidence for final devoicing in English, the constraint would still be part of the set of constraints.)

(12.3) Tableau for English *bed* [bɛd]

Input: /bɛd/	IDENT-IO(voice)	NOVOICEDCODA
☞ bɛd		*
bɛt	*!	

With the order of the constraints reversed, we get the correct results for English, a language in which the voicing faithfulness of the output to the input is more important than (the universal tendency towards) final devoicing. This importance can be seen by the fact that the correct output [bɛd] does, in fact, violate the constraint NOVOICEDCODA. Bear in mind that these are only two of a large number of constraints that would be involved in the evaluation of any candidates generated by *Gen*. It's also important to note here that [bɛt] is, of course, not just a possible word of English, it actually occurs, *bet*. However, the input for English [bɛt] is presumably /bɛt/; in other words it is a different word from *bed*, as it has a /t/ in the input.

As we have already noted, constraints in OT are held to be universal. That is, Universal Grammar (UG) makes available a set of constraints for all languages, and languages differ because of the different rankings of the

201

universally available constraints, as we just saw with final devoicing in German and its absence in English. Language change over time as well as dialect variation can result from a different ranking of constraints compared with another language variety.

12.2 The aims of analysis

Just as we've seen with derivational analysis in Chapter 11, the point of a constraint-based analysis is to get from an input to an output while capturing the phonological regularities of a language. At the same time, we want to do this without our analytical machinery predicting forms that don't occur in the language in question.

It is important to note here what is different about a constraint-based analysis, as well as what is the same. What hasn't changed with Optimality Theory is the recognition of phonological relationships: we still assume abstract, underlying representations, i.e. inputs, and the aim is still to yield the correct surface forms, i.e. outputs, from those underlying representations. We still want to express deletion, insertion, assimilation and metathesis of the kind we saw in Chapter 9. The importance of phonological structure is also still with us, whether syllables, feet, phonological words or even larger structures. Most importantly, the ultimate goal of constraint-based phonology is still to capture generalisations over sets of phonological data.

What *has* changed with Optimality Theory is how those relationships and generalisations are captured. Whereas in a derivational analysis the main instrument for expressing the relationship between an input and an output was a set of rules, Optimality Theory relies on constraints. What this means is that in Optimality Theory there are no derivations, there are no phonological rules, therefore there can be no rule ordering or rule interaction.

One other interesting difference, although we won't be exploring it in detail here, is the ability of OT to refer to non-phonological sorts of linguistic structure in ways that derivational phonology cannot. For instance, although a phonological rule may contain a morpheme boundary (+) or a word boundary (#), phonological rules don't typically refer to specific alignments of phonological material with morphological or syntactic structure. As we'll see below, however, a constraint can refer to such material; indeed, the ALIGN family of alignment constraints typically deals with correspondences between phonological structure, such as syllable, foot, coda, and morphological or syntactic material, such as suffix, prefix, noun stem, etc.

The absence of rules and rule interaction has the effect of focussing the analysis on three things: the input, the output, and the constraints that evaluate the output. As discussed above, these constraints evaluate the output in terms of faithfulness between input and output by means of faithfulness constraints, in terms of the allowable structure of the output by means of markedness constraints, and in terms of the alignment of phonological and other structure by means of alignment constraints.

In Section 12.4 we will consider an optimality analysis of English plural formation, parallel to the derivational analysis we saw in Chapter 11. Before doing that though, let us look again at the English assimilation, insertion and deletion data, along with the metathesis and reduplication we saw earlier in Chapter 9.

12.3 Modelling phonological processes in OT

12.3.1 Assimilation

Assimilation typically involves adjacent segments becoming more alike. In terms of constraints, this can be expressed as a prohibition on adjacent segments having differing values for some feature(s). As we have seen, nasal assimilation involves matching the values for [anterior] and [coronal] of the nasal segment with the values for [anterior] and [coronal] of an adjacent stop. To do this, we need a constraint which states that a nasal segment should not be followed by a stop which differs in its feature values for anterior and/or coronal. We'll call this constraint AGREEPLACE(nasal). This constraint must outrank IDENT-IO, a constraint which enforces identity between the input and the output. IDENT-IO requires inputs to match outputs. Consider the word *include* /ɪnkluːd/ which surfaces as [ɪŋkluːd], with [ŋ] in the output where /n/ appears in the input.

(12.4) Constraints

AGREEPLACE(nasal): a nasal segment must agree with a following stop in its values for [anterior] and [coronal]

IDENT-IO: output segments should match the corresponding input segments

(12.5) Nasal assimilation

/ɪnkluːd/	AGREEPLACE(nasal)	IDENT-IO
☞ ɪŋkluːd		*
ɪnkluːd	*!	

Here the prohibition on non-matching values for [anterior] and [coronal], enforced by AGREEPLACE(nasal), is more important than the identity between input and output, so the correct surface form is selected, since in [ɪŋkluːd] the [ŋ] and [k] are both [-ant, -cor], whereas in [ɪnkluːd] the [n] and [k] differ on both [anterior] and [coronal].

Note, however, that this isn't the only possible way for a language to resolve such a mismatch between the place of articulation of a nasal and a following obstruent. It is important to bear in mind – and this is one of the things that OT is particularly good at expressing – that assimilation is not the only way a language can resolve this sort of feature mismatch between adjacent segments. English happens to prefer to keep a nasal segment, but to have the surface form of the nasal match the place of articulation of the following stop. A different language might allow the mismatch (e.g. Russian, cf. [funksjə]), or might resolve the mismatch through deletion of the obstruent (e.g. Gadung Malay (Malaysia), cf. /rambut/ surfacing as [ramũᵈt]), or alternatively a language might resolve the mismatch by inserting a vowel between the nasal and the following stop. Each of these strategies has implications for the constraint ranking: allowing the featural mismatch, as in Russian, means that IDENT-IO is more important than AGREEPLACE(nasal) and therefore more highly ranked in the Russian hierarchy; deleting the obstruent, as in Gadang Malay, indicates that in that language avoiding the mismatch by incurring a MAX-IO violation (an anti-deletion constraint; see next section) is preferred to resolving the mismatch; inserting a vowel between the nasal and the stop shows that it is important to avoid a featural mismatch between adjacent nasals and stops, but that such a language prefers to do so through insertion rather than through deletion or feature matching.

12.3.2 Deletion

Recall that the examples of deletion seen in Section 9.4.2 involve a final cluster of coronal consonants in the underlying form which surfaces as a single coda consonant, e.g. 'hand' [hæn] and 'list' [lɪs]. Here we need to express the prohibition of [+cor] consonant clusters word-finally. This could be expressed through a constraint such as NoCorClust: do not have two [+cor] segments at the end of a word. This would be ranked higher than MAX-IO, the standard constraint prohibiting deletion of underlying material (input segments should be maximised in the output, that is, don't delete).

(12.6) Deletion

/hænd/	NoCorClust	Max-IO
☞ hæn	·	*
hænd	*!	

Here, as in (12.5) as well, we see that the ranking of the constraints leads to the selection of a candidate other than the one that most closely matches the input. This indicates that in both of these cases a markedness constraint outranks a faithfulness constraint.

Note that a full analysis is actually more complex than this. Insertion, too, would avoid the kind of cluster we find here, e.g. [hænɪd], yet we don't find that strategy in English. Therefore, there must be another constraint at work, such as the standard anti-epenthesis constraint DEP-IO. (Technically, DEP-IO requires the output to depend on the input for all of its segments; it can be thought of as 'don't epenthesise', i.e. 'don't add material'.)

Alternatively, deletion of the /n/ would also avoid the illicit cluster, e.g. [hæd], but again we don't find this strategy in English. This indicates that a further constraint must be operating, ensuring that deletion targets the final [+coronal] segment.

In light of these considerations, we could have included [hænɪd] and [hæd] in the candidate set and considered a further two constraints in the hierarchy. We've left them out here for the sake of simplicity (though they come up again in Exercise 5 at the end of this chapter).

This discussion highlights a fundamental difference between rule-based analyses and constraint-based accounts. Rules need only concern themselves with their immediate outputs; they are blind to the overall actions of other rules and to the ultimate outcome of their own application. Constraints, on the other hand, will always interact by their very inclusion in a hierarchy of ranked constraints. Therefore, an OT analysis must consider the broader implications of any specific operation or the effects of any particular process, including the need to exclude other possible candidates.

12.3.3 Insertion

The earlier example of insertion in Section 9.4.3 was that of [ə] insertion in some varieties of English between the members of a final liquid + nasal cluster, e.g. *film* /fɪlm/ pronounced as [fɪləm]. In terms of constraints, what we need to express is the prohibition of a [+son][+nas] cluster word-finally. Let us call this constraint NoFin[son][nas]. We will also need to refer to the constraint that prohibits insertion, Dep-IO, which says that the output depends on the input for all of its segments.

(12.7) Insertion

/fɪlm/	NoFin[son][nas]	Dep-IO
☞ fɪləm		*
film	*!	

In this tableau we see that the constraint against a word-final sonorant followed by a nasal is ranked as most important. Thus it is more important to avoid a sonorant + nasal coda cluster than it is to allow a vowel to be inserted in the output where no vowel was in the input.

Note, though, that again this is too simplistic: we also need to prevent resolution of the unwanted cluster by means of deletion of one of the sonorants, as in *[fɪm] or *[fɪl]. This can be done by means of an anti-deletion constraint, Max-IO(son): do not delete a sonorant. (This is a more specific example of the Max constraint family, of which we've already seen Max-IO.)

Including Max-IO(son) in the tableau, along with the candidates to be ruled out, *[fɪm] and *[fɪl], we see that the constraint against a word-final sonorant followed by a nasal is still ranked as most important.

(12.8) Insertion

/fɪlm/	NoFɪN[son][nas]	Max-IO(son)	Dep-IO
☞ fɪləm			*
fɪlm	*!		
fɪm		*!	
fɪl		*!	

At the same time, it is more important to prohibit deletion, through the Max-IO(son) constraint, than it is to prohibit insertion. We see this reflected in the fact that the two candidates showing deletion each have a fatal violation of Max-IO(son), while the occurring candidate violates the anti-insertion constraint Dep-IO.

Once again we see an important distinction between Optimality Theory and derivational phonology. In derivational phonology it is usually enough to propose a rule that states what change is to occur and where; there is no notion of competing candidates that must also be prevented from occurring. An OT analysis, on the other hand, must not only ensure that the right output is achieved, but must also make certain that non-occurring competing candidates are not incorrectly selected as optimal.

12.3.4 Metathesis

We saw in Section 9.4.4 the **metathesis** in many Scottish varieties in words such as 'pattern' [patəɹn] or 'modern' [mɔdəɹn] which have alternate pronunciations [patɹən] and [mɔdɹən]. In terms of OT, metathesis represents a violation of Lɪnearɪty, the constraint that requires that the linear order of elements – typically segments – in the input remains the same in the output. What we need to discover here is what constraint outranks Lɪnearɪty in these Scottish varieties so that /...əɹ.../ in the input surfaces as [...ɹə...] in the output.

The final consonant cluster in /patəɹn/ and /mɔdəɹn/ consists of two sonorants, /ɹ/ and /n/. One possible constraint would be SonDɪst, a sonority distance constraint requiring that the members of a consonant cluster in a coda have falling, rather than level, sonority distance from each other (cf. Section 6.1.3 on sonority relations in syllables).

(12.9) Metathesis in *pattern*

/patəɹn/	SonDɪst	Lɪnearɪty
☞ patɹən		*
patəɹn	*!	

Note again, as we observed in Section 9.4.4, that metathesis is a relatively infrequent process in phonology. Even when it occurs in a language, it is often very specific and may target only a very small set of segments or a very small number of words.

12.3.5 Reduplication

As we saw in Section 9.4.5, reduplication involves copying part of a word then attaching the copy in some specific way to the original word. So, main stress in Samoan occurs on the penultimate syllable. The last two syllables of a word can be thought of as a 'stress foot', that is, the foot bearing the main stress of the word (see Section 6.2). This allows us to see what's going on with reduplication: a copy of the stressed syllable (minus the stress) is inserted just before the stress foot.

In order to express this in OT terms we need two sorts of constraint: 1) a constraint to express the structure of the reduplicant, in other words, to say what should be copied, and 2) an alignment constraint to say where the copy should appear in the output. Since what we need to copy is the stressed syllable, this can be expressed by the constraint RED=ó, which tells us that the reduplicant (in other words the copied material) is the stressed syllable. In addition, we need to align this copied material to the left of the stress foot. ALIGN(red R, stressfoot L) tells us that the right edge of the reduplicant should be aligned with the left edge of the stress foot.

(12.10) Constraints

RED=ó: the reduplicant is a copy of the stressed syllable

ALIGN(red R, stressfoot L): align the right edge of the reduplicant with the left edge of the stress foot.

(12.11) Samoan plural reduplication of [ma.tu.tú.a] 'they are old'

/ma.'tu.a/ + RED	RED=ó	ALIGN(red R, stressfoot L)	DEP-IO
ma.'tu.a	*!		
☞ ma.**tu**.'tu.a			*
ma.'tu.**tu**.a		*!	*

The '+ RED' in the input states that the input consists of the stem plus a reduplicant. In this tableau the reduplicant is shown in bold for clarity. Here we see that the candidate identical to the unreduplicated part of the input, *[ma.'tu.a], is ruled out because it includes no reduplicant at all. The correct output, [ma.**tu**.'tu.a], satisfies both the reduplication = stressed syllable constraint and the alignment constraint, although it does violate DEP-IO.

As with the other phonological operations we have seen in this section, reduplication too can be expressed as resulting from the interaction of violable constraints evaluating representations. In this case, the interaction of a constraint stating the correct material to copy with another constraint stating where the copy should appear allows us to model reduplication in OT.

In this section we have considered basic OT sketches of assimilation, insertion and deletion, metathesis and reduplication first presented in Chapter 9, along with some of the implications of the analyses. In the following section we reconsider the data from English plural formation, seen in a derivational analysis in the previous chapter. Here we examine the same data in terms of a constraint-based analysis.

12.4 English noun plural formation: an OT account

Recall the data on English noun plural formation that we saw in Chapter 11:

(12.12) a. rats, giraffes, asps, yaks, moths
        b. aphids, crabs, dogs, lions, cows
        c. asses, leeches, midges, thrushes

And remember that regular plural formation in English is entirely predictable: following a voiceless obstruent (other than a sibilant) the plural marker is [s], as in (12.12a); following a voiced segment (other than a sibilant) the plural marker is [z], as in (12.12b); following a sibilant the plural marker is [ɪz] (or [əz]), as in (12.12c).

Let us consider how the analysis of English regular plural formation would look in Optimality Theory. Just as we did in Chapter 11, let us assume that the plural marker itself is a [+strident, +coronal] segment unspecified for voicing, represented as /Z/, and that the following are the underlying representations of the words *rats*, *crabs* and *leeches*.

(12.13) /ɹæt + Z/ 'rats' /kɹæb + Z/ 'crabs' /liːtʃ + Z/ 'leeches'

Let us also assume that the following constraints are those most relevant to the question of plural formation. (Of course there are many more constraints involved in the evaluation of any candidate. Given the limits of the printed page, along with our ability to process complex diagrams, typically in OT analyses only the most relevant constraints are considered in any specific tableau.)

(12.14) Constraints particularly relevant to English plural formation

NoSib-Sib: Two sibilants cannot be adjacent
Voicing: Two consonants in a cluster must agree in voicing
Align(stem R, affix L): The left edge of the plural marker aligns with the right edge of the stem, i.e. the suffix follows the noun
Left-Anchorplural: In the plural marker, the leftmost segment of the surface form is the same as the leftmost segment of its underlying form

The constraint NoSɪʙ-Sɪʙ is a markedness constraint which disallows a sequence of one sibilant segment followed by another. What it does here is to ensure that if a noun stem ends in a sibilant consonant (e.g. [s, z, ʃ, ʒ, tʃ, dʒ]), the plural marker /Z/ will not appear adjacent to it.

Voɪcɪɴɢ, a more general markedness constraint, ensures that two consonants in a cluster share the same voicing, either both voiced or both voiceless.

Aʟɪɢɴ(stem R, affix L) is an alignment constraint that operates on the structure of words to ensure that a suffix appears to the right of a stem. In this particular case it is specified that the left edge of the plural marker /Z/ is to align with the right edge of the noun stem. In other words, the suffix follows the stem. (Note that this constraint is not actually phonological, since its function is to enforce the alignment of a suffix with a noun stem.)

The last of these four constraints, Leꜰᴛ-Aɴᴄʜᴏʀ$_{plural}$, is a 'positional faithfulness' constraint involving both phonology (since it refers to segments) and word structure. The effect of this constraint is to require that the initial underlying segment of the plural marker immediately follows the final segment of the stem.

Before we can represent the analysis of plural formation in tableaux, there is one more thing we need to establish: the ranking of the constraints. We can do this through **pairwise evaluation** of candidates, in other words consideration of an occurring wordform compared with its non-occurring competitors. Take, for instance, the example of *rats* [ɹæts], the surface form of underlying /ɹæt + Z/. Bearing in mind that *Gen* produces a candidate set of forms differing from the input in random ways (as discussed in Section 12.1), let us consider the potential outputs *[ɹætz], *[ɹætɪz], *[zɹæt] along with occurring [ɹæts].

Comparing first occurring [ɹæts] with non-occurring *[ɹætz] tells us that the constraint Voɪcɪɴɢ must be important, as it distinguishes between these two forms: Voɪcɪɴɢ is violated by *[ɹætz], since [t] is voiceless and [z] is voiced, but not by [ɹæts], in which the [t] and [s] are both voiceless. Comparing [ɹæts] with non-occurring *[zɹæt] shows us the effect of Aʟɪɢɴ(stem R, affix L), since the occurring form has the plural marker as a suffix, while the non-occurring form has the plural marker as a prefix. Finally, comparing [ɹæts] with non-occurring *[ɹætɪz] allows us to see that Leꜰᴛ-Aɴᴄʜᴏʀ$_{plural}$ distinguishes between these two forms. Note here that *[ɹætɪz] does not violate Aʟɪɢɴ(stem R, affix L), since the plural marker *does* follow the noun in *[ɹætɪz]; however, it violates Leꜰᴛ-Aɴᴄʜᴏʀ$_{plural}$ simply because the [z] does not *immediately* follow the noun stem, since the [ɪ] intervenes.

This pairwise evaluation of [ɹæts] with its non-occurring competitors shows us the value of three of the constraints, Voɪcɪɴɢ, Aʟɪɢɴ(stem R, affix L) and Leꜰᴛ-Aɴᴄʜᴏʀ$_{plural}$. However, it tells us nothing about NoSɪʙ-Sɪʙ. Moreover, it tells us nothing about the relative importance of the three constraints. Consider a tableau of *rats* on the basis of what we know so far:

(12.15) Tableau for *rats*

/ɹæt + Z/	NoSib-Sib	Voicing	Align(stem R, affix L)	Left-Anchor_plural
ɹætz	*!			
☞ ɹæts				
zɹæt			*!	
ɹætɪz				*!

At this point we have evidence that Voicing, Align(stem R, affix L) and Left-Anchor_plural distinguish between the desired output [ɹæts] and various competing candidates. Nonetheless, our comparison of [ɹæts] with these competing candidates doesn't allow us to distinguish between the constraints in terms of importance. This is shown by the dotted vertical lines between the constraint columns, indicating that these constraints are of equal importance or are as yet unranked. These four constraints arranged in any order and used to evaluate the four candidates shown will produce the same results: [ɹæts] will be selected as the output.

The other thing that our comparison of [ɹæts] with its competitors has *not* shown is the importance of NoSib-Sib. This, of course, is because *rat* doesn't end with a sibilant consonant, so this constraint is irrelevant in the evaluation of *rats*. Nonetheless the NoSib-Sib constraint is included in the tableau for *rats* because of its importance for the plural marker with other wordforms. Once the importance of a constraint is established, it is shown in a tableau even when it is irrelevant for the evaluation of a specific wordform. To see the importance of NoSib-Sib, consider the evaluation of *leeches*, where the stem *leech* does end in a sibilant.

Starting again with a pairwise evaluation, this time of *leeches*, let us assume the input /li:tʃ + Z/ along with the occurring output [li:tʃɪz] and three non-occurring candidates *[li:tʃz], *[li:tʃs] and *[zli:tʃ]. We see immediately that *[li:tʃz] and *[li:tʃs] violate NoSib-Sib, since both of these forms end with a sibilant consonant followed by a sibilant consonant. Furthermore, *[li:tʃz] also violates Voicing, since [tʃ] is voiceless and [z] is voiced. The occurring output [li:tʃɪz] violates neither of these constraints. Comparing [li:tʃɪz] with *[zli:tʃ] shows us again, as we saw with the evaluation of *rats*, that the plural marker must occur after, not before, the noun. Finally, consider the correct output [li:tʃɪz]. Unlike [ɹæts], [li:tʃɪz] does violate one of the constraints, namely Left-Anchor_plural, since the plural marker does not immediately follow the noun stem – there is an epenthetic [ɪ] between the noun stem and the plural marker. Nonetheless, [li:tʃɪz] is the correctly occurring output. This tells us two things: 1) it tells us that while Left-Anchor_plural is important in eliminating *[ɹætɪz] when compared with [ɹæts], it is nonetheless violated by the correct output in the case of [li:tʃɪz], and 2) it tells us that a violation of Left-Anchor_plural is less important than a violation of the other three constraints. We can see this because the correctly surfacing [li:tʃɪz] violates Left-Anchor_plural, while each of the non-occurring competitors violates one or more of the remaining three constraints.

On the basis of this evaluation we can revise the tableau. In (12.16) we see that a solid vertical line now separates LEFT-ANCHOR$_{plural}$ and ALIGN(stem R, affix L). This indicates that a violation of LEFT-ANCHOR$_{plural}$ counts as less important than a violation of any of the other three constraints. The other three constraints appear to be equally important; they could in principle appear in any order, as long as they are all ranked higher than LEFT-ANCHOR$_{plural}$. We also see in this tableau that NoSIB-SIB does do some work, specifically when the noun stem ends in a sibilant consonant.

(12.16) Tableau for *leeches*

li:ʧ + Z	NoSIB-SIB	VOICING	ALIGN(stem R, affix L)	LEFT-ANCHOR$_{plural}$
li:ʧz	*!	*		
li:ʧs	*!			
zli:ʧ			*!	
☞ li:ʧɪz				*

We observed above that in the tableau (12.15) the constraints would yield the correct output regardless of their ranking. In (12.16) we see that this is no longer the case. It is true that NoSIB-SIB, VOICING and ALIGN(stem R, affix L) can appear in any order, but LEFT-ANCHOR$_{plural}$ must be ranked lower than these three.

Finally, if this constraint hierarchy is correct, we should also achieve the correct results with the word *crabs*, assuming the input /kɹæb + Z/ and the output candidate [kɹæbz] along with non-occurring competitors *[kɹæbs], *[zkɹæb] and *[kɹæbɪz].

(12.17) Tableau for *crabs*

kɹæb + Z	NoSIB-SIB	VOICING	ALIGN(stem R, affix L)	LEFT-ANCHOR$_{plural}$
☞ kɹæbz				
kɹæbs		*!		
zkɹæb			*!	*
kɹæbɪz				*!

Thus, the prediction is borne out that this constraint hierarchy, along with the assumption of an underspecified plural marker /Z/, yields the correct results for plural formation.

When considering the tableaux (12.15), (12.16) and (12.17), there are several things to note. First of all, given that all three tableaux represent a single language, English, the ranking of the constraints we have established is the same in each case, specifically, that LEFT-ANCHOR$_{plural}$ is ranked below the other three constraints. Thus, each of the three tableaux shows the same constraints in the same order of importance evaluating a four-member candidate set produced by *Gen* on the basis of the inputs indicated. Secondly, remember that optimal candidates can and do violate constraints: note that although the optimal candidates in (12.15) and (12.17) incur no violations (of the constraints shown), the optimal candidate in (12.16) does. The reason the optimal candidate in (12.16) is optimal despite this violation is because the constraints violated by the other, non-optimal candidates are more highly ranked.

One other thing to note at this point concerns the ranking of constraints we have established. In our discussion we have seen reason to rank LEFT-ANCHOR$_{plural}$ as the lowest constraint and the other three, NoSIB-SIB, VOICING and ALIGN(stem R, affix L) as equally ranked among themselves, but all higher than LEFT-ANCHOR$_{plural}$. However, it is possible that further evidence from other facts of English may well establish some ranking hierarchy among these other constraints as well. We will not explore that here.

12.5 Competing analyses

We saw in Chapter 11 that there may be competing derivations of a particular set of phonological facts. In the same way, there can be competing analyses couched in the same constraint-based framework.

For the sake of comparison, let us consider what it would look like to have an OT analysis of the same data from English noun plurals assuming a fully specified plural marker. So, instead of an analysis relying on /Z/ as an underspecified plural marker, let us see what would be required assuming a fully specified segment as the plural suffix, either /s/ or /z/.

First consider /s/. The following tableau shows an evaluation of *rats* using only the constraints we used above.

(12.18) Tableau for *rats* assuming /s/ as the plural marker

/ɹæt + s/	NoSIB-SIB	VOICING	ALIGN(stem R, affix L)	LEFT-ANCHOR$_{plural}$
ɹætz		*!		
☞ ɹæts				
sɹæt			*!	*
ɹætɪs				*!

Here we see the same result we had for the tableau (12.15): VOICING rules out the candidate *[ɹætz], ALIGN(stem R, affix L) rules out *[sɹæt] and LEFT-ANCHOR$_{plural}$ correctly rules out *[ɹætɪs].

Now consider *crabs*, again assuming underlying /s/ as the plural marker.

(12.19) Tableau for *crabs* assuming /s/ as the plural marker

kɹæb + s	NoSɪʙ-Sɪʙ	Voɪcɪɴɢ	Aʟɪɢɴ(stem R, affix L)	Lᴇꜰᴛ-Aɴᴄʜᴏʀ_plural
☞ kɹæbz				
kɹæbs		*!		
skɹæb			*!	*
kɹæbɪz				*!

Here again, the results are the same as we had assuming underspecified /Z/ as the plural marker. Nonetheless, something not shown in the tableau (12.19) is the fact that the correct output [kɹæbz] violates Iᴅᴇɴᴛ-IO(voice), introduced in Section 12.1, the constraint ensuring faithfulness between an input segment and its output. Ideally, we should show that violation, as in (12.20), if we are to compare analyses in terms of simplicity. In the absence of evidence to show a ranking between them, we have put a dotted line separating Lᴇꜰᴛ-Aɴᴄʜᴏʀ_plural and Iᴅᴇɴᴛ-IO(voice).

(12.20) Tableau for *crabs* assuming /s/ as the plural marker

kɹæb + s	NoSɪʙ-Sɪʙ	Voɪcɪɴɢ	Aʟɪɢɴ(stem R, affix L)	Lᴇꜰᴛ-Aɴᴄʜᴏʀ_plural	Iᴅᴇɴᴛ-IO (voice)
☞ kɹæbz					*
kɹæbs		*!			
skɹæb			*!	*	
kɹæbɪz				*!	*

Now let us consider *leeches*. Here again we assume /s/ as the plural marker and we've included Iᴅᴇɴᴛ-IO(voice) in the tableau.

(12.21) Tableau for *leeches* assuming /s/ as the plural marker

liːtʃ + s	NoSɪʙ-Sɪʙ	Voɪcɪɴɢ	Aʟɪɢɴ(stem R, affix L)	Lᴇꜰᴛ-Aɴᴄʜᴏʀ_plural	Iᴅᴇɴᴛ-IO (voice)
liːtʃz	*!	*			*
liːtʃs	*!				
zliːtʃ			*!		*
☞ liːtʃɪz				*	*

So far, so good. But, consider another plausible candidate produced by *Gen*, namely non-occurring *[liːtʃɪs], where the final segment is [s]. The tableau (12.22) includes this candidate.

(12.22) Tableau for *leeches* assuming /s/ as the plural marker

li:tʃ + s	NoSib-Sib	Voicing	Align(stem R, affix L)	Left-Anchor_{plural}	Ident-IO (voice)
li:tʃz	*!	*			*
li:tʃs	*!				
zli:tʃ			*!		*
li:tʃɪz				*	*!
☞ li:tʃɪs				*	

Tableau (12.22) shows us that the inclusion of the further plausible, but non-occurring, candidate *[li:tʃɪs] yields the wrong result, since it is selected over the correct output [li:tʃɪz]; this is because the correct output violates two constraints (of equal ranking), whereas non-occurring *[li:tʃɪs] violates only one.

There are two things to note here. First, the assumption of a fully specified /s/ as the plural marker requires the addition of a further constraint, Ident-IO(voice), but that alone is not enough to distinguish between *[li:tʃɪs] and [li:tʃɪz]. Second, assuming /z/ as the plural marker would lead to a simpler analysis, since *[li:tʃɪs] would be correctly ruled out by Ident-IO(voice), as shown in tableau (12.23).

(12.23) Tableau for *leeches* assuming /z/ as the plural marker

li:tʃ + z	NoSib-Sib	Voicing	Align(stem R, affix L)	Left-Anchor_{plural}	Ident-IO (voice)
li:tʃz	*!	*			*
li:tʃs	*!				
zli:tʃ			*!		*
☞ li:tʃɪz				*	
li:tʃɪs				*	*!

Here, assuming a fully specified /z/ as the plural marker, the violation of Ident-IO(voice) correctly rules out *[li:tʃɪs] in favour of [li:tʃɪz]. Thus, in terms of competing analyses, it would be simpler – and therefore preferable – in this case to assume an underlying /z/ as the plural marker, rather than the equally plausible /s/. We leave it to the reader to draw tableaux of *crabs* and *rats* assuming underlying /z/ as the plural marker, and including Ident-IO(voice), to compare with tableaux (12.18) and (12.20) to demonstrate the advantage of assuming /z/ over /s/.

But how does this result compare with our earlier assumption of an underspecified plural marker /Z/? The main difference is that assuming underlying /z/ crucially requires the IDENT-IO constraint to decide between an occurring wordform and a non-occurring competing candidate in a case like *leeches*, in which the noun stem ends with a sibilant consonant. Assuming /Z/, however, does not rely on IDENT-IO(voice) simply because /Z/ is not specified for [voice], which is the only feature IDENT-IO(voice) is acting on in this case. Since /Z/ is not specified for [voice], we cannot say that either voiceless [s] or voiced [z] violate IDENT-IO(voice): the features that /Z/ *is* specified for, such as [+strident, +anterior, +coronal], are also features of both [s] and [z], so there is no violation of Ident-IO(voice) relative to the features for which /Z/ is specified.

We can conclude from this that although the analysis assuming /z/ is simpler than the analysis assuming /s/, the analysis assuming underspecified /Z/ is simpler still than either of them. Therefore, the simplest and thus preferred analysis of this set of facts involves the assumption of an underspecified plural marker /Z/ for English, along with four constraints.

12.6 Conclusion

We have seen in this chapter that, just like derivational phonology, Optimality Theory relies on notions like evidence and economy. We have also seen how differing assumptions - here, for example, different underlying representations of the plural marker – can be evaluated in terms of both simplicity and generality.

The constraint-based analysis of English noun plural formation presented here shows the importance of what one assumes as the input together with the constraints used and their ranking. This analysis also demonstrates an interesting contrast with the derivational analysis in Section 11.3. In the derivational analysis, rule interaction was shown to be crucial in yielding the correct surface form. Here, on the other hand, we have seen the correct results emerge in the absence of rules and rule ordering. Instead, the analysis relies on an input form and the evaluation of potential surface forms – the candidate set – by a hierarchically ranked set of constraints. Thus, there are no intermediate levels of representation, only input and output.

In the next chapter, however, we will see that there are some outstanding problems both with derivational phonology and with Optimality Theory.

Further reading

The widely distributed manuscript that started Optimality Theory off is Prince and Smolensky (1993/2004). This is, however, not intended for the beginner and can be rather daunting. Textbooks dealing more accessibly with Optimality Theory include Kager (1999), McCarthy (2002) and McCarthy (2008).

The account of English plural formation is based on the analysis in Russell (1997).

Exercises

1   Korean (isolate; Korea)
   In the exercises to Chapter 8, we saw that Korean [s], [ʃ], and [z] are
   allophones of a single phoneme, /s/. (Please see Chapter 8, Exercise 3
   for data set.)

   From phoneme /s/

   ❑ [ʃ] appears before [e] and [i] (i.e. [+syll, +front, –low],
   ❑ [z] appears following a nasal, N
   ❑ [s] appears everywhere else

   Examples:
   satan 'division'   ʃeke 'world'   inza 'greetings'
   su 'number'   ʃihap 'game'   paŋzak 'cushion'

   To account for the same data in Optimality Theory, assume the
   following constraints and answer the questions below:

   Constraints:

   a. IDENT-IO: outputs match inputs
   b. No[NS]: a nasal cannot be followed by a voiceless sibilant
   c. SIBPAL: a non-low front vowel cannot be preceded by an [s] or [z]

   i. How must the constraints be ranked? *Justify* each ranking through
      pairwise evaluation.

   ii. Draw tableaux for   a. [su] (showing candidates *su*, *zu*, and *ʃu*),
                           b. [ʃeke] (showing candidates *ʃeke*, *seke*, and
                              zeke)
                           c. [inza] (showing candidates *inza*, *inʃa*, and
                              insa)

   Remember: the tableaux must work for all three wordforms using the
   same constraint hierarchy!

2   English *hymn* and *damn*
   Consider the words *hymn* [hɪm] and *damn* [dæm].

   i. What evidence is there (apart from writing!) that there is a final
      /n/ in both of these words underlyingly? Give at least one piece of
      evidence for each word.

   Assumptions and constraints

   a. Assume the following inputs and candidate sets
      /hɪmn/   /dæmn/
      *[.hɪmn.]   *[.dæmn.]
      *[.hɪ.mən.]   [.dæm.]
      [.hɪm.]   *[.dæ.mən.]

b. Assume the following constraints

Dep-IO: the output must contain no material not present in the input

Max-IO: all material present in the input be present in the output

SonSeq: a coda cluster must have falling sonority [i.e. not rising or equal sonority]

ii. Rank the constraints, justifying the ranking you give.

iii. Draw tableaux of /hɪmn/ and /dæmn/ using the inputs and the three candidates given above for each word.

3 **Non-rhotic English**

In Exercise (1) in Chapter 11 we saw that there are two ways of analysing the alternation between [ɹ] ~ Ø in non-rhotic English, either through insertion of [ɹ] or by deletion of an underlying /r/. Consider the words *soar* [sɔː] and *soaring* [sɔɹɪŋ] in a non-rhotic dialect of English and assume a deletion analysis. Answer questions i., ii. and iii., below.

Assumptions and constraints

a. Assume the following inputs and candidate sets:

Inputs	soar /sɔr/	soaring /sɔr + ɪŋ/
Candidates	.sɔɹ.	.sɔɹ.ɪŋ.
	.sɔː.	.sɔ.ɹɪŋ.
	.sɔ.ɹə.	.sɔ.ɹɪŋ.

b. Assume the following constraints

Dep-IO: the output must contain no material not present in the input

Max-IO: all material present in the input be present in the output

Onset: all syllables must have an onset

NoCoda-[ɹ]: the segment [ɹ] may not appear in a coda

i. Rank the constraints, justifying the ranking you give through the sort of pairwise evaluation discussed in this chapter.

ii. Draw tableaux for *soar* /sɔr/ and *soaring* /sɔr + ɪŋ/, following the conventions of Optimality Theory. Remember that the constraint hierarchy in both tableaux must be the same.

iii. Discuss what modification you would have to make in the analysis to allow for a *rhotic* variety of English, i.e. one in which *soar* is pronounced [.sɔɹ.]. Bear in mind that two varieties of the same language will differ in the constraint *ranking*, not in the constraints themselves.

4 **English past tense formation**

In Section 12.4 we looked at a constraint-based analysis of English plural formation. Consider the data in (a.–j.) below (seen before in Exercise (2) in the previous chapter) and propose an extension to the analysis in 12.4 to cover English regular past tense formation.

Make sure that your analysis rules out the ungrammatical past tense and plural forms given in (k.–p.) in favour of the grammatical surface forms. Explain whether or not NoSib-Sib is relevant to past tense formation. If not, what sort of constraint needs to be added?

Present tableaux of *walked*, *bugged*, *studded* and *cats* to show how your analysis works. (Remember, for *cats* your analysis should rule out *[kætɪz] while ruling in [kæts].)

a.	wɔːkt	'walked'	b.	houpt	'hoped'
c.	kɹiːst	'creased'	d.	ɹʌʃt	'rushed'
e.	ɹɒbd	'robbed'	f.	bʌgd	'bugged'
g.	tiːzd	'teased'	h.	seɪvd	'saved'
i.	wɒntɪd	'wanted'	j.	stʌdɪd	'studded'
k.	*feɪsɪd	'faced'	l.	*skɹætʃɪd	'scratched'
m.	*kɹuːzɪd	'cruised'	n.	*dʒʌdʒɪd	'judged'
o.	*kætɪz	'cats'	p.	*lædɪz	'lads'

5 Deletion and insertion in English
In this chapter we discussed OT approaches to deletion and insertion, presented in tableaux (12.6) and (12.7). In those tableaux, however, only the constraints relevant for deletion were included in (12.6) and only those relevant for insertion were included in (12.7). Moreover, as pointed out in the text, the candidate set considered in tableau (12.6) focussed only on the winning candidate and the non-surfacing candidate most faithful to the input; other candidates could have been included.

Now consider the following candidates and, using the constraints given, construct two tableaux, one for each correct output. Ensure that both tableaux show the (same) ranking of *all* of the constraints given to yield the correct outputs, i.e. [hæn] for *hand* and [fɪləm] for *film*.

film: input /fɪlm/, candidate set: [fɪləm], *[fɪlm], *[fɪm], *[fɪl]
hand: input /hænd/, candidate set: [hæn], *[hænd], *[hæd], *[hænɪd]

Constraints:

NoCorClust:	do not have two [+cor] segments at the end of a word
Max-IO:	inputs should be maximised in the output (i.e. don't delete)
NoFin[son][nas]:	do not have a sequence of sonorant-nasal at the end of a word
Max-IO(son):	sonorants in the input should be maximised in the output, (i.e. do not delete a sonorant)
Dep-IO:	the output should not contain material not present in the input

13

Constraining the model

We have seen throughout this book that phonology is the study of the underlying organisation of the sound system of human language. We have also seen that phonology is not simply phonetics. Recall that phonetically [t], [tʰ] and [ɾ] are distinct sounds, yet, at the same time, for American English these three sounds are related to a single underlying entity that can be symbolised as /t/. In order to make this argument, we need to assume a certain degree of abstraction. In other words, we need to abstract away from the differences between these sounds in the surface phonetics to their underlying similarities. This allows us to establish the underlying phoneme unifying these surface sounds and in the process capture the native speaker's intuition that they are related.

Throughout the phonology chapters of this book, we have dealt with this abstraction by linking the abstract phonological representations with concrete phonetic representations by means either of a system of phonological rules (in derivational phonology) or by a hierarchy of constraints (in non-derivational phonology). While these two approaches to characterising phonological regularities differ in many significant ways, the important point about both types of approach is that by abstracting away from the phonetic detail they allow us to attempt to understand the system underpinning the phonology of language.

However, this abstraction must be counterbalanced both by the concrete facts of the language and by considerations such as learnability. While abstraction allows the linguist to understand and characterise the relationships between speech sounds, if our phonological model is to be a reflection of native speakers' knowledge of their phonological system, it must be learnable. If an analysis or theory is too abstract, it may not be learnable, since learning requires available evidence. In order to learn something a learner requires evidence of what is to be learned, some indication that some relationship exists between things, in this case between two or more speech sounds.

This is the essential tension in phonology (and indeed in linguistics in general): abstractness allows us to capture insightful generalisations, but there is a danger that too much abstraction will lead to the model being too powerful, in that it will be able to do too much (and in doing so, actually say next to nothing of real worth). Recall at the very beginning of this book, in Section 1.2, we mentioned the need for a grammar to model all and only all the possible structures of a language; if the grammar is too abstract, it may well go beyond 'and only all' by making the wrong predictions and allowing, as apparently grammatical, structures which native speakers know to be ungrammatical. Conversely, too much concreteness may result in the grammar being unable to capture structures which native speakers know *are* part of the language, and may well miss important generalisations about the language.

In what follows, we will look at the ways in which the power of both derivational and non-derivational models may be restricted in order to limit their capacity to over-generate while still making the predictions and generalisations we need. Sections 13.1 and 13.2 deal with derivational phonology, Section 13.3 looks at Optimality Theory.

13.1 Constraining derivational phonology: abstractness

As we have been discussing, abstractness allows us to capture insightful generalisations, but too much abstractness serves more to show the cleverness of the linguist than to say anything interesting about the organisation of language. Abstractness must be tempered by among other things the needs of the language learner; if a set of relationships posited in an analysis cannot be inferred by a learner, then the analysis is too abstract. This section looks at a number of important issues in this connection: (1) learnability, (2) synchrony and diachrony, and (3) plausibility.

13.1.1 Learnability

Bearing in mind that our theories of phonology are intended to be models of the knowledge speakers have of their language, they must reflect the fact that languages are learnable. Learnability is thus one of the measures of an appropriate theory. That is to say, the theory must be able to express the (unconscious) knowledge of the native speaker concerning the relatedness of, for example, a set of speech sounds. Taking again the example of [t], [tʰ] and [ɾ], a native speaker of American English will say that these three sounds are 'the same', despite their demonstrable phonetic differences. This is a piece of evidence that the theoretical abstraction from [t], [tʰ] and [ɾ] to /t/ is warranted: the expression of [t], [tʰ] and [ɾ] as allophones of a single phoneme /t/ coincides with native-speaker intuition about the 'sameness' of these sounds.

A mirror image of this can be seen in German. A literate but linguistically naïve speaker of German will feel that the final [t] in [bɑt] 'requested' and the one in [bɑt] 'bath' are different; although phonetically they are identical, the final [t] in [bɑt] 'requested' is related to /t/, while the final [t] in [bɑt] 'bath' is related to /d/. This feeling is reinforced by the relationship of the [t] in [bɑt] 'bath' to the underlying /d/ in the related word ['bɑdən] 'to bathe'. In both the American English and German cases the failure of the phonologist to accept abstractness would result in a failure to account for why [t], [tʰ] and [ɾ] are felt to be 'the same' in the one case and two instantiations of [t] are felt to be 'different' in the other.

220

How might these relationships be learned? For the speaker of American English there are word pairs – such as 'atom' ['æɾəm] ~ 'atomic' [ə'tʰɑmɪk], 'metal' ['mɛɾəɫ] ~ 'metallic' [mə'tʰælɪk], 'matter' ['mæɾəɹ] ~ 'material' [mə'tʰɪɹiəɫ] and 'metre' ['miɾəɹ] ~ 'metric' ['mɛtʰɹɪk] – that lead the learner to identify [tʰ] with [ɾ]. The German speaker will learn that the [t] of [bɑt] 'requested' corresponds to the [t] of ['bɪtən] 'to request', while the [t] in [bɑt] 'bath' corresponds to the [d] in ['bɑdən] 'to bathe'. Although unifying the 't-sounds' in American English and associating [t] with two separate phonemes for German requires the phonologist to propose an abstract analysis, this seems to capture something about the intuitions of speakers of American English and speakers of German. At the same time, it can be argued that there is evidence available to the learner which coincides with the abstraction proposed by the phonologist.

What if the phonologist pushes the analysis further in the direction of abstraction? It has been proposed, for example, that words like 'right' and 'righteous' are represented underlyingly as /rixt/ and /rixt-i-ɔs/, in order to distinguish them from pairs like 'rite' and 'ritual'. This latter pair exhibits an alternation in their root vowels while 'right' and 'righteous' have no such alternation. The analysis that arrives at this conclusion is very thorough, internally consistent and highly complex. Without considering whether the analysis itself is in general correct or not, what are the implications of it? First of all, the analysis does have some historical support: the written '-gh-' did originally stand for the voiceless velar fricative [x] and the pronunciation of 'right' has changed from Middle English /rixt/ to Modern English [ɹaɪt]. But does the native speaker know this? Can the learner arrive at this? While we might argue that the American English speaker in some sense 'knows' that [t], [tʰ] and [ɾ] are somehow related (though of course the naïve native speaker won't think of it in those terms), what can we say of the relationship between an [aɪ] diphthong and an underlying sequence of /ix/? Even with the best will in the world it is hard to see how positing /x/ – a phoneme that no longer has a surface form in most varieties of English – mirrors what native speakers might be said to know about the language they speak. Although this makes for a tidy, internally consistent analysis, it seems to err on the side of being unlearnable.

For the sake of argument, let us assume that in this one case we wish to make an exception and allow a very abstract synchronic analysis of the [aɪ] diphthong in English. The problem that then arises is where to stop. Would we want, for instance, to derive 'foot' and 'pedal' from a shared underlying form because we know that they are semantically related and because historical relationships between /f/ and /p/ as well as /t/ and /d/ are well documented? Once one exception is made how are other abstract analyses to be ruled out? In suggesting that it is too abstract to derive [aɪ] from /ix/ synchronically – even if that *does* mirror the historical development – we are constraining the possible degree of abstractness of a particular analysis by invoking learnability. If a speaker cannot learn the relationship between sounds or representations from the synchronic language itself, an analysis positing such a relationship is more indicative of the complexity that the linguist has introduced to the theory, and perhaps of the linguist's knowledge of the history of the language, than it is a model of the native speaker's knowledge of the language.

13.1.2 Synchrony and diachrony

In linguistic analyses and models we need to separate synchrony and diachrony. Synchrony refers to the state of a language at a particular moment in time. Diachrony refers to the changes that occur in a language when comparing two different points in time. As mentioned in the last section, there is historical, i.e. diachronic, evidence that English once had a velar fricative [x] and the Middle English word 'right' [rixt] may well have had an underlying representation /rixt/. And it may well be that the loss of [x] from English led the vowel to lengthen (a process known as compensatory lengthening) and subsequently to diphthongise (via the Great Vowel Shift). So, in fact, we might reasonably argue that *diachronically* English did change from /rixt/ through /riːt/ to /raɪt/. Note though that this is very different from saying that Modern English [ɹaɪt] derives *synchronically* from /rixt/. Stating this relationship diachronically means that change has taken place over time, presumably little by little, and we now have [ɹaɪt], just as we now have [laɪt] for 'light' instead of [lixt], [naɪt] for 'knight' instead of [knixt] and so on. To say on the other hand that [ɹaɪt] derives synchronically from /rixt/ means that the native learner either has to know the history of the language (which infants typically do not), or has to arrive at an underlying representation for which there is no evidence at all in the language the learner is exposed to (which is a logical improbability). If we are modelling the knowledge native speakers have of their language we can only rely on available evidence and what can be inferred from available evidence; historical changes in a language are not typically available evidence for most speakers of most languages.

13.1.3 Plausibility

The tightrope that the phonologist treads is therefore this: to capture generalisations about the system underlying the speech sounds of language, while at the same time making sure that the analyses proposed are able to reflect the native speaker's linguistic knowledge.

Plausibility is a measure of the fit between an analysis and the likelihood that it reflects a speaker's knowledge of language. An analysis can be considered to be plausible to the extent that it models a learnable set of relationships between phonological objects such as segments, rules and contrasts. In Chapter 11 we suggested that deriving 'went' from 'go', for example, was implausible. Despite the semantics linking the two words, there is no other systematic linguistic connection between them, as they are morphologically suppletive (see Section 9.2.4), phonetically and phonologically dissimilar, and historically unrelated. Moreover, early learners tend to overgeneralise (compared with the adult grammar), forming the past tense as 'goed' rather than 'went'. So, while the linguist looks for generalisations, they must be *insightful* generalisations or, again, they risk merely highlighting the cleverness of the linguist without telling us anything about natural language.

13.2 Constraining the power of the phonological component

In the preceding sections we have seen that there are a number of areas in which there is a danger of excessive power lessening the overall plausibility and efficacy of the phonological theory that we have been establishing. On the other hand, we have also seen that notions like abstract underlying representations (URs) bring with them descriptive and explanatory gains that a more 'concrete' model might be unable to express. How, then, might we constrain the model to minimise the deleterious aspects of such power while maintaining those aspects we need? This is an area of considerable controversy in current phonological theory, and we do not pretend to provide an answer here. Rather, we will content ourselves with surveying some of the attempts that have been made towards limiting the power of the model.

There are three obvious areas where we might want to try to make a start at curbing excessive power: the URs themselves, the rules which affect them and the overall organisation of the phonological component. The following sections deal with each of these in turn.

13.2.1 Constraining underlying representations

In our discussion of feature geometry and underspecification in Section 10.2 we have already touched on one of the ways in which we might constrain the nature of URs. There, we saw that some of the features are dependent on others, in that they cannot occur in a tree unless the node on which they are dependent also occurs. This rules out certain combinations that would be perfectly possible in a representation comprising an unordered matrix. Under the proposals in Section 10.2, no segment can be simultaneously both [+ strident] and [+ sonorant], for example. If features aren't grouped together, we cannot formally rule such a combination out; feature geometry thus serves to reduce the number of possible segment types by automatically ruling out some of those we never find in human languages.

The discussion in Section 10.2 introduced another way in which URs can be constrained. We saw there that rather than features having the two values '+' and '-', that is, binary features, it is possible to think of features as having only a single value, that is, being unary (or monovalent). With unary features, rather than referring to '+' or '-' values of a feature, we can only refer to a feature when it is present in the tree. No negative values are available, so the number of segment types that can be postulated is correspondingly reduced; no segments defined by, for example, the absence of the [coronal]

223

node can be part of an underlying representation. As we saw in the discussion of vowel systems in Section 10.2, it has been suggested that *all* features (rather than just non-terminal, organising nodes like [coronal], for example), are unary. Under this proposal, we can only refer to segments as say underlyingly [nasal] or underlyingly [round]; we cannot have segments underlyingly distinguished by the absence of nasality or roundness, since specifications like [– nasal] and [– round] are impossible with monovalent features. Less radically, it has also been proposed that only one value for any feature ('+' or '–') is available underlyingly; URs in a language could thus only involve segments specified for say [+ voice] but not segments specified for [– voice] (or for some other language underlyingly [– voice] but not [+ voice]). The other value for the feature would then be filled in later (in the derivation) by default rules similar to those discussed in Section 10.2. Either of these moves will serve to reduce further the number of possible underlying segment types. (The use of unary features also serves to constrain the rules, as we shall see in the next section.)

Another way of constraining underlying forms is to say that they may not contain any segment not found in the phonetic inventory of the language in question. The argument is that it is difficult to see how learners might choose a UR containing a segment they have never encountered in their language. This proposal would, for example, serve to rule out a UR like /rixt/ for 'right' discussed in Section 13.1.1, since the segment [x] is not found in English (for most varieties, at least). Given the non-surface occurrence of [x] in English, any putative UR containing it must always undergo some rule to remove or change it (this is known as 'absolute neutralisation'). If this is the case, then it is difficult to see why the learner should hypothesise the presence of the segment in the first place. The presence of non-occurring segments like /x/ in a UR serves simply as a way of marking the UR as behaving exceptionally or differently in some way; in the present case, it serves to distinguish 'right' from 'rite', as these behave differently when a suffix is added (compare the root vowels in 'right' and 'righteous' vs. those in 'rite' and 'ritual'). That is, something that looks phonological – /x/ – is being used in a non-phonological way – as a diacritic, or marker – to distinguish one UR from another. To see this, note that any segment would do here: there is no particular reason for it to be /x/ – /ɣ/ or /ɲ/ would have done just as well, since all we have to do is make sure the two forms are different underlyingly – we're going to get rid of the distinguishing segment later in any case. The reason /x/ rather than any other segment was posited has to do with the history of English, as mentioned above. By outlawing such non-phonological uses of underlying segments, the degree of abstractness between UR and phonetic form (PF) is reduced, and thus the power of the grammar is constrained.

13.2.2 Constraining the rules

We suggested above that the use of unary features was one way in which the operation of phonological rules might be constrained. If we can only refer to one value for a feature (i.e. the presence of a feature, and not its absence), then the number of things that can be done in rules involving that feature is curtailed. So, if [nasal] is a unary feature, then a rule can spread [nasal] onto other segments; in this sense, it is the equivalent of spreading [+ nasal] in a binary system. A rule cannot, however, spread the absence of nasality, since there will be no feature to spread; this is very different to the situation with a binary feature, since the [– nasal] value can be referred to in a rule just as straightforwardly as the [+ nasal] specification. Given that the spreading of nasality does appear to be a common process cross-linguistically, whereas the spreading of non-nasality (orality?) does not, the use of a unary feature [nasal] seems to be preferable. It constrains the power of the model towards capturing all and (crucially) only all the phenomena found in languages, since only one state of affairs (the one that actually occurs) is possible with a unary feature while two states of affairs (one found, one not) are characterisable with a binary feature.

Another way in which the operation of rules may be constrained mirrors another of the constraints on URs outlined above. Just as we suggested URs should not contain non-surface occurring segments, so it has been proposed that the same restriction should apply during the course of a derivation; no rule may have as its output a segment which cannot occur on the surface. While this may seem obvious, a number of analyses which do exactly this have been proposed. For example, it has been suggested that to account for the non-alternation of the root vowel in words like 'cube' and 'cubic' (compare 'metre' and 'metric' where the root vowels do vary), the underlying /u/ in 'cube' should be unrounded to /ɯ/ to prevent the rules responsible for the alternation from applying (since these rules only apply to vowels which agree in backness and roundness). The /ɯ/ is then rounded again back to /u/ once the alternation rules have attempted to apply but have failed to do so because their environments were not met. This type of derivational manoeuvre is sometimes known as the 'Duke of York Gambit', after the nursery-rhyme (and historical) character who led his army up a hill to avoid a battle, and came back down once it was over. As with the /x/ in 'right' discussed above, this analysis of 'cube' involves postulating a segment – /ɯ/ – which never occurs on the surface in English (and which must thus always be removed or changed before reaching PF). Again, what we have here is something that looks phonological being used in a non-phonological way, and banning such moves restricts the range of operations rules can perform, thus constraining the overall power of the grammar.

A further way of limiting the power of the phonological grammar is to restrict specific types of outputs by means of constraints on possible forms at various levels of the derivation. We saw in Chapter 10 that the phonotactics of English disallow a sequence of labial consonant followed by [w] in the onset of a syllable, e.g. *pwell, *bwee, *vwoot, *fwite. This is a phonotactic constraint of English and as such is a constraint on both possible underlying forms and possible intermediate forms; no rule could be allowed to have as an output a form which contained an initial labial followed by [w]. Note that unlike constraints in Optimality Theory, constraints in derivational phonology are considered to be inviolable: violating such a constraint results in an ungrammatical form, which is why the forms above are starred. An ungrammatical form is either abandoned or repaired in accordance with the phonological system of the language in question; note for instance the typical American English pronunciation of the island of Puerto Rico as ['pɔɹtə 'ɹiːkoʊ] from the Spanish [pwerto]. To avoid the onset sequence [pw…], which is ungrammatical in English, the word is changed to a form that does not violate the phonotactics of English. Thus, another way of restricting possible outputs – as distinct from restricting allowable segments at the underlying level as discussed above – is through the use of constraints on allowable rule outputs.

In Section 11.3 we discussed extrinsic and intrinsic rule ordering. Recall that intrinsically ordered rules are those which order themselves, in the sense that the application of one rule creates the environment for the application of another rule or rules. Extrinsic ordering, on the other hand, refers to the ordering of rules by the linguist to arrive at a correct description of the data.

We saw examples of both of these in Chapter 11. The [ŋ]-formation and g-deletion rules were intrinsically ordered: the assimilation of the underlying nasal to the place of articulation of the following velar stop provided the input for g-deletion. It was only after the application of the [ŋ]-formation rule that g-deletion could apply, since the rule of g-deletion specifies [ŋ] in its environment of application. On the other hand, the ɪ-epenthesis rule and the /Z/ voicing specification rule do not interact in the same way. Neither rule creates the environment for the application of the other. Since either one could apply independently of the other, their ordering – ɪ-epenthesis before voicing specification – must be stipulated by the linguist. It is only when they are ordered in this sequence by the linguist that the correct result is obtained.

This raises a problem similar to that surrounding abstraction. Just as some abstraction appears to be necessary to afford insight into phonology as an organising system, some extrinsic ordering seems to tell us more than does the absence of ordering. In the plural formation discussed in Chapter 11 the absence of extrinsic ordering would allow two possible derivations for a word like 'leeches', only one of which is correct (see Section 11.3). Extrinsically ordering the rules, on the other hand, forces the correct result. However, unconstrained extrinsic ordering again runs the risk of telling us more about the cleverness of the linguist than it does about the language being analysed. A grammar without extrinsic ordering would be much more restricted, since fewer options would be open to us.

While it is difficult to do away entirely with imposed ordering, attempts have been made to limit the extent to which it can be used. As an example of this, consider the variation in the surface forms of the preposition 'to' or the definite article 'the' in English. The 'citation forms' (i.e. the pronunciation in isolation) of these words might be [tuː] and [ðiː]. However, prepositions and articles in English usually lack stress, and the normal pronunciation (i.e. when in combination with other words) of these words involves a schwa rather than a full vowel, [tə] and [ðə] respectively, as in 'go [tə ðə] pub'. We might thus propose a rule of vowel reduction which reduces a full vowel to schwa, as in (13.1).

(13.1) $[+ \text{syll}] \rightarrow \text{ə} / \underline{}_{[- \overline{\text{stress}}]}$

That is, a full vowel becomes schwa when it is unstressed. The specification [– stress] indicates that the environment is to be found in the features of the segment undergoing the rule; in this case this means that the vowel undergoing the rule must include the specification [– stress]. This is a very general rule, applying in a wide variety of environments, including word-internally – [tə'gɛðə] – and utterance- as well as word-finally: 'He really wants [tə]'. (The facts of vowel reduction in English are considerably more complex than this, but this outline will serve our purposes here.)

However, for many (though not all) varieties of English, under certain circumstances these full vowels do not reduce as far as schwa; rather, they become shorter, lax versions of the full vowel. So we get 'to' as [tʊ] and 'the' as [ðɪ] in '[ðɪ] Englishman went [tʊ] a pub'. This laxing takes place only when the next word begins with a vowel, a process which can be characterised as in (13.2).

(13.2) $\begin{bmatrix} + \text{syll} \\ - \text{stress} \end{bmatrix} \rightarrow [- \text{tense}] / \_ [+ \text{syll}]$

How do these reduction rules interact? Note first that (13.2) must be extrinsically ordered before (13.1); if this were not the case, and the 'reduction to schwa' (13.1) were applied first, it would remove all potential inputs to the laxing rule, giving, e.g. *[ðə ɛnd]. Note further that even if we correctly order (13.2) before (13.1), if (13.2) applies, then (13.1) must not consequently be allowed to apply to (13.2)'s output. If (13.1) were allowed to apply, then, since its environment is met by the intermediate form 'ðɪ', the rule would further reduce the new lax vowel to schwa, again resulting in *[ðə ɛnd]. The two rules must thus be 'disjunctively' ordered. If two rules are disjunctively ordered, this means that they are not both allowed to apply, even if their respective environments are met; the application of one of the rules precludes the application of the other.

This state of affairs can be alleviated by appealing to a general principle which we can impose on the phonological component as a whole, known as the *elsewhere condition*. This condition states that if two rules can apply to the same input, then the more specific rule applies before the more general one, and at the same time prevents the more general rule from applying. If our phonology contains such a condition, we do not need to invoke extrinsic, disjunctive ordering for our rules. The order of their application is a consequence of the elsewhere condition since (13.2) is more specific than (13.1) and so precedes it.

The elsewhere condition also allows us to account for the idea that default rules, which fill in missing values for underspecified features, occur late in the derivation, since by their nature they are general rules, applying to any underspecified form irrespective of any other conditions.

A further limit on the power of extrinsic ordering concerns the overall organisation of the phonological component, to which we now turn.

13.2.3 The organisation of phonology: Lexical Phonology

We saw in Section 9.2 that we can distinguish between at least three kinds of phonological alternation (and therefore between the rules that characterise the alternations). Some rules, like voiceless stop aspiration or flapping, are conditioned purely by phonetic environment; others, like regular plural formation, are conditioned by both phonetic environment and morphological structure; and a third set, like velar softening, are conditioned by phonetic, morphological and lexical considerations. Our discussion of derivations in Chapter 11 made no mention of these three subtypes of rule, however. The model outlined there treats all phonological rules, whatever their conditioning factors may be, as equal; and given extrinsic ordering, they can all potentially appear anywhere within a derivation. Work within the model known as **Lexical Phonology** has suggested certain refinements to this rather unstructured view of the phonological component, with the different rule types operating in blocks at different points within the phonological derivation. Rules are said to apply at different levels within the phonological component.

One basic assumption in this model is that the phonological component is split into two parts. One part of the phonology (i.e. some of the phonological rules) operates within the lexicon itself (hence the name Lexical Phonology), i.e. before the words are combined (by the syntactic component of the grammar) into sentences. The other part (containing the remaining rules) operates after the concatenation of words by the syntax, and is known as the post-lexical phonology. So which rules belong in which subpart of the phonology? In essence, the more specific and idiosyncratic the conditioning environment of a rule is, the earlier in the derivation it will appear; the more general the environment of the rule, the later it applies. Note that this organisation mirrors the elsewhere condition discussed above.

So what are the consequences of this for our three rule types? Those involving lexical, morphological and phonetic conditioning factors clearly have the most specific conditioning environments; they apply within the lexicon at the start of a derivation and are often referred to as Level 1 rules. Those rules involving morphological and phonetic/phonological conditionings also apply within the lexicon, but after the first block, since their environments are less specific – they are not restricted to particular (sets of) lexical items. These may be classed as Level 2 rules. Those rules involving only phonetic factors apply at the end of the derivation, once the syntactic structure has been specified; i.e. they are post-lexical rules, since they apply irrespective of the morphological or lexical information. Lexical rules are less general and often have exceptions, whereas post-lexical rules apply across the board, typically being exceptionless.

Organising the phonological component in this manner goes some way to eliminating some aspects of extrinsic ordering, since the nature of the rule will determine its place in the derivation. As an example, consider the derivation of a word like 'wanted' in a variety of English which deletes /t/ after /n/ and before a vowel (a common process in many varieties of English). The UR for this word might well be /wɒnt+D/ (for British varieties) or /wɑnt+D/ (for North American English). The /D/ represents the past tense suffix as a coronal stop underspecified for voice – see Exercise 1 in Chapter 11. The surface form in the varieties in question is [wɒnɪd] or [wɑnɪd], showing post-nasal 't-deletion' and 'ɪ-epenthesis' which here inserts an [ɪ] between two oral coronal stops. In a 'flat' model of phonology, with no distinction between rule types, we would need to impose extrinsic ordering on these two rules. The rule inserting the [ɪ] would have to apply prior to the deletion of the root-final /t/, since it is the presence of /t/ that triggers epenthesis. If the order were reversed, 'ɪ-epenthesis' would not apply, since the /t/ would have been deleted, and an incorrect surface form, *[wɒnd], would be predicted. The two competing derivations are given in (13.3).

(13.3)

	UR	/wɒnt + D/		UR	/wɒnt + D/
ɪ-epenthesis	/wɒnt ɪ ɪD/		t-deletion	/wɒn + D/
t-deletion	/wɒn + ɪD/		ɪ-epenthesis	/wɒn + D/
voice assim	/wɒn + ɪd/		voice assim	/wɒn + d/
PF	[wɒnɪd]		PF	*[wɒnd]

In a phonological model involving different levels of rule application this problem is avoided, since the two rules we're interested in – 'ɪ-epenthesis' and 't-deletion' – are in separate subcomponents. The 'ɪ-epenthesis' rule crucially refers to morphological information in its formulation, as it only applies across a word-internal morpheme boundary (there is no epenthesis between the [t] and [d] in 'want drink', for example). So the rule must be in the lexical subcomponent. The 't-deletion' rule, on the other hand, applies irrespective of the morphological structure; the final /t/ of 'want' is also lost in 'want it', for example, and the presence of a following vowel in this environment is a result of a syntactic operation. Given this, 't-deletion' must be a post-lexical rule, and so automatically applies after the lexical rule of 'ɪ-epenthesis'. We might, in fact, use a similar argument with respect to voicing assimilation too, since it also does not refer to morphological structure. It too could thus be argued to be post-lexical and so automatically to apply after 'ɪ-epenthesis'. Note that this would also serve to avoid the need for extrinsic ordering in the analysis of the plural forms, since the two rules concerned, ɪ-epenthesis and /Z/ voicing assimilation, would be in the lexical and post-lexical components respectively, and so ordered by the model, not the linguist.

Having a more structured model of the phonology thus allows us to dispense with (at least some instances of) extrinsic ordering, and so gives us a further way of curbing the overall power of the phonological component, since fewer options are open to us.

A further way of reducing the power of the model is by limiting specific operations to particular parts of the phonology, for instance constraining what sorts of operations can occur where. One such restriction on the Lexical Phonology model is the constraint called **structure preservation**. Structure preservation states that only segments belonging to the set of underlying phonemes of a language may be referred to by phonological rules at the lexical level, i.e. in the lexicon. This means both that only phonemes (not allophones) may be referred to by a phonological rule at the lexical level and that surface allophones cannot be introduced at that level. In other words, segments that are not part of the phonemic inventory, i.e. allophones, can only be introduced at the post-lexical level. Take as an example the aspiration of voiceless stops in English. As we've seen, [tʰ] is an allophone of phoneme /t/; but English has no phoneme */tʰ/. As a consequence, the operation deriving [tʰ] from /t/ cannot occur in the lexicon, since this would fall foul of the structure preservation constraint. This is because [tʰ] is not part of the phonemic inventory of English and therefore cannot, according to structure preservation, result from the application of a phonological rule in the lexicon. Consequently, the derivation of [tʰ] from /t/ must occur post-lexically.

13.3 Constraining the power of OT

Despite the massive interest in OT since its inception in 1993, there are a number of issues and challenges to the model that continue to be investigated in ongoing phonological research.

As with derivational phonology, one of the areas of concern with Optimality Theory is its excessive power. As we have stressed in the later sections of this textbook, a theory that is too powerful ends up telling us nothing. A theory must therefore, in principle, be restrictive; it must spell out very clearly the predictions it makes and must also make clear what sort of data would count as evidence against a particular prediction. This is an area that OT has not been very quick to address: it is an extremely powerful theory and a number of its claims are not open to falsifiability (see Chapter 11). For example, the constraints of OT are claimed in principle to be universal, that is, the phonologies of all languages share the same constraints, though the ranking of those constraints differs from language to language. But consider a constraint that is not operative – that is, not highly ranked – in a particular language, e.g. final devoicing in English. Within OT, a constraint for which there is no evidence of its operation in a particular language is said to be ranked so low in the constraint hierarchy that its effects cannot be seen. This, however, raises a serious question: if the effects of a constraint cannot be seen, how do we know that it is ranked too low rather than simply being absent? The answer is, we don't.

Over the next few pages we will look at some of the issues that have arisen with OT, including questions about constraint writing, difficulties posed by the absence of intermediate representation and considerations surrounding learnability.

13.3.1 Constraining constraints

Another issue of a more practical nature concerns constraints, in terms of how they are expressed and how they are justified. We have seen with rules and rule writing (Section 9.3.1) that there is a set of conventions on proper rule writing, in other words, there are formal guidelines governing how rules can be written and what counts as a proper phonological rule. With Optimality Theory there is no set format for constraints, neither for how they are written nor even for what sorts of structural elements they refer to. They may refer to features or segments, to syllables, to other structural elements (coda, onset, foot, word), they may refer to phonology or word formation (e.g. Align(stem R, affix L) seen in Chapter 12), some combination of phonology and word formation (e.g. Left-Anchor$_{\text{plural}}$); they may refer to relationships between inputs and outputs (the faithfulness constraints, also called Input-Output correspondence constraints), or relationships between outputs (called Output-Output correspondence constraints). In the absence of agreed rules about constraint writing, or even the objects constraints may refer to, a powerful theory is made more powerful still.

This was certainly the case with early OT. In recent years, however, some attempts have been made to constrain the constraints, i.e. to try to define what a proper constraint can do, how it should be expressed, and how it can be independently justified. One such kind of justification has been to appeal to *functional* considerations: a constraint is justified to the extent that it expresses some state of affairs for which there is independent, often articulatory, evidence. A markedness constraint such as AgreePlace(nasal) seen in Section 12.3.1 is an example of a constraint supported by functional, articulatory considerations: phonetically, it is often the case cross-linguistically that adjacent segments come to resemble each other, particularly when one of the segments is a nasal. AgreePlace(nasal) is thus the phonological reflection of this articulatory tendency.

A different sort of support for a particular constraint can be thought of as *formal* justification. As we have seen in Chapter 12, Optimality Theory recognises three basic types of constraint or constraint family: the faithfulness constraints, the markedness constraints and the alignment constraints. Formal justification of a specific constraint means that the constraint in question fits clearly into one of the recognised constraint families. It is therefore supported on formal grounds because it is of an established constraint type. As with the functionally supported AgreePlace(nasal), we have also already seen a formally supported constraint in Chapter 12, namely Max-IO(son) in Section 12.3.3. This constraint, though specific to the preservation of a sonorant in the input, is clearly of the same constraint family as the other Max constraints we have seen, such as Max-IO. Since

231

Max-IO(son) is of an established constraint type, it can be said to have greater formal support than some proposed constraint that clearly does not fit into a recognised OT constraint family.

In phonological theory in general, there is a tension between phonologists who accept the sort of functional explanation appealed to with AgreePlace(nasal), and those who prefer a more formal, and therefore less phonetically based, account, as exemplified by Max-IO(son). This is not the place to go into detail about formalism vs. functionalism, though the two positions can be seen throughout linguistics.

The third main sort of evidence for any particular constraint is *typological*. As we discussed in Section 12.1, NoCoda (the standard constraint prohibiting coda consonants) and Onset (the standard constraint requiring syllables to have onsets) reflect universal, cross-linguistic tendencies. NoCoda expresses the universal tendency for languages to prefer syllables without codas; Onset expresses the cross-linguistic tendency for languages to prefer syllables with onsets (see also the discussion of these tendencies in Chapter 6.1.5). Thus, NoCoda and Onset are typologically grounded constraints, in that they reflect the tendency for all languages to allow syllables without codas and for no language to disallow syllables with onsets.

Although the formalisms for constraint writing are not as stringent as those for writing rules, there are, nonetheless, various considerations and various pieces of evidence that may be brought in to support the proposal of a specific constraint. As we have just seen, the evidence may be functional, formal or typological. Ideally, the evidence may be all three.

13.3.2 Opacity

One of the more vexing problems facing OT surrounds the question of *opacity*. It has long been noted that phonological operations sometimes appear to occur even though their environment for application appears not to be met. This is referred to as *overapplication*. In other cases, we find phonological operations failing to occur even though their expected environment for application is met. This is referred to as **underapplication**. Overapplication and underapplication result in opacity, as we'll see in a moment. Note that the terms derive from rule-based phonology, where a rule is said to overapply if its environment for application was not immediately obvious at the surface, or to underapply if it failed to apply despite the requisite environment being present.

As an example of overapplication, recall the data from Quebec French from Exercise 3 in Chapter 11. There we saw the interaction of several processes, including the affrication of /t/ and /d/ when followed by a high front vowel, and the loss of specific high vowels, known as vowel syncope. Thus, in a word like /tipik/ 'typical' we find that the surface form is [tˢpɪk], i.e. the initial /t/ has affricated to [tˢ], the first /i/ in the word has not surfaced and the second /i/ in the word surfaces as lax [ɪ]. Since the first /i/ has not surfaced, there is no *obvious* reason for the affrication of /t/. That is why affrication is said to have overapplied here – the affrication rule has applied although the triggering high vowel is not present at the surface. Nonetheless, in a rule-based derivational analysis we have a ready answer to the apparent paradox: the affrication rule preceded the vowel syncope rule. That is, affrication occurred and subsequently the vowel was deleted. So, the overapplication is only apparent, since when affrication applied the vowel had not yet been deleted and was thus able to trigger affrication.

However, remember that OT is non-derivational – there are no rules and no rule ordering, so there are no intermediate steps between input and output. This means that we cannot account for overapplication by appealing to some intermediate stage in the derivation where the relevant environment was present. That is why overapplication is said to be **opaque** in OT, and that's why opacity is a problem.

The second type of opaque operation mentioned above is under-application. As an example of underapplication, consider English. Typically in English a vowel lengthens before a voiced obstruent, so we find a lengthened vowel in 'led' [lɛˑd], but a comparatively short vowel in 'let' [lɛt]. Now consider American English, in which an underlying /t/ and /d/ may surface as a flap, [ɾ], between two vowels when the first vowel is stressed (see Section 9.3.1).

A flap is a voiced obstruent, so we might expect a vowel occurring before a flap to be lengthened in both 'latter' and 'ladder', since both have [ɾ] on the surface. However, in some varieties of American English, the vowel length depends not on the flap, but on the underlying voicing of the following /t/ or /d/. So, 'latter' ['læɾəɹ] surfaces with a short vowel and 'ladder' ['læˑɾəɹ] surfaces with a lengthened vowel. As with overapplication, a rule-based approach allows a straightforward analysis of this underapplication: the vowel lengthening rule applies first, followed by the flapping rule. This means that despite the occurrence of the flap at the surface in a word like 'latter', the flap does not provoke vowel lengthening, since when the vowel lengthening rule had the opportunity to apply voiceless /t/ was still in place.

The derivational account of underapplication again relies on rule ordering, as did the account of overapplication. But rule ordering is not available as an analysis tool in standard OT. Therefore, underapplication is opaque, i.e. not predicted by what we find at the surface. Such opacity is widespread in the phonological systems of the world's languages and is, thus, a serious challenge to Optimality Theory. The problem of opacity has not yet been solved for OT, but there have been various approaches to it. One approach, which we discuss in the next section, is Stratal OT, combining some of the insights of lexical phonology (discussed above in Section 13.2.3) with constraint interaction.

13.3.3 Stratal OT

Recall above that we characterised Lexical Phonology as dividing the rule component of the phonological grammar into distinct levels, so specific rules are associated with specific levels of interaction – or strata – between the phonology and word formation or the phonology and syntax. Given the underlying assumptions of OT, we cannot easily separate out the constraints that are purely phonological (e.g. the faithfulness constraints or some of the markedness constraints) from those that interact with word formation or syntax (in particular the alignment constraints). However, it has been suggested that the notion of levels might still be relevant to phonological analysis and Stratal OT has been proposed as a solution to the problem of opacity.

Stratal OT proposes that distinct constraint rankings are associated with specific levels, or strata, much like the distinct rules associated with particular levels in Lexical Phonology. These strata are distinct levels of evaluation, each with its own constraint hierarchy and with the output of one level serving as the input to the next level of evaluation. The way that this addresses the problem of opacity is as follows. Imagine with the overapplication of affrication in Quebec French, where for the word *typique* 'typical' underlying /tipik/ yields surface [tˢpɪk], that there are two relevant markedness constraints: the first constraint states that /t/ and /d/ affricate before a high front vowel; let's call this AFFRICATE. The second constraint states that specific stressless high vowels do not surface; let's call this NoStresslessV[+hi]. These interact with the faithfulness constraint Max-IO. (A complete analysis, however, is much more complex than this, and we'll ignore here the vowel laxing of the second /i/ that surfaces as [ɪ].)

At an initial stratum the constraints are ranked such that AFFRICATE is highly ranked and NoStresslessV[+hi] is low ranked, with Max-IO in between them. At this level the satisfaction of AFFRICATE yields [tˢ] and [dᶻ] for underlying /t/ and /d/; being relatively unimportant at this level, below Max-IO, NoStresslessV[+hi] is violated and the underlying high vowels remain in the output. But this 'output' is not the surface form. Rather, the output from the first stratum of evaluation provides the input to a subsequent level of evaluation. In this case, the winning candidate from the first level, [tˢipɪk] – with the affricated [tˢ] or [dᶻ] in place – now serves as the input for a further evaluation. And at this second level the constraints may be in a different ranking. So if at this level the constraint prohibiting specific high vowels from surfacing, NoStresslessV[+hi], is now more highly ranked than Max-IO, the result from this second evaluation will yield a surface form like [tˢpɪk], with the affricated [tˢ] and the syncopated high vowel.

Let us look at this schematically. At the first level of evaluation AFFRICATE » Max-IO » NoStresslessV[+hi], (where '»' means 'ranks higher than'), but at the second level AFFRICATE » NoStresslessV[+hi] » Max-IO.

(13.4) The structure of Stratal OT – overapplication

a. At Level 1: AFFRICATE » Max-IO » NoStresslessV[+hi] ; input /tipik/ from lexicon

/tipik/	AFFRICATE	Max-IO	NoStresslessV[+hi]
tipɪk	*!		*
☞ tˢipɪk			*
tˢpɪk		*!	

b. At Level 2: Affricate » NoStresslessV[+hi] » Max-IO; input /tˢipɪk/ = output from Level 1

/tˢipɪk/	Affricate	NoStresslessV[+hi]	Max-IO
tipɪk	*!	*	
tˢipɪk		*!	
☞ tˢpɪk			*

Thus, Stratal OT provides a constraint-based analytical tool for the analysis of overapplication. Let us also take a brief look at how a stratal account would approach underapplication.

As we saw above in the case of American English vowel lengthening before a flap, vowel length appeared to be sensitive to the underlying voicing value of the post-vowel obstruent. Thus, vowel lengthening fails to apply – underapplies – when followed by a flap derived from voiceless /t/, as in 'latter' ['læɾəɹ] surfacing from input /'lætəɹ/. The problem for OT is that at the surface, which is where constraints are assumed to apply, flap is a voiced obstruent, yet a pre-flap vowel is not lengthened here.

Stratal OT again provides a means of analysing underapplication while relying on constraint interaction. Although a complete analysis would be much more complex that this, the following gives an indication of how the facts could be analysed. In this case, let us assume two markedness constraints: the first constraint states that intervocalically following a stressed vowel /t/ and /d/ appear as [ɾ]; let's call this constraint Flap. The second constraint states that a short vowel cannot appear before a voiced obstruent; let's call this constraint NoShtV-C[+voi]. These interact with Ident-IO, and with Dep-IO; vowel lengthening is here interpreted as a violation of Dep-IO.

(13.5) The structure of Stratal OT – underapplication ['læɾəɹ]

a. At level 1: Ident-IO » NoShtV-C[+voi] » Dep-IO » Flap; Input /'lætəɹ/ from lexicon

'lætəɹ	Ident-IO	NoShtV-C[+voi]	Dep-IO	Flap
☞ 'lætəɹ				*
'læɾəɹ		*!		
'læ·ɾəɹ			*!	

b. At level 2: Flap » Dep-IO » Ident-IO » NoShtV-C[+voi]; input /'lætəɹ/ = output from Level 1

'lætəɹ	Flap	Dep-IO	Ident-IO	NoShtV-C[+voi]
'lætɔɹ	*!			
☞ 'læɾəɹ			*	*
'læ·ɾəɹ		*!	*	

Recall that in this dialect of English the vowel is lengthened before a flap derived from an underlying /d/, as in 'ladder' ['læ·ɾəɹ]. Using these same constraints in the same hierarchies for Level 1 and Level 2, and assuming /'lædəɹ/ as the input from the lexicon, the correct surface form should result. We invite the reader to test this with a candidate set consisting of candidates with either [d] or [ɾ] and with short [æ] or lengthened [æ·].

As we can see, the introduction of strata into Optimality Theory gives us a way to account for opacity, while at the same time representing phonological operations as the result of constraint interaction.

While this is a way round at least some instances of opacity, the introduction of different levels of evaluation in Stratal OT, in fact, reintroduces derivation into Optimality Theory. And derivation was something originally explicitly rejected in OT. Some advocates of OT are therefore not happy with this sort of solution.

Before leaving this section on Optimality Theory there is one more issue we would like to briefly discuss, learnability.

13.3.4 Learnability

Earlier in this chapter we touched on the question of learnability, specifically with regard to using diachronic evidence for a synchronic analysis. There we suggested that although English diphthongs in words like 'night' and 'right' derive historically from sequences of /...ix.../, it was too abstract, i.e. unlearnable, to suggest synchronic analyses in which the diphthong [aɪ] is derived from /ix/ in Modern English.

OT, however, takes a different approach to abstractness, leaving it not with the analyst but with the learner. OT confronts the question of abstractness of underlying representations directly by positing *lexicon optimisation*, a principle which states that (in the absence of alternations) a learner will assume that an output is identical to an input. Thus, in the absence of evidence to the contrary, a learner will assume that the input for 'right' [ɹaɪt] will be /ɹaɪt/. In other words, an input can only be as abstract as is recoverable by the learner from an output.

There are, however, other aspects to learnability of interest to Optimality Theory. Before concluding this section, we'll consider just one, the relationship between the acquisition of phonology and OT as a model of phonology. In OT, not only has the question of learnability not gone away, language acquisition itself is used as evidence in support of the theory.

With rule-based phonology it was assumed that the learner's task was to acquire the rules specific to the phonology of a particular language. Moreover, the rules of child grammar might be very different from those of the adult phonology; there was no necessary continuity between child phonology and adult phonology. With OT, the assumption is that the constraints are part of Universal Grammar and that what the learner needs to learn is the ranking of those constraints for the language he or she is learning. There is thus assumed to be a continuity between child and adult phonology and an assumption that the adult phonology develops from the child's phonology. Furthermore, this continuity is expressed straightforwardly in OT whereas it is not reflected at all in derivational rule-based phonology.

The expression of continuity from child to adult phonology in OT comes from the assumed initial ranking in UG of markedness constraints over faithfulness constraints. Children tend to produce words with onsets and without codas, for example, before they produce words without onsets and with codas. They tend to simplify onset and coda clusters, even when the ambient language – the language of the adults the children interact with – has onset and coda clusters. As the child's phonology develops, the child learns to rerank the constraints. Thus, when a particular faithfulness constraint in the adult language overrides some markedness constraint, the child learns to rerank that faithfulness constraint over the markedness constraint.

As a concrete example, imagine a young child learning English who pronounces 'cat', 'dog' and 'apple' as [kæ], [dɔ] and [pə], respectively. This is not too surprising, if the markedness constraints NoCoda and Onset are initially ranked higher than the faithfulness constraint Max-IO. However, during the acquisition process the child will be exposed to input from adult English that contains syllables and words with codas, e.g. 'cat' and 'dog', as well as vowel-initial syllables and words, as in 'apple'. Thus, the child will learn that – expressed in OT terms – it is more important to produce coda consonants (thereby satisfying Max-IO) than it is to satisfy NoCoda and Onset. As a consequence, during the acquistion of English Max-IO will be promoted in the child's constraint hierarchy to dominate NoCoda and Onset. That is, the faithfulness constraints of the adult language will, where necessary, come to dominate the markedness constraints. Thus, in OT, the child and the adult have the same set of constraints, but the difference between a child's phonology and the adult phonology resides in the ranking of those constraints. This is in stark contrast to rule-based phonology, where there is no necessary connection between the rules of a child's phonological system and the rules of the ambient adult phonology.

13.4 Conclusion

As we have seen throughout the second part of this book, the aim of a generative model of phonology is to characterise formally the knowledge native speakers have of their language. We wish to be able to characterise the relationships speakers recognise between individual sounds – like [t], [tʰ] and [ʔ] – and between words as a whole – like [dɒg], [dɒgz]. We have suggested that within a derivational framework, this is best done in terms of a model involving two levels – an underlying level and a surface level – with a set of rule statements which link these levels by specifying the relationship between a UR and its various surface realisations. Without choosing between a derivational and a non-derivational framework (both because the jury is still out and because the model continues to develop), we have also indicated how the underlying/surface relationship is approached within OT. It may turn out, of course, that a model may emerge incorporating both derivational rules and constraints.

In this book we have considered the nature of phonological structure, and seen that there is rather more to this than simply a sequence of separate speech sounds; we need to be able to refer both to elements smaller than speech sounds, such as features, and to elements of phonological structure which are larger than individual speech sounds, such as the syllable and the foot.

We have also seen that there is a danger that a model of phonology – whether derivational or non-derivational – may in fact be too powerful. Whilst it may be able to characterise and describe the phonological phenomena we wish it to (those found in human languages), it may well also be capable of characterising and describing a whole range of phenomena we do not want (because they are not found in languages). In Chapter 12 we saw how the relationship between underlying form and surface form – i.e. input and output – can also be modelled in terms of constraints in Optimality Theory rather than by using rules in a derivational framework. In this chapter we have seen that there are issues surrounding any sort of phonological theory, including questions of evidence, learnability and formal vs. functional justification of phonological analysis.

Issues of power or, indeed, whether derivational or non-derivational phonology is ultimately to be preferred, are by no means resolved in current phonological theory, but having reached this far, you should at least be in a position to start considering more detailed treatments of such controversies.

Further reading

For an overview of Lexical Phonology see Kaisse and Shaw (1985).

For accessible discussions of developments in derivational models, over and above the textbooks referred to in previous chapters, see the collections of the papers in Goldsmith (1995), Durand and Katamba (1995) and de Lacy (2007).

McCarthy (2008) is an accessible textbook on Optimality Theory. See also Archangeli and Langendoen (1997), Kager (1999) and Dekkers, van der Leeuw and van de Weijer (2000). Hayes, Kirchner and Steriade (2004) explores various issues with regard to functionalism in phonology. For a critical assessment of OT, see McMahon (2000) and the papers in McCarthy (2004). For stratal OT see Kiparsky (2002).

Glossary

Acoustic phonetics: the study of the physics involved in speech sounds

Active articulators: the lower lip and tongue

Affricates: sounds produced by the slower release of air through the narrow channel between the articulators (the first and last sounds in '<u>ch</u>ur<u>ch</u>' for example)

Alignment constraints: in Optimality Theory, the constraint-family that ensures structural alignment between different linguistic structures

Allophones: the predictable surface speech sounds of a language

Alpha-notation: a means of capturing feature-matching generalisations through the use of 'Greek letter variables'

Amplitude: the size or intensity of a sound wave, resulting in the perception of loudness

Articulatory phonetics: the study of how speech sounds are produced

Aspiration: a delay in the onset of voicing. Cf. Voice onset time

Assimilation: when the production of a sound is influenced by the character of a neighbouring sound

Association lines: in autosegmental phonology, the lines that directly link relevant features to timing slots

Auditory phonetics: the study of how speech sounds are perceived

Autosegmental phonology: an approach to phonological structure which treats features as potentially independent of one another, rather than as part of a feature matrix

Breathy voice: the 'murmured' sounds, found in languages such as Hindi, that result from the vocal cords being apart but the force of air still causing some vibration

Broad phonetic transcription: a type of phonetic transcription that lacks fine detail, for example, of phenomena such as aspiration in English

Candidate: in Optimality Theory, one of an infinite set of forms produced by *Gen* for evaluation by a constraint set

Candidate set: in Optimality Theory, the infinite set of forms produced by *Gen* for evaluation by a constraint set

Cardinal Vowel chart: a standard way of representing vowel space, in terms of a quadrilateral showing the positions of idealised vowels

Class nodes: in feature geometry, a node type such as [supralaryngeal] or [manner]

Click: stop produced by a dual closure in the oral tract, one velar and one forward of the velum, trapping a body of air. Subsequent to release of the oral closure, the release of the velar closure results in the click

Close approximation: when the articulators are close together, but without complete closure

Coda: consonant(s) following the nucleus in a syllable

Commutation test: substitution of one sound for another in a specific position in a sequence, yielding a different lexical item

Complementary distribution: state in which two sounds do not occur in the same environment; characterises allophones. Cf. Constrastive distribution, Free variation

Consonant: a sound made with some sort of obstruction in the oral tract

Constraint set: in Optimality Theory, the hierarchically arranged constraints used to evaluate a candidate set

Contour tones: tones exhibiting pitch variation during their production

Contrastive distribution: state in which two sounds can occur in the same environment thereby yielding different lexical items; characterises phonemes. Cf. Complementary distribution, Free variation

Corpus external evidence: evidence from outside the language under consideration, i.e. evidence from another language

Corpus internal evidence: evidence from within the language under consideration

Default rules: in underspecification theory, rules that assign values to those features not specified in the underlying tree

Deletion rule: a phonological rule that removes an entire segment, as distinct from a feature-changing rule, and is expressed in terms of a segment 'becoming zero'

Derivation: a step-by-step process yielding a surface form from an underlying form through the application of rules

Diachrony: comparison of language states at two or more different points in time

Diphthong: classification of vowels determined by the movement of the tongue during production

Ejectives: stops produced by the glottis being closed then raised, with the air above it (in the vocal tract) being pushed upwards and compressed, then released

Elision: the loss of a speech sound

Elsewhere condition: states that if two rules can apply to the same input, then the more specific rule applies before the more general one, and at the same time prevents the more general rule from applying

Eurhythmy: the alternating pattern of a stressed syllable followed by an unstressed syllable

Eval: in Optimality Theory, the operation of evaluating a candidate set by means of a set of ranked constraints

Faithfulness constraints: in Optimality Theory, the constraint family that seeks to ensure that outputs are faithful to inputs, in the sense that output segments match input segments

Feature-changing rules: rules which affect individual features or small groups of features, such as nasal assimilation

Feature geometry: organisation of phonological features in terms of a tree structure

Foot: a phonological structure consisting of a stressed syllable (often known as the head), plus any associated unstressed syllables

Formal justification: linguistic justification based on linguistic theory

Formants: resonant frequencies associated with specific vowels; these appear on a spectrogram as dark horizontal lines emphasising certain frequencies

Free variation: state in which two sounds can occur in the same environment, yielding different pronunciations of the same lexical item; characterises allophones. Cf. Complementary distribution, Contrastive distribution

Fricatives: the sounds produced when the articulators are close together, but without complete closure, so the air is forced through the narrow gap between the articulators, causing some turbulence (the first and last sounds in fez, for example)

Functional justification: linguistic justification based on language use

Fundamental frequency: for voiced speech sounds, the frequency at which the vocal cords are vibrating

Gen: in Optimality Theory, standing for *Generator*, that function in the grammar that produces the candidate set from a particular input

Generative grammar: a discipline with the aim of capturing formally the unconscious knowledge speakers have of their native language

241

Generative phonology: the identification of alternations, the phonological processes behind them, and the formalising of the most appropriate means of capturing them

Glides: non-vowel sounds produced with the articulators wide open and the air flowing out unhindered (the initial sounds in <u>y</u>ak and <u>w</u>arthog, for example). These are sometimes known as 'semi-vowels'

Glottal stop: sound produced at the glottis from closed vocal cords, causing a build-up of pressure behind the cords, which when opened is released in a forceful outrush of air

Glottis: the space between the vocal cords

Grammatical: permissible combinations of linguistic elements such as phonemes or words

Homophones: words that sound the same

Implosives: stop produced with ingressive airflow where the glottis is lowered, drawing the air in the vocal tract downwards, then released

Intonation: pitch variation over structures such as phrases or sentences

Intonation languages: languages that use intonation meaningfully over larger structures

Insertion rule: a phonological rule that inserts an entire segment, as distinct from a feature-changing rule, and that is the mirror-image of the deletion rule, so inserting a segment

Intrusive 'r': the occurrence in non-rhotic accents of a word-final 'r' which is not there in the spelling (compare 'tuna' ['tjuːnə] pronounced in isolation with 'tuna alert' ['tjuːnəɹə'lɜːt])

Laterals: 'l' sounds, involving airflow over one or both sides of the tongue

Level tones: tones where the pitch is maintained at the same level for the duration of the syllable

Lexicon: the storage component for all the idiosyncratic, non-predictable information in a language, including words, stems, affixes, meaning, grammatical categories, etc.

Lexicon optimisation: in Optimality Theory, the principle according to which a learner assumes that an input is identical to an output in the absence of evidence to the contrary

Linking 'r': in non-rhotic accents where a word-final orthographic 'r' precedes a vowel sound, and the 'r' is pronounced. Compare 'far' [fɑː] pronounced in isolation with 'far away' ['fɑːɹə'weɪ]

Liquids: sounds produced when there is both contact between the articulators and the free passage of air (for example, the first and last sounds in 'rai<u>l</u>')

Manner of articulation: the vertical relationship between the active and passive articulators, i.e. the distance between them which creates different types of speech sound, e.g. stop, fricative, affricate, glide, etc.

Markedness constraints: in Optimality Theory, the constraint family that deals with specific structural configurations, for example NoCoda expresses the universal tendency for languages to prefer syllables without codas

Metathesis: the reversal of adjacent segments in a word

Minimal pair: a pair of words that differ by just one sound and which are different lexical items; cf. Commutation test and Contrastive distribution

Monophthong: a class of vowels determined by the fact that the tongue remains still during production

Mora: a structural unit of quantity referring to syllable 'weight'; typically a light syllable equals one mora, a heavy syllable equals two moras

Morphology: the study of word formation

Nasal sound: the sound resulting from a lowered velum, with air flowing out through the nose (the first and last sounds in 'man' for example)

Nasal vowel: vowel produced with a lowered velum regardless of surrounding consonants; cf. Nasalised vowels

Nasalised vowel: a vowel which is underlyingly oral, but which acquires nasality from some nasal segment or feature (as in 'bean' [bĩːn]). Cf. Nasal vowel

Nasality: characterised by airflow through the nasal passage

Native speaker competence: the idealised unconscious knowledge a speaker has of the organisation of his or her language

Node: a point connected by a branch in a tree diagram; specifically, feature organisation points in a feature geometry tree

Non-derivational: a phonological model characterised by producing an output from an input without intermediate steps or stages. Cf. Derivation

Non-rhotic accents: accents in which no 'r' sound is pronounced in words like bear [bɛː] and cart [kɑːt]: a major dialect division in the English-speaking world

Nucleus: the most sonorant segment in a syllable, typically a vowel

Obstruent consonants: class of consonant where the airflow is restricted, with the articulators either in complete closure or close approximation

Onset: consonant(s) preceding the nucleus in a syllable

Opacity: the occurrence of a phonological operation in the absence of apparent motivation, or the failure of a phonological operation to occur despite apparent motivation

Open approximation: where the articulators are wide apart and air flows out unhindered

Optimal: in Optimality Theory, that candidate selected by a constraint set as best satisfying the constraints

Optimality Theory: a theory that dispenses with phonological rules and proposes that the relationship between an underlying form and its surface realisation is not derivational in nature. It proposes instead that underlying forms are linked directly to surface forms by means of a set of constraints

Oral sounds: the sounds produced when the velum is raised, so that air can only flow through the mouth (all sounds in 'frog', for example)

Overapplication: the occurrence of a phonological operation in the absence of an apparent trigger

Pairwise evaluation: in Optimality Theory, consideration of an occurring word form compared to its non-occurring competitors

Passive articulators: the upper surfaces of the oral tract

Phonemes: the abstract phonological units underlying the surface sounds of a language

Phonetics: the study of physical aspects of speech sounds

Phonology: the study of the way speech sounds are organised into patterns and systems

Phonotactics: the statement of permissible combinations of segments in a particular language

Pitch: the frequency of vocal cord vibration; the higher the frequency the higher the pitch

Place of articulation: the horizontal relationship between the active and passive articulators, specifying the position of the highest point of the active articulator in relation to the passive

Reduplication: copying all or part of a word, then attaching the copy to the original word, as in 'weewee'

Retroflex sound: sound produced with the tongue tip curled towards the back of the mouth

Rhotic accents: accents that have a rhotic in words such as bea<u>r</u> [bɛɹ] and ca<u>r</u>t [kɑɹt]: a major dialect division in the English-speaking world

Rhotics: 'r' sounds

Rhyme: syllabic constituent comprising the nucleus and the coda

Root: the highest node in a feature geometry tree, representing the segment as a whole

Rounding: vowel sounds made with protruding or rounded lips

Semantics: the study of linguistic meaning

Semi-vowel: an alternative term for a glide

Sonorant consonants: class of consonants where there is no air flow restriction in the oral tract, or the nasal tract is open, resulting in the free passage of air through the vocal tract

Sonority: a property of every speech sound, determined by features such as its loudness in relation to other sounds, the extent to which it can be prolonged, and the degree of stricture in the vocal tract. The more sonorant a sound, the louder, more sustainable and more open it is

Sonority hierarchy: a scale of relative sonority of speech sounds, ranging from least (voiceless stops) to most (low vowels) sonorant

Spectogram: the output of a spectrograph

Spectograph: a machine that measures and analyses frequency, duration, transitions between speech sounds, and the like

Spoonerism: a speech error that consists of the onset of a syllable being exchanged with the onset of another syllable in a phrase

Stops: consonant sounds produced when the articulators are pressed together (known as complete closure) and a blockage to airflow is produced. A stop may be oral (velum raised, as in the first and last sounds in 'b̲a̲d̲') or nasal (velum lowered, as in the first and last sounds in 'm̲a̲n̲')

Stress: a measure of prominence associated with the syllable

Structure-building rules: an alternative term for default rules

Structure preservation: in Lexical Phonology, a principle that states that only segments belonging to the set of underlying phonemes of a language may be referred to by phonological rules at the lexical level, i.e. in the lexicon

Suppletion: the introduction into a set of alternatives (a paradigm) of a form that is not phonologically related

Syllable: a phonological grouping of segments into a unit consisting of a nucleus and (for English) an optional onset and optional coda

Synchrony: the state of a language at a particular moment in time

Syntax: the study of the structure of phrases and clauses

Tableau: in Optimality Theory, the representation of an evaluation of a candidate set by a set of hierarchically ranked constraints

Terminal node: the lowest node in a tree diagram; in feature geometry, a node type such as [round] or [strident]

Tone languages: languages that use pitch levels to distinguish word meanings

Tone: individual pitch pattern associated with words or syllables

Typological justification: linguistic justification based on cross-linguistic frequency

Underapplication: the failure of a phonological operation to occur despite an apparent trigger

Underspecification: a model of underlying structure in which predictable features are not specified

Ungrammatical: combinations of linguistic elements, such as phonemes and words, that are not permissible

Velar softening: the alternation of [k] with [s] or [ʃ] in word pairs like 'electric' ~ 'electricity', and 'magic' ~ 'magician'

Velum: soft palate – the muscular flap at the back of the roof of the mouth

Vocal tract: mouth and nose

Voice onset time: a feature associated with stops, the interplay between stop closure and voicing that results in the difference between aspirated and unaspirated stops

Voiced sound: sound produced when the vocal cords are brought close together and air is passed through, causing the vocal cords to vibrate

Voiceless sound: sound produced when the vocal cords are apart and the air flows through unhindered

Vowel: sound type produced when the articulators are wide apart and the air flows out unhindered (the middle sounds in 'cat' and 'dog', for example)

Vowel harmony: where all the vowels in a single word 'harmonise', that is, share some feature or features

Vowel height: classification of vowels determined by the distance between the articulators, the higher the tongue, the higher the vowel

Vowel length: classification of vowels determined by how long the vowel lasts

Waveform: a record of the variations in air pressure associated with speech sounds; a waveform shows the pulses corresponding to each vibration of the vocal cords

References

Akmajian, Adrian, Richard A. Demers, Ann K. Farmer and Robert M. Harnish. 2001: *Linguistics: An introduction to language and communication*. Cambridge, MA: MIT Press.

Anderson, John and Colin Ewen. 1985: *Principles of dependency phonology*. Cambridge: Cambridge University Press.

Archangeli, Diana and D. Terence Langendoen (eds.). 1997: *Optimality Theory: An overview*. Oxford: Blackwell.

Ball, Martin J. and Joan Rahilly. 1999: *Phonetics: The science of speech*. London: Arnold.

Carr, Philip. 1993: *Phonology*. London: Macmillan.

Carr, Philip. 1999: *English phonetics and phonology: An introduction*. Oxford: Blackwell.

Carr, Philip. 2008: *A glossary of phonology*. Edinburgh: Edinburgh University Press.

Catford, John C. 2001: *A practical introduction to phonetics*. 2nd edn. Oxford: Oxford University Press.

Chomsky, Noam and Morris Halle. 1968: *The sound pattern of English*. New York: Harper & Row. (Paperback edition 1991, Cambridge, MA: MIT Press.)

Clark, John, Colin Yallop and Janet Fletcher. 2008: *An introduction to phonetics and phonology*. 3rd edn. Oxford: Blackwell.

Clements, George N. and Samuel Jay Keyser. 1990: *CV phonology: A generative theory of the syllable*. Cambridge, MA: MIT Press.

Cruttenden, Alan. 1997: *Intonation*. 2nd edn. Cambridge: Cambridge University Press.

Dekkers, Joost, Frank van der Leeuw and Jeroen van de Weijer (eds.). 2000: *Optimality Theory, phonology, syntax and acquisition*. Oxford: Oxford University Press.

de Lacy, Paul (ed.) 2007: The Cambridge Handbook of Phonology. Cambridge: Cambridge University Press.

Delattre, Pierre. 1965: *Comparing the phonetic features of English, French, German and Spanish: An interim report*. Philadelphia: Chilton Books.

Denes, Peter B. and Elliot N. Pinson. 1963: *The speech chain: The physics and biology of spoken language*. New York: Bell Telephone Laboratories.

Dumas, Denis. 1987: *Nos façons de parler. Les prononciations en français québécois*. Quebec: Presses de l'Université du Québec.

Durand, Jacques. 1990: *Generative and non-linear phonology*. London: Longman.

Durand, Jacques and Francis Katamba (eds.). 1995: *Frontiers of phonology: Atoms, structures, derivations*. London: Longman.

Ewen, Colin J. and Harry van der Hulst. 2001: *The phonological structure of words: An introduction*. Cambridge: Cambridge University Press.

Fromkin, Victoria, Robert Rodman and Nina M. Hyams. 2006: *An introduction to language*. 8th edn. Boston, MA: Heinle.

Giegerich, Heinz J. 1992: *English phonology: An introduction*. Cambridge: Cambridge University Press.

Gimson, A.C. 2008: *The pronunciation of English*. (7th edition, revised by A. Cruttenden). London: Hodder Arnold.

Goldsmith, John A. 1990: *Autosegmental and metrical phonology*. Oxford: Blackwell.

Goldsmith, John A. (ed.). 1995: *The handbook of phonological theory*. Oxford: Blackwell.

Gussenhoven, Carlos and Haike Jacobs. 2005: *Understanding phonology*. 2nd edn. London: Arnold.

Gussmann, Edmund. 2002: *Phonology, analysis and theory*. Cambridge: Cambridge University Press.

Halle, Morris. 1992: Phonological features. In W. Bright (ed.), *International encyclopedia of linguistics*, vol. 3, 207–212. Oxford: Oxford University Press.

Handbook of the International Phonetic Association. 1999: Cambridge: Cambridge University Press.

Harris, John. 1994: *English sound structure*. Oxford: Blackwell.

Hayes, Bruce, Robert Kirchner and Donca Steriade (eds). 2004: *Phonetically based phonology*. Cambridge: Cambridge University Press.

International Phonetic Association. 1999: *Handbook of the International Phonetic Association*. Cambridge: Cambridge University Press.

Johnson, Keith. 2003: *Acoustic and auditory phonetics*. 2nd edn. Oxford: Blackwell.

Kager, René. 1999: *Optimality theory*. Cambridge: Cambridge University Press.

Kaisse, Ellen and Patricia Shaw. 1985: On the theory of Lexical Phonology. *Phonology Yearbook* 2, 1–30.

Kaye, Jonathan. 1989: *Phonology: A cognitive view*. Hillsdale, NJ: Lawrence Erlbaum.

Kenstowicz, Michael. 1994: *Phonology in generative grammar*. Oxford: Blackwell.

Kiparsky, Paul. 2002: *Paradigms and opacity*. Stanford, CA: CSLI (Distributed by University of Chicago Press.)

Kuiper, Koenraad and W. Scott Allan. 2008: *An introduction to English language*. 2nd edn. London: Palgrave Macmillan.

Ladd, Robert. 1997: *Intonational phonology*. Cambridge: Cambridge University Press.

Ladefoged, Peter. 1996: *Elements of acoustic phonetics*. 2nd edn. Chicago, IL: University of Chicago Press.

Ladefoged, Peter. 2001: *Vowels and consonants: An introduction to the sounds of language*. Oxford: Blackwell.

Ladefoged, Peter. 2005: *A course in phonetics*. 5th edn. New York: Harcourt Brace.

Ladefoged, Peter and Ian Maddieson. 1996: *The sounds of the world's languages*. Oxford: Blackwell.

Laver, John. 1994: *Principles of phonetics*. Cambridge: Cambridge University Press.

Lodge, Ken. 2009: *A critical introduction to phonetics*. London: Continuum.

McCarthy, John J. 2002: *A thematic guide to Optimality Theory*. Cambridge: Cambridge University Press.

McCarthy, John J. (ed.). 2004: *Optimality Theory in phonology: A reader*. Oxford: Blackwell.

McCarthy, John J. 2008: *Doing Optimality Theory*. Oxford: Blackwell.

McMahon, April. 2000: *Chance, change and optimality*. Oxford: Oxford University Press.

Napoli, Donna Jo. 1996: *Linguistics: An introduction*. Oxford: Oxford University Press.

O'Connor, J. D. 1973: *Phonetics*. Harmondsworth: Penguin.

O'Grady, William, Michael Dobrovolsky and Francis Katamba. 1997: *Contemporary linguistics: An introduction*. London: Longman.

Picard, Marc. 1987: *An introduction to the comparative phonetics of English and French in North America*. Amsterdam and Philadelphia: John Benjamins.

Quilis, Antonio and Joseph A. Fernández. 1972: *Curso de fonética y fonología españolas*. Madrid: Consejo superior de investigaciones científicas.

Rand, Earl. 1968: The structural phonology of Alabaman, a Muskogean Language *International Journal of American Linguistics* 34 (2), 94 103.

Russell, Kevin. 1997: Optimality Theory and morphology. In Archangeli and Langendoen (eds.), pp. 102–133.

Spencer, Andrew. 1996: *Phonology: Theory and description*. Oxford: Blackwell.

Tallerman, Maggie. 1987: Mutation and the syntactic structure of Modern Colloquial Welsh. PhD dissertation, University of Hull.

Trommelen, Mieke. 1984: *The syllable in Dutch*. Dordrecht: Foris.

Trudgill, Peter and Jean Hannah. 2008: *International English: A guide to the varieties of Standard English*. 5th edn. London: Hodder Education.

Wells, John C. 1982: *Accents of English*. 3 vols. Cambridge: Cambridge University Press.

Wolfart, H. Christoph. 1973: *Plains Cree: A grammatical study*. Philadelphia: Transactions of the American Philosophical Society, N.S. vol. 63, part 5.

Yip, Moira. 2004: *Tone*. Cambridge: Cambridge University Press.

Yule, George. 2006: *The study of language*. 3rd edn. Cambridge: Cambridge University Press.

Subject index

Varieties of English index

Language Index